TOOLS FOR TRANSFORMING TRAUMA

TOOLS FOR TRANSFORMING TRAUMA

Robert Schwarz

Routledge
Taylor & Francis Group
New York   London

Routledge is an imprint of the
Taylor & Francis Group, an informa business

Published in 2002 by
        Routledge
29 West 35th Street
New York, NY 10001

Published in Great Britain by
        Routledge
27 Church Rd.
Hove, East Sussex BN3 2FA

Printed in the United States of America on acid-free paper.

10 9 8 7 6 5 4

Library of Congress Cataloging-in-Publication Data is available from the Library of Congress

ISBN 1-583-91341-6

CONTENTS

ACKNOWLEDGMENTS

There are many people who have been involved in the creation of this book, some more directly and some more indirectly. I want to give particular thanks to my teachers and mentors Jeffrey Zeig, Stephen Lankton, Harry Aponte, Robert Dilts, Steve de Shazer, Insoo Kim Berg, and David Calof, who have been sources of inspiration and wisdom. In many ways their voices are clearly heard on the pages of this text.

To my colleagues: Yvonne Dolan, Fred Gallo, Stephen Gilligan, Kurt Ebert, Bessel van der Kolk, Maurice Prout, Bill O'Hanlon, and Sandy Bloom for the many lessons and suggestions that they have provided throughout the years.

To Milton H. Erickson, who has influenced so many who have influenced me.

To Marc Tracten, who originally encouraged me to submit a proposal for this book many years ago.

To my patients, who have been my greatest teachers.

To my wife Kim and son Daniel, my family and friends for their love and support.

INTRODUCTION

This book is the outgrowth of 20 years of experience with Ericksonian and solution-oriented approaches to hypnosis and psychotherapy in general and 10 years of specific work with trauma and abuse. The purpose of this book is to provide the reader with both an integrative framework and practical tools for transforming the negative effects of trauma. As opposed to some books (including a previous book that I authored) that make brief references to specific interventions, this book includes many detailed instructions, rationales, and examples of specific tools.

As is stated in chapter 2, the problem with trauma is that it disconnects people from their resources. Therefore, therapists need to cultivate their own resourcefulness in what can sometimes be demanding, yet rewarding, work. The majority of the tools described in this book do not require formal training in hypnosis. Nevertheless, I have found my training in neurolinguistic programming (NLP) and hypnosis, especially in the Ericksonian tradition, to be invaluable with all of my patients. It has been particularly important in helping me work with severely traumatized individuals. I certainly recommend that therapists who plan to work with traumatized patients get advanced training in these areas.

One of the decisions that I had to face in writing this book was to decide between the terms *client* and *patient*. I confess to some ambivalence on this point. While I use and like the term "client," which connotes a collaborative effort that is necessary in this work, in the end I chose the term "patient," since it means "one who suffers." Certainly, many of the people with whom I have worked have suffered. What I do think is most important is to treat the people who come to see us with the utmost respect. Now the problem here is how each person translates the word *respect*. What I think of as respectful may not be what someone else thinks. It certainly will vary from patient to patient.

There is a classic Milton Erickson story about a woman who calls Erickson up and hesitantly asks for his help even though she believes that she is beyond hope. Erickson agrees to see her. She comes into his office and Erickson ends up saying to her that she has completely underrated how bad she really was. He proceeds to tell her how she is obese and she is wearing a polka dot dress that just emphasizes her weight problem. Her nose is over toward one side of her face. He goes on and on for a while pointing out every thing wrong with her that he can notice. (For those unfamiliar with Erickson stories, this is referred to as *the set-up* [Zeig, 1985]. Every great Erickson story has a set-up, where Erickson will do something very unusual *to meet the patient at his or her model of the world*.) He then asks, "Now that you know that I understand your situation and can tell you the whole truth, are you ready to get down to business?" The patient responds well to this intervention.

This is a story about respecting patients' model of the world. It means really understanding the inner world of people. I have considered myself very fortunate to know these stories, because they have empowered me to realize that people who have undergone terrible trauma often have highly idiosyncratic ways of being in the world. This has sometimes re-quired me to behave and think differently than I would tend to on my own aesthetics in order to be respectful. I am not suggesting that we should all go around talking like Milton Erickson. Part of Erickson's legacy has been the message for therapists to go beyond dogma and reified theories and really *be with* patients. I have used the many stories of uncommon Ericksonian practice as permission to be more present and transparent in the room with patients. Part of the training I have had in the Ericksonian approach and NLP has been to be very specific. Erickson was also a man who did not hesitate to practice and refine a tool. For instance, he would write out 30-page hypnotic passages and refine and condense them down to 15 pages then to 10, and then to 5 pages. I do not intend for the tools described in this book to become dogma. I do suggest that once they have been well learned, they can be changed and tailored to the needs of a given patient. Once a tool has been mastered, then the unique presence of the therapist using a tool with a patient becomes as important as the tool itself.

I have always been interested in integrating approaches rather than in filial loyalty to a given approach. As we will see later in the book, the concept of "yes, and" is far more adaptive than the concept of "either/ or." This text attempts to integrate a number of diverse approaches both explicitly and implicitly. There are many great books on different aspects of treating trauma from the point of theory as well as technique. It is my hope that readers will integrate the ideas presented in this book with the ideas of others in the field of trauma, Ericksonian, and neo-Ericksonian approaches to treatment and beyond.

Helping people overcome the effects of trauma and abuse is an honor-able profession. I remember being an idealistic college student wanting to change the world. I gradually decided that this was a rather grandiose idea of late adolescence, so I eventually decided I could help create a world to which one would want to belong[1] one person at a time by becoming a therapist (well, that's what I thought consciously at least). I was content with this for many years. Then, starting in 1991, I began to organize the Advances in Treating Abuse and Trauma Conferences. We held two events a year for 4 years. In that time we trained over 6,000 therapists. After the first year I began to realize that these conferences were having a much bigger impact than me alone in a room with a patient or a group of patients could have. I began to think about how helping a therapist learn therapeutic skills that he or she could then use with hundreds of people over the next several years would affect all of those lives and potentially the lives of children and so on.

In addition, I became aware of the work of Ruppert Sheldrake (1988) on morphic fields, commonly known as the 100th monkey effect. The story of the 100th monkey effect is that there were scientists studying the behavior of monkeys native to certain islands off of Asia. One day a monkey discovered that if she washed the roots she had dug up in the sea, they got clean and tasted better because of the salt. Over time, she taught her family. Gradually other families on the island learned the knowledge. In the meantime, none of the other monkeys on the other islands engaged in this behavior. Then one day, all of the monkeys on all of the islands were washing the roots in the salt water. The 100th monkey had learned the behavior that generated a wave through the invisible morphic field that connected the species, and the information was transmitted. So I would like to suggest that we (therapists who work with trauma patients and the patients themselves) are engaged in creating a morphic field through which the effects of trauma can be overcome. I hope you find this book helpful in that endeavor.

It is not necessary for the reader to have knowledge of hypnosis in order to benefit from this text. Nevertheless, training in hypnosis will add a level of appreciation to some of the nuances described in these pages. Furthermore, I cannot imagine working with trauma patients and not knowing hypnosis. Even if one never does formal trance work, understanding the power of language to communicate with more impact is one of the benefits of hypnosis training.[2]

---

[1]I first heard this expression, "creating a world to which you want to belong," at a NLP master practitioner training session with Robert Dilts and Todd Epstein. If stealing is the most sincere form of compliment, ...

[2]Excellent training in hypnosis can be found in a number of places. Two resources are the American Society of Clinical Hypnosis (130 East Elm Court, Suite 201, Roselle, IL 60172-2000; Phone 630-980-4740; Fax 630-351-8490; e-mail info@asch.net) and the Milton H. Erickson Foundation (Phoenix, AZ 85016; Phone 602-956-6196).

Finally, I want to comment on how to read this text. I see everything written in this book as interdependent. Unfortunately, we have to write in a linear fashion. So, I have chosen a given linear order to the chapters that makes sense, but it is by no means the only order that makes sense. Depending on the needs of the reader, there may be different ways to read this book to get the most out of it. I am not going to presume I know what that order is. I am merely opening up the possibility of reading the book in whatever way makes sense to you.

CHAPTER 1

Understanding How Trauma Leads to PTSD

In order to be able to help clients transform trauma, it is important to understand how trauma affects people. A traumatic or stressful event does not necessarily lead to formal post-traumatic stress disorder (PTSD) or to other trauma-based psychological problems. The process that creates this change is highly dynamic. There are many interactions with many variables. The person is the passive recipient of certain events, and at the same time is never truly passive, but rather always actively processing information, creating responses, and creating meaning. The process occurs over time. The time involved can be on the microlevel of the time it takes to process visual stimuli and develop an immediate cognitive appraisal of danger. Or the time involved can be on a macrolevel consisting of days, months, or years in developing a view of self and other, creating behavioral patterns, and so on. The process is depicted in Figure 1. The figure does not adequately depict the time dimension.

If we look at the extreme left of the figure, we see that some type of traumatic event happens. If we look at the right-hand side, we see the end of the process. We see that there are two possible directions that a given person can eventually take. In one direction, the person will eventually have a positive resolution either with no residual effects or coping well with any effects that do occur. Optimally, the person's life remains rich. In the other direction, a person has a poor adaptation in which there are many symptoms and in which the person's life becomes impoverished and/or focused in one of several limiting manners.

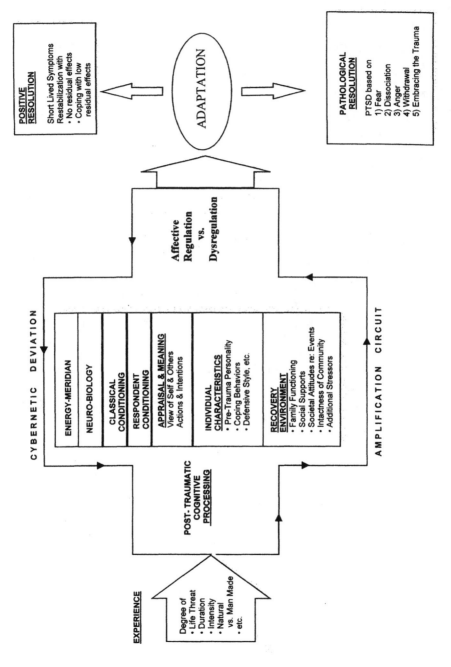

Figure 1.1. Eco-systemic model of PTSD.

2

We will spend the rest of this chapter looking at what happens in between the precipitating event(s) and the resolution to learn how one path is chosen over another. A thorough understanding of all of the different interactive elements that create PTSD will allow us to design different tools to help transform a negative resolution into a positive one.

☐ The Qualities of the Traumatic Experience

The nature of the traumatic event(s) does have a significant impact. First, the duration and intensity of the event or events matters a great deal. A single event of childhood sexual abuse can have tremendous effects. However, years of repeated sexual abuse will have a far greater impact, all other things being equal.[1] Being held captive for a day in jail is likely to be less traumatic than being held captive in a Nazi death camp for a year. All things being equal, the longer and more intense the experience, the more likely it will be to overwhelm the individual's ability to cope, resulting in greater PTSD. If a person perceives the likelihood of serious injury or death, there is a far greater likelihood of PTSD developing (Kilpatrick et al., 1989). If the traumatic incident is perceived as natural and without malicious intent or manmade negligence, it is less likely to lead to PTSD. Quarantelli (1985) has noted that survivors of natural disasters such as hurricanes and tornadoes do not have relatively high levels of PTSD given the amount of devastation. If abuse is inflicted with sadistic intent, it will tend to create different reactions in the victim than if the intent were nonsadistic (Salter, 1995).

Big "T" and Little "t" Traumas

This is a good point to discuss the difference between *"big T" traumas* and *"little t" traumas*. Big T traumas all meet the criteria in the DSM (APA, 1980, 1994) for PTSD. They include violent attacks, rape, war, and so on. A little t trauma is any event that is beyond a person's ability to master at the time of the event. It can be something as simple as a child getting lost for a few minutes, or a child being overwhelmed with fear

---

[1]For any given person, one cannot predict the future impact of a trauma just by the nature of the event alone. It is well within the realm of probability that one person can have a single event of childhood abuse and fare far worse than someone else who has had years of abuse. However, if all the remaining variables are held constant between two such events (which of course is not possible), then longer, more intense events tend to cause more problems.

after a nightmare and no one comforting the child. These little t traumas often are left unprocessed in the unconscious. They create areas of vulnerability that become part of a negative spiral when a Big T trauma occurs. In the case of a major trauma, the person may be able to stand the impact of the main event. However, he may be so weakened that it is a small t trauma that finally collapses his coping abilities. For instance, when I recently watched the movie *Saving Private Ryan*, I was barely able to stand the first 30 minutes when the soldiers attacked Normandy. This was not to be the scene that haunted me. It was the scene where the Nazi slowly kills one of the soldiers in a knife fight while "hushing" the man like you would a baby. This was more than I could take. There was something about the smallness of this event (compared to the massive trauma of the assault on the beach) that allowed the trauma to get through. Some of these small t traumas are inevitable in life. When caretakers allow too many of these small t traumas to occur, neglect is present.

The Role of Neglect

The role of neglect is often underrated in working with trauma and abuse. If a person is raped as an adult or sexually or physically abused as a child, it is easy to point to "The TRAUMA." These are capital T traumas. But, it is often the shear number of small t traumas in a neglectful family that can create such havoc. (This is not a legal definition of childhood neglect, which usually includes lack of appropriate physical care.) In many cases, therapists as well as clients pay too much attention to the big T traumas because they are easy to identify. In many cases it was the neglect or the acts of omission that individually or cumulatively caused so much dysfunction.

Neglect forces a child to attempt to self-regulate before the child is able to do so effectively. Therefore, the child will become overwhelmed, perhaps chronically so. The child will be forced to make adaptations, such as increased use of dissociation and denial. The child will make certain assumptions verbally or preverbally about the nature of the world. There is evidence that neglect may lead to actual brain changes that may make it more difficult to self-regulate later in life.

Neglect also means that the child will probably not learn more successful and adaptive coping strategies. Nor will the child have effective internal representations (states of consciousness, SoCs) of love and positive affect to call upon in times of stress. Children who have histories of significant to extreme abuse by definition live in families that are highly dysfunctional. It is not just the events of abuse that occurred. These families "neglect" to teach their children adaptive coping strategies or belief systems. There are almost always huge problems with boundaries. For instance, the child is often made to feel it is his or her fault that the abuse occurred. Some of this belief comes from the developmental ego-centricity of the child. But oftentimes, the child is told this directly and indirectly. These children are almost always deprived of loving, warm, and safe interpersonal transactions. It is not just that you were raped as a child, it is that very few times were you hugged or told "I love you" (without it leading to some abuse).

☐ Post-Traumatic Cognitive Processing and Affect Dysregulation

Once an external event happens to a person, that person must process it. Technically, we can speak of the event from an external perspective, such as, "A yellow car traveling at 35 miles per hour impacted a green car traveling at 10 miles per hour at an angle of 25 degrees at 9:15 a.m. on Tuesday, April 22, 1998." We can speak of specific physical injuries and so on. These are so-called objective facts. However, from the perspective of the people in the car, we cannot speak about the accident as an external event independent of their processing.

Over time the person must process the experience and all of its ramifications. Horowitz (1986) has described this process as a cognitive information model. He suggested that the main reason for the phenomenon of intrusion of traumatic symptoms (e.g., flashbacks) is that the individual keeps trying to think about the event to understand and process the event. During those times the brain is attempting to assimilate the experience. If during the process the person becomes overwhelmed again, the cycle shifts and the person moves into a numbing phase. The cycle continues until the traumatic experience has been assimilated. The problem is that many times this never happens. In more severe cases it would be more accurate to say that instead of the person assimilating the trauma, the trauma assimilates the person.

As the post-traumatic cognitive processing is occurring, a parallel process occurs in the affective system. Part of the overwhelming nature of the trauma is that the person is flooded with intense affect. Fear states are the main feeling. This can include fright, anxiety, panic, and terror. Other common affects are helplessness, shame, anger, guilt, and grief. The person attempts to regulate the amount of affect and feeling they are having. The more a person can maintain a connection to positive or resourceful feeling states, the more they can cognitively process the event.

For example, Michael lives through a devastating hurricane. His house is destroyed and he and his family are almost killed. He feels intense fear as he remembers the event. He feels grief that he has lost his house. He feels even more fear and helplessness as he ponders the possibility that everyone he loved could have been killed. So his unconscious mind begins to search for something resourceful and positive to help regulate the feelings as well as process the event. He thinks about other difficult challenges he has overcome and feels some pride and mastery. He reflects on how he did certain things during the storm that were helpful and feels some decrease in helplessness. He attends to the fact that this happened to his entire community and knows he is not alone in this, so he feels some belonging. He also remembers his connection to God and is grateful that no one got hurt, so he begins to feel safe and loved. In this manner his affect is regulated so that he can continue to process the experience.

The affect itself is one additional variable that must also be processed cognitively. To put it simply, people often have fear after a trauma. The person must make sense of this feeling. In the example of Michael, it seemed perfectly normal to him that he felt fear. Everyone else felt fear. The entire community was demolished. Furthermore, the entire country was galvanized to help. So there was no loss of face for having fearful reactions in the face of such devastation. Let us quickly compare this to a child who is being sexually abused by her father at night. She also has intense fear. But when she comes downstairs the next morning and everything seems perfectly normal, her fear now does not make so much sense to her. She begins to doubt herself. Every person I have ever seen who has not adjusted well after a car accident is always tremendously upset about his or her emotional reactions to the car crash. They are traumatized by the fear they felt postcrash.

To summarize to this point, during and after any novel event, a person has some emotional reaction to the event and must make sense of the event. The affective regulation and cognitive processing systems work interactively to achieve this goal. Traumatic events are traumatic because they tax and overwhelm the parameters of this system. The system will eventually adapt. One path of adaptation is healthy; the other adaptation is unhealthy. We now move to the variables that affect this outcome.

☐ The Recovery Environment

The single biggest factor in how a person adjusts to a traumatic event is the recovery environment. The recovery environment includes the amount of social support a person has, the reactions of the family, the reactions and intactness of the community, societal attitudes, and the responses of helping professionals (doctors, Red Cross, police, courts, etc.). To put it simply, the more these variables help soothe and comfort the person (regulate affect) and help the person stay connected to positive and resourceful contexts, the more adaptive the resolution is likely to become.

On the other hand, the recovery environment is the arena where a person can also be hit with any number of small t traumas. The individual is especially vulnerable. His or her shields are down. A relatively small problem can do serious damage. I have repeatedly worked with people whose symptoms were not tied to the actual incident, whether that was an accident or rape. Rather, it was something that someone said to them in the emergency room. Or, it was something that a police offer said when questioning the person that haunts him or her. With abuse cases, it is often a small t event that is so hurtful psychologically.

When Vietnam vets came home, they were not welcomed as heroes. They were treated as villains and baby killers. World War II veterans were treated as heroes. This difference in the recovery environment was a huge factor in some Vietnam vets' poor adjustment to coming home.

Paradoxically, a small gesture of support and kindness at these times of vulnerability can make a world of difference. For instance, Tom had been in a serious auto accident and had lost his arm. As he was entering the emergency room, a nurse came up to him and talked to him in a very soothing voice. He reported that she said, "I know you are scared. That is completely normal. We are going to make you comfortable. We are going to take good care of you. The surgeons will try to reattach it. Let your body relax. That will help the surgeons. Let your body know that you are safe. Everything will work out for the best." Tom reported that this event is the one thing that he clearly remembered in the blur. He also reported that he did in fact calm down. He stated that he had a task to do in order to help the doctors, so his perceived helplessness lessened. In fact, the doctors could not save his arm. While this did cause Tom some psychological issues, he often thought of the nurse and what she had said. It always was a comfort.

Trauma cascade refers to the fact that traumatic events do not just happen to individuals but to their families as well. In some circumstances, the effects of the traumatic event(s) spread from family member to family member, creating a cascade of increasing trauma and decreasing resourcefulness. This phenomenon often occurs in traumatic deaths of children. Each individual in the family is affected and reacts poorly, which further stresses other family members. Parents begin to fight and blame each other instead of supporting each other, and so on. Another example is in the case of rape. A husband or father may be unable to get a picture of the rape out of his mind. He reacts with rage at the perpetrator. He is not able to manage his feelings. He is not able to be supportive to the rape victim, who then becomes more upset. In some cases, he may even act out and attempt to kill the perpetrator, which places him in legal trouble, and so on.

Nowhere is the impact of a poor recovery environment seen more clearly than in the case of long-term incest. In the best-case scenario, the child is induced to have sex at various times, while at other times the family is "loving" and acts as if nothing is going on. In the worst-case scenario, the child is forced to have sex every night, and during the day is neglected or even physically and emotionally abused. In either case the healing potential of family is seriously compromised. The child cannot ask for help. In many cases the child does ask for help and is not believed or appropriate steps are not taken. This response must also be processed and managed by the child. The response of the family system itself becomes part of the overall process that occurs over time.

Consider for a moment the following scenario that occurs repeatedly in such families. The child is forced to have sex with one parent or sibling at night. Suppose further that there has been ample evidence that something inappropriate is going on, which is being ignored by the rest of the family. The next morning everyone sits around the breakfast table eating corn flakes as if nothing has happened. Imagine this repeating over and over. Consider what this child would be thinking and feeling. Ponder the potential manner in which this child would be able to process the overall situation. The acts of sex at night actually become a relatively small part of the overall dynamic.

One of the most important factors that determines resiliency in children is the presence of at least one supportive person in childhood. One of the reasons this is so important is that the supportive person prevents some of the effects of the neglect. The child gets some measure of love, some measure of comfort and support that helps the child regulate affect. The child is given some better coping strategies. The child gets some resourceful and positive experiences. These experiences and learnings are available to the child to internalize. Unconsciously, children realize it is better to light a candle than curse the darkness.

The role of the mental health professional in impacting the healing power of the recovery environment cannot be understated. Obviously, a therapist becomes part of the recovery environment. In the best circumstances, the mental health professional remembers that his or her client is not just the patient. The client is the patient and everyone else in the recovery environment. It is often helpful to point out to family members that they have been traumatized too.

☐ Individual Characteristics

Historically, traumatic reactions were seen as a reflection of the personality flaws of the individual. Since the inclusion of PTSD as a formal diagnosis, this has shifted. Traumatic reactions are now seen as a function of the overwhelming nature of the traumatic event itself. But, as we have just discussed, the person must make some sense of the trauma and must regulate his or her affect. Two people will not experience the same traumatic incident in the same way. The individual characteristics of the person are one of the factors in determining the final outcome of the processing of the event. The subfactors include the person's life history, defensive style, coping mechanism, and so on. For example, virtually every person I have ever seen who did not adjust well following a car crash shared one common personality characteristic. Without exception, these people have counterdependent defensive styles. They have tremendous difficulty with asking for help or feeling vulnerable. Their number 1 coping strategy is to be in control at all times. They felt out of control in the crash. They attempt to control their fear reactions postaccident and fail. They become very upset with themselves for feeling so upset. They feel more out of control.

Another subfactor is the person's previous history of trauma and neglect. Clinical experience has shown that a significant percentage of people who have a negative resolution to a single traumatic event (e.g., a terrorist bombing) appear to also be reacting to previous trauma in their lives. It is as if the big trauma that is current activates big or small traumas in the person's past.

The quantity, quality, and accessibility of the resourcefulness of the person are other individual characteristics. As I will discuss later, it is not just the raw size of the trauma that counts. A more accurate predictor of an outcome of a "traumatic event" is the ratio of the destructive power of the trauma to the available resources of the person. The term "resource" is used very loosely here. It can include any experience the person has ever had. Resources that may be particularly helpful can include any experience of mastery, memories of being supported and loved, and flexible beliefs about being safe in the world even if bad things happen.

☐ Appraisal and Meaning

There is the story of the three baseball umpires. The first umpire says, "I call them as they are." The second umpire says, "I call them as I see them." The third umpire says, "They ain't nothing till I call them." We are creatures of meaning. Until we make some appraisal of the meaning of something, we do not respond. It may be that we do this in less than a second at an unconscious level and at an animalistic level of our nervous system, but we do it nonetheless. We assign meaning to a "traumatic event" as it is happening. Most importantly, we appraise how dangerous it is. Kilpatrick et al. (1989) found that the likelihood of a person developing PTSD was 800 times greater if that person had the thought that they were going to either die or be seriously injured.

But it is not just the event itself. We assign meaning to the event after it has happened. How does this event fit in with the rest of our life? What is the lesson of this event? What does it bode for the future? We also assign meaning to how we responded to the event itself. We look at how we are responding to the postevent period. One common problematic appraisal is, "I should be doing better than I am. Something is wrong with me." We give meaning to how others respond to us. What does their response tell us about other people and ourselves? Of course, we have our conscious meaning making. We also have our unconscious meaning making. Do the traumatic event and its sequelae reinforce a dysfunctional belief? For instance, a survivor of incest gets raped; she now has further proof for the belief that she is bad and dirty. Does the traumatic incident blow away an unconscious belief in personal invulnerability (Janoff-Bulman, 1992), for instance, the consensual delusion that when it comes to driving no one is going to cross the double yellow line?

☐ Spirituality

As we go deeper into the appraisal and meaning a person gives to an event, sooner or later we get to the following question, "Where was God?" The answer to this question often has a huge impact on the eventual outcome of the experience. If a person feels or believes that God was with them and helping them during the event, he is likely to have a better adjustment. If the person believes or feels that God abandoned them or punished her, she is less likely to have a positive adjustment.

In the former case, the experience of feeling connected to God is a powerful resource that has an almost unlimited ability to calm and regulate affect. If that connection is maintained, it sends the person on a path of strengthening that spiritual bond. In the latter case, not only does the person not have the tremendous calming support from a spiritual connection; the person has the additional burden of feeling abandoned and/or punished. In all likelihood, a person who has this reaction already has that belief (although it may be unconscious). Such a person is highly vulnerable to a negative spiral. The person can react with anger toward God and himself. The fear associated with the trauma itself becomes part of a much larger scope of fear about being alone in a hostile universe.

The more serious the event is in terms of its consequences for people, the more likely it is that issues of spirituality will be activated. As clinicians, we tend not to see the cases where people adjust well to a traumatic event. So we do not see the people who have spiritual support. As I have begun to be more open to these matters, I have discovered that most of my patients with negative outcomes have significant spiritual issues with their relationship with God.

☐ Classical Conditioning

The creation of intrusive symptoms is partly based on classical conditioning. For instance, Anthony was mugged at a specific street corner. If he walks by that street corner, he becomes anxious. Anthony has become conditioned to associate the street corner with danger. As with many PTSD patients, the conditioning does not just stop there. There is a generalization gradient, so that when he even thinks about this street corner, he becomes anxious. The mental picture is conditioned. Anthony also would become anxious for no apparent reason at other times. It took a while to figure this out. It turned out that just before he was mugged, a bus was driving by. The sound of the bus became a conditioned stimulus not unlike the bell in Pavlov's experiment. When a bus drove by, Anthony would become anxious. His case is a good example of how variables interact. He did not realize the connection between the sound of the bus and his anxiety. Since he did not know why he became anxious, he would become very upset with himself. His anger increased and even began to spread into his relationship with his girlfriend. He did not tell her he was anxious. She just saw him become agitated and angry. Once we discovered what the connection was, Anthony instantly felt better (without treating the problem). He knew what his problem was. He knew he was "not some scared mouse who would be frightened of anything."

Survivors of sexual abuse, especially sadistic abuse, often have their sexuality conditioned. Patients find this symptom particularly shaming. In the more extreme cases, pain becomes sexually arousing because the child was repeatedly hurt and then aroused to orgasm.

☐ Respondent Conditioning

Anything that reduces anxiety is reinforced (Dollard & Miller, 1950). Much of the avoidance and numbing associated with PTSD fits into this paradigm. Furthermore, if patients try to face their fears, but leave the feared situation too soon, before their anxiety diminishes, they are inadvertently reinforcing their avoidance. In either case, the attempt to solve the problem actually leads to a more negative outcome. One of the dangers of exposing patients to traumatic memories is that they will not calm down sufficiently during that exposure. If the treatment ends without the patient being calm, the patient is likely to be retraumatized and to have their avoidance defenses reinforced.

The responses of family and friends to the patient often fall under the respondent conditioning paradigm. Allison was raped and wanted to be able to talk with her husband about it. However, every time she tried, he would become so upset and angry (at the rapist) that she could not continue to talk to him. She then began to feel less close to him. He sensed this and became more upset. They each perceived the other as getting upset when the topic of the rape came up. They each did not want that outcome to happen. So, they stopped talking about the rape. The anxiety was avoided. However, their intimacy suffered.

Family members and friends can also be conditioned. Tina had been abused as a child and had developed a coping strategy of being tough and angry. She also had developed a strategy of acting out sexually so that "she was the one in control." Both approaches were reinforcing with respect to keeping her vulnerability and pain out of her conscious mind. She was also being conditioned to feel worse and worse about herself. Everyone around her was being conditioned to stay away. Mary, on the other hand, would talk with people about her feelings about being raped. She would feel better after talking and people felt that they were helping. Everyone was being reinforced for talking and working through the problems.

☐ Biology and Energy

The important aspect of these two factors is that they involve bodily systems that directly affect the experience of the individual but are not easily influences by the conscious intentions of the person. Once either of these systems is changed, it tends to stay changed. This makes it more difficult for the person to gain control over his or her functioning.

There is a significant body of work that describes the biological changes that accompany trauma, especially longstanding trauma (van der Kolk, 1988; van der Kolk, Greenberg, Boyd, & Krystal, 1985; van der Kolk & Greenberg, 1987; van der Kolk & Saporta, 1993). Changes in brain activity and the neurochemistry associated with affective regulation can make it difficult for people to regulate their affect.

There is now a growing awareness that the biological system is not the only system of the body that is affected by trauma. The meridian system of ancient Chinese acupuncture appears to be an important aspect of mediating the affective regulation system. Traumatic experiences and their memories appear to leave a lasting impact on the energy system of the body. It is postulated that the disruptions in the meridians that occur when a person accesses the problematic memory is responsible for the negative symptoms. No matter how hard a person tries to think himself or herself out of the problem, he or she is not able to influence the energetic pattern that keeps the problem stuck. Just talk with anyone who is suffering from PTSD, and you will hear energetic descriptions of symptoms. People will readily endorse the fact that they can feel a different kind of energy when their symptoms are present. Newer energy therapies (e.g., thought field therapy, see chapter 6) that appear to rapidly reduce the symptoms of trauma lend constructive validity to these ideas.

☐ The Amplification Circuit

All of the aforementioned variables interact over time. There are two paths that the person can take. One path leads to an adaptive resolution, the other to a maladaptive resolution. The person has the possibility of ending up on either path. In some cases the person may vacillate between the two paths. As time passes, various interactions amplify each other so that the person moves more and more firmly onto one of the paths. As the circuit gains strength, it becomes more and more redundant. This redundancy means that even if one or several variables were to change, the overall circuit would remain the same. This explains the importance of early intervention. The sooner intervention occurs, the less likely it is that the circuit will have redundancies. Small changes early on can quickly move a person from a maladaptive path to an adaptive one.

It is most important to understand the quantum nature of the interaction of factors over time. The interaction of the above variables creates new realities. These realities then create other realities. In many ways traumatic memories are like physical pain. Physical pain has a special ability to capture attention, so the patient focuses on more and more pain. Chronic pain patients tend to stop doing activities, so they are left with a void in their life, and the awareness of pain fills that void. Vets and other trauma victims who are not filling their life with positive actions (work, love, and play) are highly vulnerable to traumatic symptoms capturing their attention, which of course makes it harder to fill your life with positive experiences.

The person suffering from PTSD cocreates certain realities that are often problematic. For instance, problems with agitation and anger make it hard to keep a job. This constrains and limits the development of more preferred ways of being, such as good feelings about success at work as well as having adequate amounts of income. These new realities further constrain healthy developments as time continues to move on. This might include continued failure at work and stress from money problems. This in turn may lead to increased dependence on drugs and/or violence in the family. After enough time passes, the person's original trauma is no longer the factor that is limiting the person's life. It is the maladaptive adjustments that have evolved over time that are limiting further development. Many Vietnam veterans are in this situation. Even if the individual is still having flashbacks about the war, the elimination of those flashbacks and/or the processing of what happened during the war 30 years ago may have little impact on the vet's current functioning.

I was consulting with a PTSD unit in a veterans' hospital. The standard treatment had included helping the vets talk about all of their experiences during Vietnam as a "walk through the war." The idea was that the vets were developmentally fixated because of unprocessed trauma during the war. While this formulation may have been accurate at one point, it seems dubious to me to assume that talking about something that happened 30 years ago would resolve the 30 years of poor choices, problems with employment and relationships, and so on. The new unit coordinator had instituted a number of changes including a heavy emphasis on coping skills for here-and-now problems such as anger management and relationship issues. As part of the consultation, I asked the patients on the unit what they thought had been most helpful. The answer was unequivocal. It was the coping skills they had learned. Many of the patients had been on the unit before, and they too noted that learning life skills was much more helpful than talking about the war. In fact the unit had two types of groups. One group focused on the walk through the war; the other group focused on solving current problems. The nurses on the unit reported that there was a clear difference in the amount of medication that was used after each group. The group focusing on the traumatic events required much more medication. This is one example of the maxim that I will describe in detail later, which is that it is often more important to focus on building resources and solutions than to try to resolve past traumas.

☐ Adaptive Resolutions

There are a number of adaptive resolutions to a traumatic event. The first is that the symptoms are relatively short lived and the individual has essentially no perceptible long-term consequences of the event. Memories of the event do not bring up significant amounts of emotional pain. A second type of adaptive resolution is that the individual copes well with any long-term consequences that exist. For instance many World

War II vets appear to live well-adjusted lives. However, they rarely talk about the war. If they do start to talk about it, it is clear that there is a great deal of pain still unresolved. There are many survivors of abuse and rape who have leftover emotional scars, but who continue to have fulfilled lives in terms of working, loving, and creativity. They may have to cope with anniversary reactions. They may limit their contact with the people who hurt them, and so on. But all in all, their lives are rich. The key to an adaptive resolution is that the person does not become defined by the trauma. His manner of being in the world is relatively uninfluenced by the trauma. The person does not organize his perception of the world and his beliefs based on the traumatic event. The person with the adaptive resolution finds a way to connect with his resources both internally and externally. The person who adapts well continues to enjoy life.

☐ Maladaptive Resolutions

The central point in a maladaptive resolution is that the person's life is largely influenced by the trauma. The beliefs of the individual and the perceptions of the individual are strongly colored by the trauma or the defensive reaction to the trauma. "In many people with PTSD, trauma-related conceptions of themselves and the world come to dominate their every day existence" (van der Kolk, McFarlane, & van der Hart, 1966, p. 432). Ironically, it is often the reactions to defend against the effects of the trauma that become the problem. The maladaptive resolution is based on disconnection—disconnection from pain, followed by disconnection from comfort, love, and people. Borrowing from Epstein (1990), I have categorized five different maladaptive resolutions (Peterson, Prout, & Schwarz, 1991).

Fear: In this scenario, the person is chronically fearful. She suffers from anxiety or panic. The world is seen as a dangerous place. People are scary and potential threats. The person sees herself as relatively weak and vulnerable. This individual is likely to have many obvious and not so obvious flashbacks and felt memories of the trauma. The archetype of this person is the woman who is scared of her own shadow. She will tend to be dependent and anxious.

Withdrawal: In its most pure form the person will be hermit-like. Contact with people and the world is limited. Underneath the withdrawal is fear. However, unlike the fear-based person, the withdrawal-based individual will be much more numb and aloof. Anxiety will not necessarily be felt consciously. The archetype of this would be the silent war veteran who does not talk much, nor share his feelings. He works and comes home. Perhaps he has a solitary hobby. He does not have a rich life with his family.

Anger: This person is angry at the injustice in the world. She might want revenge. She will tend to obsess on the traumatic event(s) and how it should have been different. This individual will often be agitated. This is a counterdependent stance. The person says I will never be vulnerable again. The archetype of this approach is a person with borderline personality disorder (PBD). In fact, it is more accurate to understand BPD as a person who has this long-term maladaptive adjustment form of trauma (see Herman & van der Kolk, 1987).

Dissociation: The archetype of this adjustment is the person with dissociative identity disorder (DID). The use of dissociation to manage affect becomes a way of life. Even if a person does not meet the criteria for DID, he may still have very different aspects of himself that will surface in given situations. Many people with this style of adaptation can lead highly successful professional lives. However, their personal lives are often in a shambles. People who use dissociative defenses will tend to oscillate between all of the maladaptive styles.

Embracing the Trauma: There are two main ways a person manifests this type of adjustment. In the movie *The Deer Hunter*, the character portrayed by John Voight was forced by his captors to play Russian roulette. Later in the movie, we discover that he does the very same thing as a free man, only now it is for money. Similarly, many prostitutes and people in the pornography industry were sexually abused. They now embrace similar aspects of the abuse, but now "they have the control." Most people who become abusers were themselves abused. In this adjustment, the person literally identifies with the aggressor.

Each adjustment is rarely so clearly demarcated. For instance, many people who do embrace the trauma also use dissociative mechanisms. Such a person dissociates from the vulnerable victim role and associates into the invulnerable perpetrator role. Many angry people also withdraw. Many withdrawn people are also aware of their fear. Tremendous fear and pain underlie all of these adjustments, whether the person is consciously aware of them or not.

A thorough understanding of the dynamic process that transforms a traumatic event that happens to a person into a PTSD that can cripple a person for life helps us to recognize that there can be multiple entry points for therapeutic measures. Any change in this dynamic system has the potential to create a significant difference in the final outcome. It is also rather obvious that early intervention would be one of the most efficacious methods of preventing the development of full-blown PTSD (Schwarz & Prout, 1991).

☐ Basic Approaches to Treatment: The Consensus View

Since the beginning of the formal inclusion of PTSD as a diagnostic entity in the DSM-III (APA, 1980) there has been an explosion of research and writing about the theory of trauma (Courtois, 1988; Danieli, 1985; Figley, 1985; Herman, 1992; Horowitz, 1986; Janoff-Bulman, 1992; McCann & Pearlman, 1990; Terr, 1994; Wilson, 1994), the assessment of trauma (Briere, 1992; Horowitz, 1986; Litz & Weathers, 1994; Scurfield, 1985; Wilson & Keane, 1997), and the treatment of trauma (Briere, 1992; Courtois, 1988; Dolan, 1991; Herman, 1992; Kluft, 1984, 1994; Ochberg, 1988; Peterson, Prout, & Schwarz, 1991; Putnam, 1989; Ross, 1989, 1995; Schwarz & Prout, 1991; van der Kolk, McFarlane, & van der Hart, 1996). Different approaches may emphasize different aspects of treatment. Nevertheless, over the last 10 years, a common pathway has become the accepted norm for the treatment of trauma

In 1991, Peterson, Prout, and Schwarz categorized 10 major different schools of thought about the nature and treatment of PTSD. Using an integrative approach, Wilson (1994) pointed out that each of these theories implicitly or explicitly focuses on how trauma impacts the person in the following five dimensions: (a) changes in psychobiology, (b) changes in learned behavior, (c) changes in cognitive processing, (d) changes in self structure and object relations, and (e) changes in interpersonal relations. Van der Kolk and McFarlane (1996) echoed these same dimensions and added the dimension of problems with affect regulation.

Schwarz and Prout (1991) looked at six major treatment approaches: psychodynamic, family therapy, hypnosis, flooding, stress inoculation training, and systematic desensitization. Five common treatment patterns were observed across approaches. These were:

- decreasing avoidance (of affect, knowledge behavior, and interactions with others),
- ego support (including reducing aversive symptoms),
- decreasing perceived helplessness and providing resources to cope with traumatic memories,
- normalizing the abnormal (usually with education),
- altering negative or limiting attributions of meaning, and
- facilitating integration of the self, including connections with others.

In their general approach to trauma treatment, van der Kolk, McFarlane, and van der Onno (1996) used somewhat different language but describe a similar list of important variables:

- education to help patients understand what is happening to them,
- identification of feelings through talking,
- decreasing of avoidance through dissociation of memory,
- restructuring trauma-related cognitive schemes,
- re-establishment of social connections, and
- accumulation of positive emotional experiences (i.e., stop avoiding the world and live a decent life).

At the beginning of the 21st century a central tenet of trauma treatment is the concept of treatment coming in phases (Bloom, 1997; Herman, 1992; Horowitz, 1986; Phillips & Frederick, 1995; van der Kolk, McFarlane, & van der Hart, 1996). The consensus view is that trauma treatment has three main phases. Phase 1 involves stabilization, building safety, and appropriate ego support. Phase 2 focuses on working through traumatic memories and experiences as well as the associated disturbances in cognition and social relationships and work life. It also involves helping patients focus on building positive life-affirming experiences rather than focusing on past trauma or the avoidance of dealing with life. In describing their Ericksonian and hypnotic work with dissociative patients, Phillips and Frederick (1995) use a four-step model, where Phase 2 of other models is broken into two parts. Nevertheless, we can see a great deal of agreement across authors for the different meanings. Phase 3 deals with helping the patient integrate the changes of the first two phases into his or her ongoing life, including family and friends. It also focuses on increasing positive experiences. In Figure 1.2, several models are depicted across the phases of treatment.

The emphasis on making sure that in the first part of treatment patients are stable and sufficiently safe and comfortable has been, in part, an outgrowth of learning from mistakes that were made previously. All too often, far too much emphasis was placed on the patient working on the traumatic memories without sufficient resources in place in order to cope with the intense affect. The result was that it was impossible to detoxify the traumatic material. Patients often were retraumatized by the therapy. Sometimes they would decompensate. Problems in treatment are often linked to faulty assumptions about whether or not sufficient safety and stabilization are in place in a patient's current life context or the current therapy context. If treatment is not going well, it is a good rule of thumb to reasses the stage a patient is in (with particular attention to safety). The concomitant rule of thumb is to assume that one needs to go back to safety and stabilization if there is doubt about what is going on.

The importance of adding the third stage of integrating the material into an ongoing life as well as building a life was based on the fact that

	Phase 1	Phase 2	Phase 3
Herman (1992)	Developing safety	Reconstruction of memories	Reintegration of social connections
Schwarz and Prout (1991)	Ego support (including reducing aversive symptoms Normalizing the abnormal (usually with education),	Decreasing avoidance (of affect, knowledge behavior) Decreasing perceived helplessness and providing resources to cope with traumatic memories), Altering negative or limiting attributions of meaning, and	Decreasing avoidance (interactions with others) Facilitating integration of the self Facilitating connections with others
van der Kolk, McFarlane, and van der Hart (1996)	Education to help patients understand what is happening to them, Identification of feelings through talking,	Identification of feelings through talking, Decreasing of avoidance through dissociation of memory, Restructuring-trauma related cognitive schemes.	Re-establishment of social connections and Accumulation of positive emotional experiences (i.e., stop avoiding the world and live a decent life)
Bloom (1997)	Developing the boundaries of a therapeutic milieu for biological, psychological, social, and moral safety	Reconstruction of memories. The use of inpatient setting to provide structure, diagnose and counteract trauma reenactment within the milieu.	Reconnection through community spirit. The importance of play and lightheartedness
Phillips and Frederick (1995)	Develop safety & stabilization	Stage II: Access trauma material by alternating uncovering sessions with ego strengthening sessions. Stage III: Resolving traumatic material Continued working through, processing and connecting dissociated BASK of memories to ongoing awareness	Stage IV: Integration and new identity Integration of personality Integration of identity and future visions of the self.

Figure 1.2. Phase oriented approaches to treating PTSD.

working with the past is not enough. In many cases the client's traumas were many years past. The biggest part of the client's ongoing clinical problems was how he or she did not cope with current life issues (see the discussion on Vietnam vets in chapter 7).

At the end of each section of this book I will discuss how each tool can be used in the different stages of treatment. While I have no disagreement with a phase-oriented model, I want to emphasize several points that may not be obvious.

The first is that the notion of stages should be considered a general approximation of the territory of trauma recovery. It is not etched in granite. Second, even if we assume that there are stages of treatment, it does not tell us a great deal about the length of those stages and how quickly a given patient will move through those stages. In some cases of acute trauma, a patient can move through the three stages in one or two sessions. In some cases of chronic childhood abuse, a person may take years to move through the stages. Kluft (1994) has suggested that DID patients recover in one of three trajectories from low to middle to high, the former being the slowest transitions through the phases and the latter being the quickest. Third, the movement through stages is often nonlinear. In many cases patients are in more than one stage at a time. Patients can also move forward and regress back through stages based on the issues with which they are working.

Finally, it can be useful to think of the concept of stages as being on both macro and micro levels. The macro level refers to the overall treatment timeline. Micro levels can refer to a given session hour or the flow of a given intervention. In delivering an intervention the first step is to help the client feel safe to accept and participate in the intervention, and the second step is the intervention itself, followed by linking the outcome of the intervention to the client's social network. Zeig (1985) described how Erickson would seed an intervention, deliver the intervention itself, and follow through on the intervention. The acronym SIFT (setup, intervene, follow-through) is useful to remember. Successful application of the three stages in microcosm tends to build safety, trust, and ease of movement at the macro level, whereas violations of the SIFT protocol tend to decrease overall safety and trust.

2

CHAPTER

A Neo-Ericksonian Framework for Treating Trauma

Perhaps the biggest misunderstanding about trauma is the emphasis on the direct damage or injury caused by traumatic events. The more important impact on life is caused by trauma's ability to disconnect a person from his or her resourceful states of being. (The same principle applies for families, nations, and the planet as a whole.)

The tools described in this book come from a number of different schools of therapy. The schools include Ericksonian hypnosis, solution-oriented therapy, neurolinguistic programming (NLP), energy psychology, and narrative therapy. In addition, the work is informed by many of the basic principles that apply to psychotherapy in general and to the therapy of trauma.

There are five principles or presuppositions about the nature of human experience and the nature of therapeutic interactions by which a patient's trauma is transformed. Each of the schools embraces some, if not all, of these principles, though each may emphasize one over another. Or, each school may have its own interpretation of a given principle. By understanding the principles, the therapist can have an eclectic "toolbag" while remaining centered on basic principles.

Principle 1: Social reality is constructed. There are few absolute truths. Any given knowledge base is contextualized by the culture and language from which it springs. This applies to patients, therapists, and the schools of thought about therapy. The implication of this principle is that it allows us to take useful tools from different schools of thought and eclectically reorganize them according to our use of principles. There is nothing inherently "true" about any given school of thought, including the words on these pages. The key is to do what works.

Principle 2: Psychological experience is constructed and maintained in an ongoing, moment-to-moment manner. Energy is used to maintain or change a given psychological moment of experience. There are a multitude of variables that interweave to form the fabric of experience. These include the influence of biology, narrative memory, implicit memory, family systems, community systems, cultural systems, language, expectations about the future, attentional filters, and focuses, identity stories, and the phenomenological coding of experience.

Principle 3: Psychotherapy is based on changing at least one of the variables of constructed experience so that "felt experience" changes. The emphasis on what to change and how to change it is usually the thing that separates different schools of thought. Since the goal is changing "felt" experience, any specific school of thought does not limit us. We choose our interventions by making decisions about which variable will most likely help the patient's "felt experience" to change in the direction the patient desires.

Principle 4: At the very least, patients should be treated with respect and dignity. Patients should be viewed as greater than their given problem (even if they do not believe this). In other words, the therapist should provide hope for an expanded range of possibilities in one form or another. This principle might seem absurdly self-evident. Nevertheless, it is so important that it should be made explicit.

Principle 5: It is the therapist's job to be (a) as flexible as possible in identifying the variables that keep a patient locked into a problematic experience; (b) skilled in using tools that impact on those variables; (c) skilled at tracking the effects of their interventions while (d) remembering to treat patients in a respectful, dignifying manner; (e) hopeful that solutions and positive outcomes can be constructed for people who are suffering; and (f) humble about the "truths" of their own hypotheses and ideas about the people with whom they work. Erickson did not articulate a theory of therapy, which has forced people to create different theories to support the techniques Erickson described. Along the way, new techniques and approaches have arisen that can be traced to Erickson's work. This book is written with the goal of integrating the ideas of a number of different schools of therapy that can be described as neo-Ericksonian. It is not my intention to create a new school of thought based on this integration. It would be more accurate to say that I wish to clarify a more generalized way of thinking. While I do want to maintain the flexibility of technical eclecticism, I think it is important that therapists have some theoretical understandings that orient their attention, thinking, and decision making. These can be found in the different schools of thought from which this work is derived.

The orientations that inform this work include a resource-based therapy orientation, a future orientation, a solution orientation, a systems orientation, a states of consciousness (SoCs) model of experience and an hypnotic orientation. It is my goal in this chapter to show how these orientations are connected to each other in a consistent manner. It is my hope that underscoring the consistencies will act as a guide to orient the clinician through the myriad of choices that he or she must make.

☐ Resource-Based Therapy Orientation

One of the linking threads between all of the approaches described throughout this book is the overriding emphasis on describing, emphasizing, eliciting, and building the resources of individual patients as well as the systems in which they live. Solution-oriented language emphasizes the importance of exceptions to problems and solutions (de Shazer, 1985, 1988; Dolan, 1991,1998; O'Hanlon & Weiner-Davis, 1987); Ericksonian and NLP language emphasizes "eliciting and building resources" (Dilts, 1990; Erickson, 1980; Lankton, 1985; Lankton & Lankton, 1983; 1987); narrative language (Epston, 1988; White & Epston, 1990) refers to "unique outcomes" and "overcoming the influence of problems"

It is not that problems, pain, and pathology (the three Ps) are denied (which would be either/or thinking). It is that the three Ps are always seen in context with resources. However, if given a forced choice between attempting to reduce the three Ps or attempting to increase resources (which luckily is rarely the case), the default setting is to choose increasing resources rather than decreasing trauma. I often refer to this as the "numerator principle." Resources are considered the numerator and pathology the denominator of a fraction. And we have a person who is really suffering, so that the fraction equals 1/100. If you were allowed to increase or decrease a number 1 point, which would you choose? The only realistic choice is to increase the numerator by 1, thereby cutting suffering by 50%. This fictitious ratio suggests what trauma therapists have learned. It is only worthwhile to start dealing with the trauma or pathology when the patient already has many resources, in other words, once safety and coping skills have been established. Mathematically speaking, if one limited to only adjusting one point, which clinically corresponds to a situation in which there is a lot of difficulty in creating a change, it never pays to touch the denominator until the ratio of trauma to resources is at least in even balance.[1] (See the discussion about the VA and coping skills on page 14.) This principal has significant implications for working with abuse and PTSD in the era of managed care.

☐ Solution and Mastery Orientations as Resources

Despite the myth that hypnosis means losing control, psychotherapy utilizing hypnosis usually involves the injunction to have more mastery over one's own experience. The same is true with NLP, solution-oriented therapy, and narrative therapy. These therapies are active and involve the direct or indirect alteration of perception, sensation, and meaning. Patients can be asked to make mental images and then alter the images or their sensations. Patients are asked to consider questions that they have rarely considered. Patients learn that they can change their understanding of something or their responses to a situation that previously was unchangeable. They actually learn to regain control of their own functioning.

Perhaps the most important resource for any person with any problem is a well-formed description of the solution to the problem. As we will see in a moment, a well-formed description of the solution is the "royal road to health." It is not the easiest thing to achieve. Before one can arrive at a well-formed description of a solution, there are several more basic resources that are needed. First, a person needs to be open to believing that a solution is possible at all. Second, a person needs to be open to the possibility that they could know what the solution might look like. Third, the person needs to be open to the possibility that he or she deserves to achieve and is capable of achieving the solution once it is described.

☐ Well-Formed Outcomes

An intrinsic part of both future and resource-based approaches is having a good idea of the outcomes one wants to achieve in the future. The description of an outcome is considered well formed when it has certain characteristics. These characteristics make it easier for someone to get

---

[1]Compare the following ratio transformations: 1/10 becomes either 1/5 or 1/9. 1/4 can become either 1/2 or 1/3. In fact the only time it makes sense to work on trauma is when the ratio of trauma to resources is equal to or in favor of resources. 2/2 becomes either 3/2 or 2/1.

from where they are to the desired outcome. There are several variations of the characteristics: Dilts (1980) described the NLP version of the rules as follows.

1. *The outcome must be stated in positive terms.* In other words, well-formed outcomes cannot be described as the cessation or decrease of something (e.g., "less depressed" or "no more flashbacks"). Instead of "getting rid of flashbacks," the outcome could be remembering what happened as a distant memory while remaining calm.

   A solution-oriented version of this criterion would emphasize that: (a) *The goal should be small.* This allows for an increased chance of building a string of small successes. The behaviorists call this shaping behavior. (b) *The goal should be seen as the beginning of something rather than the end of something.* It allows the therapist and the patient to focus on the beginning of the solution occurring. A question to ask is, "What would be the very first things that would let you know that you are on your way to getting to the solution?"

   There are several hypnotic qualities to this question. First, the ending of something connotes stopping. The ending of X does not necessarily lead to the beginning of Y. However, the beginning of Y does connote getting to the full elaboration of Y. Second, a good testable sensory description of the full elaboration of the outcome may be out of reach for a patient. But a testable sensory experience of the very first thing a patient would notice on the way to the outcome may be in reach. Third, once the patient gets to the first step, it will be easier to describe the testable sensory aspects of steps 2 and 3 and so on.

2. *The outcome must be testable in sensory experience.* In other words, the outcome must be described in specific detail that one could see or hear or feel it. O'Hanlon used the idea of "video talk." The patient is asked the question, "If we made a video of this outcome, what would we see and hear on the video?" In addition, sensory experience can include internal auditory dialogue, internal visual pictures, and kinesthetic feelings. The therapist can ask, "What would need to be different for you to remember what happened as a distant memory? What would let you know that you were calm?" The patient might eventually say, "I would see it as a picture far away from my body. I would not be in the experience or see it happening all around me as if it was happening right now. I would be breathing comfortably and my muscles would be relaxed. I would hear myself say that this happened 10 years ago."

   It is crucial to understand that the very act of describing an outcome in such detail increases the representation in the brain of the outcome, thereby significantly increasing the probability of it actually happening. The elicitation of a positive and testable goal can take considerable time and effort but is always worth it. In fact, most books or theories of personal leadership (Covey, 1990) suggest that having a clear, detailed image of one's goal is an essential aspect of excelling.

3. *The outcome must be contextualized.* The criterion deals with the issue that a specific state of mind is not likely to be useful in all situations. Furthermore, patients often need to recognize that they are in a different context with different resources available, so that different outcomes are possible (see Dolan, 1991). For instance, remembering the fact that a certain person raped you and remaining calm might not be appropriate if that person were walking toward you on a dark street. One might want a different emotion, such as fear, in order to motivate running away. Many abuse patients need to be able to access and express anger. However, the time and place of this expression should be contextualized to an appropriate place and time. In addition, the type of expression should also be tied to the situational context.

4. *The desired outcome must be initiated and maintained by the patient.* The most common violation of this rule in general therapy is complaining about other people, for instance, "I want my wife to be more affectionate." The therapist would need to help the person describe what they do that leads to their wife being more affectionate. Dilts (1980) pointed out that this criterion is designed to help return the locus of control to the patient, which is particularly relevant to trauma patients who have had things happen to them. There is one final criterion for a well-formed outcome.

5. *The desired outcome must be ecologically sound.* When change occurs in the targeted aspect of a patient's life, there are likely to be consequences in other aspects of a patient's life. A desired outcome is ecologically sound when the consequences are not perceived to be unduly negative. In the area of domestic violence, the consequences of a woman becoming more assertive may be an increased level of violence from her partner. The consequence of a dissociative patient becoming aware of traumatic material too soon can be an overwhelming degree of affect, leading to an increase in self-harm. These negative consequences would make these otherwise positive goals not well formed. Negative or positive consequences can be intrapersonal or interpersonal. If a patient truly accepts the degree of abusiveness of her family, the intrapersonal consequence can be the loss of the hope for things to change. The interpersonal consequence may be the recognition of the need to sever ties, followed by angry or demanding responses from the family. For most patients losing hope would be

unacceptable. Many patients would also find severing family ties unacceptable. These violations of the well-formedness conditions would undermine motivation and movement toward these goals.

Ecological soundness is the criterion that is involved in a large number of so-called "resistant" or "difficult" problems. If a company wants to build a factory, there may be a variety of different effects on the ecology of the surrounding habit, including plants, animals, people, property values, and so on. There may be a vociferous objection to the factory being built. There are only two ways to healthfully resolve the conflict and build the factory. One is to provide sufficient information to change the perception of the people objecting. The other is to acknowledge that the ecological impact is real or probable and to provide an alternative that meets the needs of the people objecting. The same is true in psychotherapy. The problem that occurs is that the therapist may not recognize the existence of the objection or appreciate its importance to the patient. Of course, in many cases the patient also does not consciously recognize these issues. Self-harm is an excellent example.

Symptoms of self-harm often serve multiple functions (Calof, 1995). Therefore, there will often be multiple objections as to the ecological soundness of letting go of the symptom. One such objection might be that the relinquishing of self-harm strategies may lead to the loss of coping strategies to reduce aversive affect (Briere, 1992). The job of the therapy is often to work though and respond to all of the objections so that this last criterion is met. Once this happens, the "resistant" problem resolves.

☐ The Relationship Between Solutions and Problems

I think it is important to state that believing in solutions and making efforts to describe the details of those solutions are acts that are important for therapists as well as patients. Furthermore, assuming that therapists believe in the possibility of solutions, they need to recognize that their theoretical descriptions of the relationship between problems and solutions will affect their understandings of what needs to happen in therapy.

The brief therapy of a Mental Research Institute (MRI) approach (Watzlawick, Weakland, & Fisch, 1974) emphasized that problems have reached the status of a clinical problem that merited therapy as a function of an interactive pattern where the attempted solution actually kept the problem going. Therefore, this approach advocated that the way to get to a solution was to find the stuck pattern and interrupt it. Pattern interruption approaches have been a mainstay of a variety of Ericksonian and strategic therapists.

A number of authors (de Shazer, 1985, 1988; Dolan, 1991; O'Hanlon & Weiner-Davis, 1987) maintained that the description of a solution to a problem does not need to have anything to do with a description of the etiology of the problem or even the reason why a problem continues (e.g., homeostatic function). Furthermore, the position would state that even if the solution to the problem does have something to do with the etiology, it is not particularly helpful to focus attention, time, and effort on that connection. It would be far more useful to focus just on building the solution. The goal of the therapy is to orient the patient and the therapist toward a picture or verbal description of what it would be like to have the solution. The very act of cocreating that solution in the future increases the probability that the solution will become manifest. The "numerator principle" mentioned earlier flows from this perspective. It does not necessarily matter why the ratio of resources to trauma is in favor of trauma. It is crucial to begin to increase the number of resources or solutions any way one can. It is not essential to consider the strategic and solution-oriented approaches mutually exclusive (Quick, 1995). It is helpful to understand that the theories suggest different relationships between problems and solutions.

☐ Building Maps to the Future

More classical therapies orient to the past. The question to be answered is, "What was the cause of the problem?" Considerable effort is spent to describe in detail what the past was like. The progressive approaches in this book (NLP, Ericksonian, and solution oriented) share a strong future orientation. The questions to be answered are, "What would the solution to this problem look like, sound like, and feel like? What would be the steps to get to a more resourceful future?" Therapists have certain ideas about how one overcomes trauma. Also, patients might have certain ideas about what they will be like once they overcome the trauma.

One of the problems that patients have is that they do not pay attention to their own ideas about what a solution might look like and sound like; they may not even think it is possible. This is usually called a lack of hope. One of the jobs of the therapist from this progressive frame is to help patients regain hope by becoming aware of their own nascent descriptions of a positive future and the methods to get there. A second job is to help support patients on their path toward the future.

What is known about how people heal from trauma? Interestingly enough, there is almost no research that can answer the question. Clinically and theoretically, most persons who overcome traumatic situations and return to a well-functioning life describe some or all of the following aspects of recovery:

1. Regain access to resources and apply them to appropriate contexts. They regain access to good feelings, relatively positive belief systems, and good self-images. These are applied to and maintained by supportive relationships to other people, satisfying life tasks, and so on.
2. Maintain appropriate boundaries.
3. Honor and value previously dissociated parts of the self and (a) associate back into devalued and dissociated parts with resources, and (b) do and be in the present in manners that value and honor all parts.
4. Learn to place the trauma in a larger context so that they can (a) dissociate from the abused self and associate into a larger self, (b) shift attention from past to present and future, and (c) learn from the trauma.

Therapeutic intervention should be geared toward these ends. Therapists should not dictate in an authoritarian manner that these are the exact goals toward which the patient should be working. Nevertheless, therapists can resemble navigators of a sailboat and keep directing patients toward these or similar goals. Of course, sometimes, if the desired goal requires heading right into the wind, it will be necessary to "tack" (to move at an angle to the wind away from the direct route, and then later make a course correction).

Schwarz and Dolan (1995) conducted an unpublished pilot study to begin to get answers to this question. Twenty survivors of sexual abuse who considered themselves far along in the healing process were asked solution-oriented questions about their recovery. Below are some of the questions:

- What limiting beliefs that were formed as a result of the abuse have you overcome? How have you done that?
- What do you do to nurture yourself [that you believe diminishes the effects of the abuse]?
- What do you do [day to day] that maintains or amplifies your healing?
- Most people have ways of motivating themselves to get over problems or do difficult or new things. They often use images, or talk to themselves, or imagine the voices or presence of significant others. What do you do?
- Many survivors have experienced problems with trust. What aspects of trust have you recovered? How did you do this?

- If someone you truly cared about were abused and you could give them three lessons that you have learned, what would they be?
- What do you do to let others help/know you?
- What activities are important in your life now?
- If we assume that everyone has a reason to be on the planet, what would you say is your reason to be on the planet?
- Has there been a particular creative, personal, or professional goal that has been helpful in deemphasizing the abuse and overcoming the effects of the abuse?
- How would you describe your identity? Who are you today?
- What would significant others say that you have done or are doing that has diminished the negative effects of the abuse?
- Many people have the experience, "If only I knew then what I know now." What do you know now that has been helpful to you in your healing? How have you come to know this?

There were 18 women and 2 men in the study. As a group they had undergone a great deal of abuse as children, including multiple perpetrators with substantial amounts of violence and sadism present in the sample. The average level of self-reported recovery on a scale of 0–10, where 10 was completely recovered, was 8.5. No one rated themselves a 10.

While part of the intent of this study was to get narrative data about people's experiences, a number of interesting patterns began to emerge. The first finding was that the subjects reported a large quantitative drop in symptoms. Twenty-eight different symptoms were assessed. The average degree of improvement from the lowest point to the current point of symptoms ranged from 200% to 350% improved ($P < .001$). A second finding was that not a single person, when asked, "How would you describe your identity? Who are you today?" made a reference to being a sexual abuse survivor. We see this finding as an important clue about the direction treatment should take. A third finding also has implications for treatment and recovery. We asked a series of questions about how the subject actively overcame the effects of abuse. These questions included, "What do you do to nurture yourself that you believe diminishes the effects of the abuse?" or "What do you do day to day that maintains or amplifies your healing?" When the answers to these questions were taken as a group, a pattern emerged. The solution to horrific abuse was to increase the positives in one's life to such an extent that the abuse did not have much of an effect. It was as if everyone figured out that they could create an ocean of resources and positive life events that could dissipate the toxicity of the abuse. It is of interest to note that to a person, there was a sense of personal agency regarding taking direction and control in one's life toward positive and meaningful experiences. To a person, references were made to taking care of their bodies through some form of exercise or physical activity. This is striking in that it suggests that these individuals have revalued their bodies. Almost everyone made references to taking time to connect with nature as a source of feeling connected to something larger than oneself.

We took these findings as evidence that supports our solution-oriented view of recovery. Of course, the hardcore scientist would have problems with this study from a number of perspectives. A casual look at the questions we asked reveals that they point a person toward a certain domain of answers. Therefore, one might criticize the study by saying that there is a demand characteristic (Orne, 1969) to answer in the direction of solutions. The reply to this is, "Yes! You are absolutely right. Thank you." We were specifically pointing people to think about what they have done to solve their problems. We wanted to elevate and privilege those types of narratives. The questions were fairly open-ended toward solutions in general. It is fascinating that common threads did develop. The concept that one can be "an objective observer of the truth" is itself a highly biased frame of reference. As therapists and healers, we ought to elevate patients' sense of personal agency in their lives. We ought to privilege a patient's solutions, resources, and positive stories.

☐ A States of Consciousness Model of Trance and Trauma

Lankton (1985) described a States of Consciousness (SoCs) model of hypnosis that is particularly well suited to understanding the treatment of PTSD from a hypnotic perspective. A SoC is considered to be a "unique, dynamic pattern or configuration of psychological structures, an active system of psychological subsystems" (Tart, 1975 p. 5). It can be helpful to think of a SoC as a molecule consisting of various atomic substructures. These substructures can include feeling states, patterns of attention, degree of sympathetic and parasympathetic arousal, quality of internal dialogue and mental images, memories, and so on.

During everyday life people use different SoCs to adapt to varied roles and situations.[2] "Various SoCs contain discrete as well as overlapping sets of resources and limitations. The use or misuse of these sets determines the utility or liability of any particular SoC" (Lankton, 1985, p. 28). For instance, a child may have learned to use a set of SoCs that

---

[2]The concept of discrete SOCs appears in a variety of therapy models including transactional analysis (Berne, 1977) and ego state therapy (Watkins & Watkins, 1997).

include alterations in sensation, changes in perceptual orientation, and hallucinated visual images in order to escape from the experience of trauma. The child may call this "going into the rabbit hole" or some such name. (This is often called dissociation.) This SoC may have been useful during the abuse, but becomes highly problematic in everyday life as an adult. A more common example was depicted in a movie with Clint Eastwood. He was a rough, tough drill sergeant for the Marines. His SoC for being a drill sergeant was excellent for solving the problems associated with training Marines. Unfortunately, he would try to use this SoC to solve the problems associated with maintaining closeness to his wife. Needless to say, this did not work well.

We have been discussing SoCs as a single entity, such as the SoC that Clint Eastwood's character used. It is more accurate to state that he used a combination or chain of SoCs to solve his problem. The shifting and combining or recombining of SoCs is rule governed. In other words, some mental states are strongly connected, while others are weakly connected or not connected at all. For instance, a victim's visual memory of the trauma may easily lead to fear or sadness, rather than feelings of security. The person certainly has SoCs that contain security, but they are usually not readily accessible from the SoC that contains the visual memory of the trauma.

From an Ericksonian point of view, the goal is often to create a new association between that resource and the trauma, even if it is not "natural" or usual for one to exist. According to Erickson (1980b), recovery or cure takes place as a function of a re-association and reorganization of the patient's inner experiences, learnings, and associations. In other words, therapy changes the rules of recombination either within a SoC or between SoCs.[3]

A specific symptom state can be made up of a variety of atomic components such as negative internal dialogue, hyperactivity in the sympathetic nervous system, mental pictures with both negative content and structural properties that act as cues for danger, and internal feeling of powerlessness. Therapy involves changing some or all of these components. Just as in chemistry, altering a molecule changes its properties. The "trick" to efficient therapy is to know which components relate to the biggest change in the patient's state. For example, Dolan (1991) suggested creating a symbol of comfort by helping the patient elicit a resourceful SoC and then linking it up to a physical object. By looking at or holding this symbol the patient can feel comfort while dealing with painful or difficult memories or feelings (SoCs).

Finally, one must keep in mind that both problems SoCs and solution

---

[3]This within-SoC and between-SoCs distinction is not unlike the difference between intrapersonal and interpersonal variables.

SoCs evolve over time. Among the variables in a SoC that make a big difference as to whether a problem or a solution develops is the locus of attention. The shifting of attentional patterns from problem to solution is one of solution-oriented therapy's greatest contributions to changing the pattern of SoCs in general.

The idea that rules govern the recombining and shifting of experience within and between SoCs supports Shor's (1959) ideas about consciousness and trance. Shor postulated that each person has a generalized reality orientation (GRO) that is a network of associations, memories, and learning that supports, interprets, and gives meaning to all experiences. In other words, the GRO is the set of rules that govern how we organize our various SoCs. They let each of us experience a "normal" or familiar reality. Trance occurs when the rules of GRO either have been rendered nonoperational or have been significantly altered in some manner. A traumatic experience significant enough to meet Criteria A of the DSM-IV (APA, 1994) for PTSD is quite likely to be beyond the flexibility of the GRO; thereby rendering it at least partially nonoperational. As a result, the person's consciousness becomes altered. Hypnosis is present when the GRO is rendered at least partially nonoperational and there is the construction of a special temporary orientation to a limited range of experience (Shor, 1959). To put it simply, in hypnosis, normal reality is suspended and a new special reality becomes operational. In trauma situations, the new reality in operation is usually one of danger, lack of personal resources, and uncontrollability. Perhaps this is one of the reasons why the perceived threat of significant harm increases the chance of the development of PTSD by 800% (Kilpatrick et al., 1989).

State-Dependent Aspects of Trauma

Erickson (1980b) viewed trance as a particular psychological state that made it easier to reassociate and reorganize one's inner experience. While these facets make it useful for therapy, the knife alas cuts both ways. Trauma by its very nature breaks the GRO and therefore induces a trance. The same psychological mechanisms that make it easier to reassociate and reorganize SoCs toward flexibility and resourcefulness can also produce highly limiting and rigid SoCs that become dysfunctional. During a traumatic event, not only is the person overwhelmed by the stimuli, he or she is in a nonresourceful state and is susceptible to ideas and suggestions (helpful or nonhelpful) from others as well as him- or herself. In other words, an abuser may directly or indirectly tell the person that he or she is no good. An accident victim may believe that he or she is no good, because he or she should have been stronger.

Rossi and Cheek (1988) stated that the individual's reactions to the trauma become state dependent. In the language of this chapter, the physiological reactions, emotions, thoughts, meanings, and so on become linked together in a traumatic SoC. Even though this SoC may be partially or completely dissociated (and therefore partially or completely out of awareness), it can influence the individual in dramatic ways, not unlike a powerful posthypnotic suggestion.

Systemic View of Trauma and States of Consciousness

The importance of taking a systemic view of understanding trauma has been discussed by a variety of authors (Green, Wilson, & Lindy, 1985; Peterson, Prout, & Schwarz, 1991; Trepper & Barret, 1989; Wilson, 1994). One must always take a systemic view when working with people. Even if you are working with just an individual, it is a good idea to keep the family and the social context in mind. Lapses in application of this principle are one of the variables that have fueled the false memory debate. The net outcome of a trauma is determined by many more variables than just the intensity or duration of the trauma.

The term *states of consciousness* sounds like it refers to something inside the person. In addition, the metaphor of atoms and molecules also suggests a structuralist view. Nevertheless, it is of absolute importance that we remember that the intrapsychic aspects of a person's SoCs cannot be separated from the social and interpersonal contexts in which a person lives. As we will see later on, the therapist can focus certain interventions on the "structures of association" in a given patient's problematic SoC as a means to interrupt one source of stuckness in the social construction of the patient's problems. This does not mean that the therapist loses sight of the other socially constructed variables.

Lankton's model stresses that SoCs are partially induced, maintained, and systemically reinforced by the social stimuli. Not only do family members, friends, and social networks elicit and support certain responses and SoCs from a traumatized individual, but different types of responses made by the traumatized individual will elicit different responses and SoCs of the environment. For instance, a crying patient who tells people about the intrusive traumatic memories that are occurring tends to elicit different types of behaviors and SoCs from family members than a person who is yelling, angry, and avoids telling anyone what is happening. It is also important to recognize that these influences occur over time in many different interactions. Returning to Figure 1.1, all points are somehow interactive with the other points. So, for instance, the social support system's response will be put on some type of reinforcement schedule partially determined by the cognitive appraisals of the patient. These appraisals may be highly colored by past transactions, especially in highly disturbed families. While considering this may be daunting for the therapist and the patient, it allows the therapy to look at any point of the system from any other point.

For example, a patient told one of her best friends that she had been in a satanic cult. The friend responded by becoming upset and somewhat less available. The patient then concluded that this meant that the friend had abandoned her, and she stopped calling her friend. This contributed to the patient destabilizing. Luckily the friend rebounded and challenged the patient about how the patient had unfairly judged her. This then became a focus of the individual therapy. The question put to the patient was to have the patient look at how her actions influenced her friend and how her friend's actions influence the patient. In addition, the patient was asked to look at how the patient's meaning-making activities influences her choice of actions. She was also asked to assess how this particular interaction was a sample of a broader way of coping with people, including the therapist.

The issues of transference and countertransference in working with severely traumatized individuals can be viewed as special cases of SoCs that interact through the therapeutic system. Transference is a set of SoCs that color and distort a patient's view of himself or herself as well as his or her relationship with others based on old SoCs. These SoCs exert a real influence on other people. They effectively act as hypnotic inductions. The power of these SoCs is evident by their ability to elicit affective and behavioral responses in others that reinforce the underlying structure of the SoC. If the therapist is fully inducted, the problem is that the SoC to which the therapist will be inducted will (a) not be resourceful, (b) complement and reinforce the patient's trauma-based SoC. One of the main points of analyzing the transference (that is less often explicitly discussed) is to prevent the therapist from becoming hypnotized and then interactionally reinforcing the patient's view of the world.

☐ Solution-Oriented Therapy and a SoC Model

Solution-oriented therapy (de Shazer, 1985, 1988; Dolan, 1991; O'Hanlon & Weiner Davis, 1987) has its historical roots in Erickson's work. De Shazer (1985) traced his model to a nonhypnotic form of Erickson's crystal ball intervention. The essential feature of the solution-focused therapy (SFT) model is that there is an explicit awareness that the type of information the therapist seeks and the questions used to find that information drastically alter the social construction of the therapy. The conscious and strategic use of language to build a certain social construction is highly hypnotic. Erickson and Rossi (1976, 1979) described repeatedly and at length the use of questions to focus a patient's awareness as a specific type of indirect hypnotic suggestion. In SFT, there is a deliberate attempt for the therapist to think and behave in a manner that creates a social construction that quickly leads the patients and the therapist toward finding or creating a solution to the problems that are being discussed in the therapy room. In other words, the therapist is helping cocreate states of consciousness that support solutions as opposed to problems.

Consider the following example:

Therapist: *When have you been able to see your spouse as someone who could support you in dealing with the trauma* (instead of not talking to spouse)?

Patient: *Well, one night I was so upset that I just told him.*

Therapist: *What made this possible?*

Patient: *First, I really needed to talk to someone. Then I thought about a couple of times that my husband was really helpful and I just decided to talk to him?*

Therapist: *What did you notice happening between him and you after you talked to him?*

Patient: *Hmm. Instead of him burying his face in the paper he talked to me. Even after we talked and I felt better, he seemed to be more attentive to me. Of course, I was not hiding in my room and feeling bad, so that may have had something to do with it.*

Therapist: *If you compare and contrast the talking strategy versus the holding-in-your-feelings strategy, does this outcome of talking work better for you than keeping things to yourself?*

Patient: *Well, when you put it that way, it sure seems that talking to my husband works better.* (Patient begins to look off into space thinking.)

Therapist: *So when you can remember that your husband can be supportive of you, you find that you can just decide to talk to him. As a result of talking to him you and he are closer to each other, maybe partially because you stay out of your room and maybe partially because he is being closer to you, or perhaps both of these things build on each other like a snowball effect. So when you are next confronted with feeling bad, you can really remember to compare and contrast the strategies of holding it in versus talking to your husband. You can remember the outcome of holding it in and you can remember the outcome of talking to your husband. And with that awareness either in the front or back of your mind, you can make the best choice for you.*

The therapist used an exception-finding question to begin to elicit the patient's solution. If the patient is creating a solution, he or she must have a SoC that supports that solution.

When a solution is only an exception, one or several of three problems is occurring:

1. The solution SoC itself is not stable.
2. The solution SoC is not stably linked up to the patient's problem-solving strategies at either a conscious or unconscious level.
3. The solution SoC is not being sufficiently supported and reinforced by the patient's social structure.

In this example, the internal stability of the SoC was strengthened by the questions and responses referring to the patient remembering when her husband was supportive. Her being able to compare and contrast different outcomes strengthened the stability of the link of this SoC to the patient's problem-solving ability. The social reinforcement of this SoC was strengthened by the interview itself because it brought this awareness into the foreground of the patient's experience and methodically linked up each step. The therapist's last recapitulation of what happens is essentially a hypnotic suggestion. It is also assumed that if the patient is more likely to talk to her husband, he will then positively respond and reinforce her use of the talking-about-your-feelings SoC.

The importance of the therapist noticing, eliciting, and expanding exceptions or resources cannot be understated.

☐ Principles of Hypnotically Based Therapy: Eliciting, Building, and Linking Resources

One of the oldest and still common protocols for treating trauma asks the patient to tell the story of the trauma event in order to have a catharsis. But an iatrogenic problem can occur when the patient goes back to the trauma without the resources he or she needs and simply becomes traumatized again. If one is to use the integration of traumatic experience via the catharsis and review method, it is very helpful if the review occurs with a resourceful state in the foreground of experience. In many therapeutic modalities, the therapeutic relationship is considered to be the important resource that makes the difference. While it is true that the therapeutic relationship is an important resource in itself, the degree of resourcefulness can be significantly increased by accessing the patient's own resourceful states. The inability to keep resources in the foreground of experience when remembering or working through traumatic material is perhaps the single biggest impediment to recovery from trauma when using a model of reviewing the material.

What defines a resource, or more precisely a resourceful state? A resourceful state is a SoC that allows the person to have an effective, empowering, and adaptive choice as to how to respond. For any given situation, the patient decides the needed resources. When traumatized people are asked what resource or emotional state would have made the events or memory of the events less traumatic, they cite common themes of safety, security, strength, mastery, competence, or "knowing that I will survive." It is important to note that relaxation is generally not one of the resources this author's patients pick. Therefore, hypnosis or desensitization using relaxation as the main resource does not meet these criteria.

An initial job of the therapist is to elicit these needed resources. Sometimes patients know exactly what they need. Other times, therapists need to use their own experiences, either in general terms or as empathic responses to the patient's story, to generate possibilities. These are then offered to the patient in a "20 questions" manner to negotiate the needed resources (e.g., "Do you think you would have needed a feeling of power?") Patients usually do not name dissociation as something they think would be useful. Nevertheless, it is perhaps the most important resource.

The next job of the therapist is to find or build these resourceful states. It does not matter if the resourceful state comes entirely from another context. For instance, the resource of safety may come from a memory of being with one's dog, and competence may come from experiences of winning a race. Once built, these states must be associated or anchored to specific cues so that they can easily be activated and maintained.

Under "normal" circumstances, these resourceful states would not be available during a trauma and would fade into the deep background. Trauma overwhelms the system. The entire genre of action films is based on the wish to be able to remain resourceful in traumatic situations. In all of these films the hero is in situations that should cause intense PTSD. No matter how many times the hero is beat up, attacked, or tortured he or she remains strong and resourceful. This is the need that these stories fulfill. On occasion the story has a twist in that the hero is suffering but somehow overcomes it. The prime example of this is Sigourney Weaver's character, Casey, in the movie *Alien* and its sequel *Aliens*. In the first film the monsters all but kill Casey. Virtually the entire viewing audience leaves the theater with a case of mild PTSD. In the second film, Casey is found and suffers from full-blown PTSD symptoms. She is scared out of her mind and only reluctantly returns to the planet. The rest of the movie is about how she reconnects to her resources. Of course, we in the audience begin to connect to our resources, vicariously. In the final scene she dons a powerful exoskeleton and faces the alien to protect her surrogate child. In the end, the alien is defeated; Casey and we are all redeemed.

By using trance, associational cues (anchors), and focusing of attention, therapists assist patients in keeping their resources in the foreground, while dealing with traumatic material. The specific tool to use in achieving this goal is trauma reassociative conditioning (TRC) (see chapter 5).

The principles of building and linking resources can be generalized far beyond the specific approach of reviewing a given traumatic incident. The hypnotically oriented therapist is guided by these principles whether or not formal trance is used. The therapist will tend to maintain an awareness of the mix between resources and problems. The goal is to make sure that enough resources are present to move from problem to solution. For instance, Marci, a patient with multiple personality disorder (MPD), was working on a problem having to do with an intense phobia about bugs that came from being left alone on purpose in a bug-infested room. An attempt was being made to link up the resources of safety and belonging while dealing with the memory (using TRC). It became clear that the resources were not going to be sufficient to deal with this memory, and time was running out in the hour. Clearly the goal was too big. Hypnotists prefer that their subjects succeed. Therefore, at an appropriate moment the entire enterprise was halted, and the therapist changed the subject to the holiday that Marci had been using to access the resources of safety and belonging. The patient was engaged in a series of questions that would lead her back into the positive feelings. Then a smaller goal was attempted. The goal was to link up the positive feelings to current moments in the patient's life (sidestepping the traumatic memory for the time being). We had already elicited a SoC of positive feelings by having Marci remember a July 4th party where she felt happy and safe. This was accomplished conversationally by saying, "Wouldn't it be nice to feel that safety when you were talking to co-workers? You know you would be talking to Aretha, but in the back of your mind you would be feeling the feeling of being back at that July 4th party." A variety of situations were chosen. Each topic was discussed using an interspersal approach (Erickson, 1980d). Marci's reaction indicated that this smaller goal of linking the resources to relatively neutral to mildly stressful situations was working.

This strategy had several goals. The first was to end the session in a resourceful manner with some sense of success (as opposed to failure). The second was to increase the strength of the linkages between safety and belonging and other aspects of Marci's life. If successful, this increases the felt sense of belonging and safety. Belonging and safety will not just be at the July 4th celebration. It will be felt while talking to coworkers. This increases the strength of the neural net of this resource. It gives it more "mass" as well as more "connectivity of the resource." The more nerve cells and the more dendrites a neural net has, the more powerful it is. As the neural net gains power, it can be used to solve more difficult problems.[4] The strategy of "growing and cultivating resources" becomes a central strategy in longer term cases. The micropattern of this one session becomes one example of a growing macropattern in the entire therapy. The idea of building safety and belonging will keep recurring in Marci's treatment. For instance, the ideas of safety and belonging will be used to help her connect the split between her alters. This may be done explicitly in a given intervention. However, it will begin to happen on its own as this "neural net" gets stronger.

☐ The Utilization Principle

The utilization principle (Erickson, 1980b, c) suggests that any behavior, emotion, or psychological mechanism that the patient brings in to the therapeutic situation can and should be utilized by the therapist as part of the therapy. Whatever psychological mechanism a patient uses to produce psychiatric symptoms can also be utilized as a resource to solve the problem (Zeig, 1985). One of the chief aspects of the response to trauma is dissociation. Following the utilization approach, dissociation becomes one of our chief resources in resolving PTSD.

The utilization principle can be seen as a key component of solution-focused therapy (de Shazer, 1985, 1988). The emphasis in this model is on utilizing exceptions, as well as patients' motivations and goals. In NLP the focus of utilization is on the micropatterns of the structure of experience such as representational systems, submodalities, and so on.

The treatment of severely abused people, especially dissociative disordered individuals, is often difficult for many therapists because of the extreme and often bizarre (compared to average functioning) nature of their symptoms. The very idea that a person can perceive himself or herself to have 20 different personalities is strange at best to many people, including many in the helping professions. The utilization principle suggests that these mechanisms be accepted and utilized regardless of their "veracity."

---

[4]This is the same principle in the therapy of MPD/DID, where angry or destructive alters are gradually enlisted to help the system as a whole (Putnam, 1989; Ross, 1989).

☐ **Dissociation and Its Utilization**

A primary defense mechanism utilized by trauma victims and others with PTSD is dissociation. The process that occurs in trauma victims is that the person is overwhelmed with information; some of it is dissociated and left unprocessed. Intrusive symptoms are an attempt of the psyche to process the split-off or dissociated material (Epstein, 1989; Horowitz, 1986; see Figure 2.1.)

What is dissociation? The term usually refers to a splitting off of information or consciousness. Let us look at it another way. This chapter suggests a relativistic view. In a hypothetical world, there are only two states of mind, A and B. If a person is dissociated from state A, then that

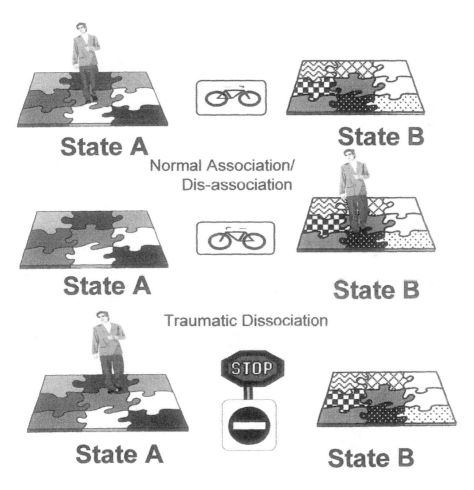

Figure 2.1. To where is a person associated?

person must be associated to state B. Conversely, if a person is associated to A, then that person is dissociated from B.

In this artificial world, it becomes clear that one is associated to one place or the other. This extreme dissociation is seen in the pathological condition of multiple personality. If patient is associated to one alter, she is dissociated from the others. The two are not integrated. But dissociation also comes in many more benign if not helpful forms. If an individual had a bad day at the office and wants to be able to have a romantic evening, he might find it helpful to dissociate from the office and associate into a romantic mood. He would not think that he is dissociated in this circumstance. But in fact, he is "disassociated" from the office SoC and is associated into the romantic mood SoC. In other words, dissociation is actually an illusion based on a point of reference.

Therefore, the more germane questions are, From where is the person disassociating and to where is she associating? Of course, in the real world the actual SoC a person can be in can be very complex and essentially mixed. The bicycle in Figure 2.1 represents the idea that in healthy circumstances one can move from one state to the next as is required. Traumatic dissociation is represented by the stop sign. In this case one is stuck in a state and cannot move to another one.

So, if a woman is being raped or sexually abused, it might be a good idea for her to use dissociation. The problem is that in the danger of the moment she (and others) tends to associate either into a relatively non-resourceful state of consciousness (e.g., a black hole in the back of the closet). Alternatively, she may not succeed completely, remaining in a mixed state of current trauma, plus feared consequence, plus helplessness, plus past experiences of helplessness, and so on. Frankle (1990) described how he minimized the effects of the Nazi concentration camps by disassociating from his current time and associating into a resourceful future that included the potential for making meaning out of his Holocaust experiences—a classic example of associating into a resourceful state!

When people are having full-blown hallucinatory flashbacks, they are associated to a SoC of the trauma and are not associated to current time and space. More often, patients having flashbacks are involved in a mixed SoC, where they are partially associated to current time and space and partially associated to the experience of being in the trauma.

In contrast, once a person is no longer bothered by a traumatic event, they stay fully associated to the present in a resourceful manner and can "think back" to the event that is "over there" in the past. It is like standing in a museum looking at a picture of a war, rather than being in a war. Occasionally, some people can do an inverse flashback, where they partially associate "back into the picture," but they bring so many resources from their current life that the relived memories are not traumatic.

The recognition of the dissociation/association mechanism as a dynamic process is crucial to understanding the general hypnotic pattern of treatment of PTSD. The therapist works to create and maintain resourceful SoCs. With these resourceful SoCs in place, the patient can either successfully problem solve current life demands or digest and transform the effects of the past trauma experiences on how the patient understands the self so that he or she can function better in the world.

☐ The Narrative Approach

Narrative therapy as first described by White and Epston (1990) and later by Freedman and Combs (1996), Zimmerman and Dickerson (1996), and Durrant and White (1990) has several key elements that are highly relevant to working with trauma and abuse. The first element is the goal of separating the identity of the person from the problem. The majority of child abuse survivors have significant difficulty separating who they are from what happened to them.

The second component is the emphasis on helping create a sense of personal agency for the patient. Personal agency is the experience of knowing and feeling that one is the subject of the sentence rather than the object: "I am the agent that makes things happen or not happen." The narrative approach is much more concerned with reconnecting the individual to an identity story that is resourceful than it is about working with the trauma itself.

The third element is the emphasis on the paramount importance of the narrative stories about and around the "facts." A person's life is more like a book, rather than a collection of events. It is the stories about the facts that determine the nature of the work. Not only will the plotline change, but also the very nature of the work is affected. Is the book a tragedy or a comedy? Is it a story of triumph or despair? There is a recognition that there is more than one narrative in a person's life. People who seek therapy are under the influence of dominant stories that are limiting. Therapy often involves finding and elevating the nondominant narratives that are nascent.

The fourth element of narrative work is an emphasis on the influence of culture and politics on the lives of individuals. This would include the importance of the family culture on the individual child in the family. It also includes all of the broader cultural contexts that would influence the family and the individuals. For instance, Jenkins (1990) looked at the social influences on men and referred to "male ways of being" that influence men to be violent toward women. The goal would be to help a man oppose those influences. Wade (1996) helped women who have been the victims of violence to look at their actions in terms of manners in which they have "resisted," as if they were resistance fighters in a war. White and Epston (1990) described narrative therapy as a therapy of opposition.

The fifth component of narrative work is the specialized questions that are used to achieve the previous goals. Externalizing questions are a key feature of the narrative approach. The first aspect of this approach is that the patient is asked to name the symptoms. Once they have a name, the therapist begins to talk about symptoms as if they were separate entities. Questions are asked about how the problem influences the patient, for example, "How does self-blame influence you in your relationships with people?" "How do the flashbacks trick you into thinking you are in Vietnam?" "Does self-blame have any allies in its attempt to convince you of your worthlessness?"

☐ Integrating Narrative and the SoCs Model

It is clear that these questions are highly hypnotic in that they influence the patient toward more resourceful SoCs and away from nonresourceful SoCs. In fact, when you first listen to White interview a patient, you become rather disoriented. The patient also becomes a bit disoriented as well. This is because the questions are linguistically very different from the types of questions with which most of us have experience. Furthermore, the type of thinking required to even consider the question takes people in directions they have rarely, if ever, considered. The result is a gentle disruption in the GRO of whoever is listening. Therefore, a natural light trance state begins to develop. The narrative approach emphasizes the use of meaning and story as an important aspect of a person's consciousness. Epston (1988) has specifically acknowledged the importance of crafting questions in such away as to help create resourceful plotlines for patients. The emphasis on finding people in the past and people in the present and future that will support the new narrative is completely congruent with the recognition in the SoC model of the systemic influences on SoCs. Externalizing the problem can be viewed as a therapeutic use of dissociation. It helps the person disassociate from an identity of being the problem and associate to an identity of being a person who is opposing the influence of a problem. The processes of externalizing the problem, finding unique outcomes, and then building narratives is parallel to the basic hypnotic pattern of eliciting building and linking resources.

☐ Framing, Deframing, and Reframing Experience

We have already seen how the adjustment to trauma is a highly dynamic process with many variables and interaction effects. From a constructivist or Ericksonian point of view, any given SoC or unit of mentation is the result of the interplay between many intrapersonal and interpersonal variables. Part of therapy is to attend to this process with the goal of influencing it in a manner that will lead to better adjustment. Simply thinking about experience as constantly under construction and reconstruction helps to orient the therapist to achieve this goal. The specific approach to help to accomplish this goal involves the *repunctuating* of experience. Repunctuating experience refers to the idea that changing the emphasis of some aspect of experience will change the entire meaning of the experience. Consider the string of words in the box.

> That that is is that that is
> not is not is that it it is

By adding punctuation, you can discover the meaning of this string of otherwise nonmeaningful words: That that is, is. That that is not, is not. Is that it? It is.

In order to effectively repunctuate experience, the therapist needs to look for opportunities that have a high degree of potential leverage. The therapist must ask the following question regarding the patient's description of his or her experience. "Is this a potential resource that when elaborated will lead to a more adaptive SoC?"

If the answer is "No" or "Don't know," the therapist then performs the following operation: Scan the patient's verbal and nonverbal expressions, the therapist's internal experience, and the interaction between the patient and therapist for more data. Then reask the question. An additional question can be, "Is this a potential resource that the patient is failing to notice or value?" As long as the answer is "No" or "Don't know," the therapist keeps scanning. Once the answer is "Yes," the therapist can begin the intervention. (See the discussion about TOTE in chapter 3.)

A fruitful area to attend to is the distinction between important or significant change versus unimportant or nonsignificant change. Many trauma survivors routinely discount the positive steps they make. The effect is that forward momentum is often undermined because it is not noticed or elaborated. From a narrative perspective, the plotline of the story is not advanced in the direction of growth and positive change.

Consider the following example. Leslie had come for her next appointment after a previous session that had utilized eye movement desensitization and reprocessing (EMDR; Shapiro, 1995) to process some of her "weird sexual ideas and feelings," which involved a great deal of self-blame, self-punishment, and isolation. When asked what changes or effects she had noticed, she replied, "Nothing significant." The word "significant" seemed a likely place to check for potential resources that when elaborated would lead to a more adaptive SoC. When asked about even "small" changes, she said that she had gone out with her friends and gone dancing and had sex with her husband. These were actually large behavioral changes that were important to her. Somehow she did not think that I would have thought them important or relevant, because they were not directly related to the work that had been done the session before. At such a point there are a number of options the therapist could choose to help elaborate a more positive story (compared to "nothing was different").

Using narrative and hypnotic approaches, the following interaction occurred. We discussed how the positive changes she reported were the result of the work from the previous session and the fact that perhaps some space for new things were opening up. Perhaps this was the beginning of a positive loop. I asked Leslie if looking at things in this manner might increase the odds of the good things continuing and stabilizing. Leslie's eyes became fixed and far away for a moment (a sign of naturalistic trance). She started to smile and reported that she had never really thought about things in this way. It did feel helpful. She had always considered the self-blame and self-punishment and the symptoms she experienced as a whole, as just ways to be. She had never considered that that she could separate them from the "weird symptoms." An externalizing conversation ensued that continued to separate her as a person from the thinking pattern. The conversation led to the following formulation. The self-blame, self-punishment, and isolation seemed to oscillate with feelings of wanting to avoid the "whole thing" with the "weird sexual ideas and feelings." If she were willing to decrease the avoidance, perhaps she would be less susceptible to being influenced by self-blame, self-punishment, and isolation. She consciously agreed with this idea. Leslie was asked to focus inside and check how it felt. She said that she had a firm idea that this would be good. Two weeks later Leslie reported many positive changes in her behavior. She also reported that she was thinking differently. She was able to separate herself from the problem. She could see the positive steps and what she did to get there.

☐ Opportunities Are Everywhere, You Just Have to Notice Them

The artistry of therapy has to do with finding the most opportune moments to intervene as well as methods of intervening to achieve the greatest amount of impact with the least amount of effort. This aspect of therapy is often more crucial when dealing with problems that have longstanding duration, such as the substantial cognitive-affective distortions that occur as a result of the chronic neglect and abuse of children. For example, A patient with a DID diagnosis had been asked to check with her system about what needed to happen to more effectively deal with some flashbacks that had begun to recur at night. The message that she got back was that "nothing much was going to happen until she stopped blaming herself." The rather forceful no-nonsense wording of this answer suggested that a potential turning point had developed. So the therapist began to talk with her about this issue. During this process there was an ongoing discussion of what it would mean to no longer blame herself and instead hold her abusers accountable. In addition, there was a discussion of how previous therapy had not helped her and that here was further proof that she was a failure and no good.

At one point during this process an important difference emerged: The patient was crying gently, sitting without agitation and reporting that she was having flashbacks. She was asking why the flashbacks were happening. The implication that the therapist took from the way the patient was talking was that she was thinking that she had failed again. It was also evident that in addition to the frame of "Here is more evidence that I failed," the patient seemed to be failing to notice the rather substantial differences in her SoC that were apparent.

The therapist then began an informal "induction" of the idea that there were some fairly important differences happening, including the fact that the patient probably had already begun to not blame herself, but she did not notice this yet. The therapist asked the patient whether or not she was having a flashback that she was "in" or having a memory of the past while she was associated to the present. The latter was the case. Her attention was drawn to the fact that her body was calm and she was crying gently (both behaviors highly different from being "in" a flashback). The patient was asked to compare and contrast her current experience to the night before when she was having flashbacks. She was then asked to account for the difference. She reported that the major difference was that now she was being "honest" about what happened. We then unpacked the word "honest," which included the idea that she was not to blame.

This example reveals a crucial "trick of the trade" for therapists. Patients are usually terrible at noticing positive changes. The more traumatized and abused and neglected a patient is, the more powerful this tendency becomes. In the above example the patient stated she was having a flashback. This was inaccurate and hid the change that was happening. Therapists need to keep scanning for possible positive changes occurring even when patients report that something bad is happening.

☐ A Therapy of Action and Interaction in the Real World

Another guiding principle of Ericksonian therapy is an emphasis on helping patients create action and interaction in the world that supports health and adjustment rather than maladjustment. Action can be overt, as in overt behavior, or it can be covert as in creating specific types of thinking patterns and internal images. Furthermore, human behavior is always seen as goal driven to solve some type of problem. A problem can be on the order of, "How do I have more closeness with my children?" or "How do I get in the best state of consciousness to write this chapter?" Symptoms are also seen as attempts to solve problems in current time. Flashbacks are not just repetitions in order to understand what happened during the trauma. Flashbacks may be repetitions, but they are in the context of current needs.

As will become apparent throughout the book, one of the aspects of the various tools is that they help patients generate new action that will lead to new information and new experience. This new experience will lead to additional action so that a positive feedback loop develops that leads the patient to more healthy adjustment.

It is vitally important that therapists spend time helping patients situate their symptoms and struggles in their attempts to make satisfactory adjustments in the here and now. Sometimes this can be achieved by asking the question, What do your symptoms prevent you from doing now that you would like to do? For example, in response to this question, a Vietnam vet who was still struggling with flashbacks and hypervigilence said that he would be more relaxed. The answer "relaxed" is not yet connected to anything in the man's life. The therapist asked him if he spent as much time as he wanted with his children. At this point, the man laughed a little, relaxed his body posture, and answered that he did not. It seems reasonable to hypothesize that this man was trying to solve the problem, How do I really know that the war is over and relax so that I can have fun with my children?

☐ A General Pattern for Treating Trauma

The general pattern of treatment follows the basic three-phase model described at the end of chapter 1. The main distinction in a neo-Ericksonian model is that the therapist attempts to apply those phases on a microlevel within each given intervention. In step 1 the therapist works to discover, elicit, create, strengthen, and maintain resourceful SoCs in the patient. The therapist does this in a variety of manners, including deconstructing meaning, reconstructing meaning, generating new experiences, and emphasizing or deemphasizing certain experience. The therapist can focus on any level of the patient's experience. In step 2 the goal is to establish and stabilize a sufficiently resourceful SoC so that the previously unresourceful SoC associated with the problem (e.g., traumatic material or life circumstance) can now be replaced with the new resourceful SoC so that the problem can be solved. From an Ericksonian point of view the goal is to generate new positive experience around contexts that previously led to negative experience. The final aspect of the intervention is to integrate the changes into the client's ongoing view of self or the client's social context. This last step is again designed to generate new experience that is usually perceived in relation to either self-concept (the experience one has when thinking about who he or she is) or self-efficacy (the experience one has when thinking about what and how to respond to the environment). This last step helps to insure that at a minimum the change will generalize to other contexts. At a maximum the hope is that the change will be generative.

These stages can be clearly seen in the single intervention of TRC discussed in chapter 5. These phases are also carried out across time through the treatment and through the therapeutic relationship. The importance of safety and stabilization are seen throughout this model with the emphasis on building resourceful states of mind. Therapy cannot proceed without a resourceful context intrapsychically and interpersonally. The therapeutic relationship is a necessary and crucial foundation for psychotherapy. The therapeutic relationship itself is a reflection of the same three-step model of building safety, remembering, and reconnection. The relationship between therapist and patient must be a resourceful SoC for both therapist and patient. In the second phase of treatment the patient begins an encounter with the past and the self. "One of the ironies of abuse focus psychotherapy is its requirement that the client approach a state he or she has spent much of life avoiding" (Briere, 1992). There is, of course, the parallel process in the therapeutic relationship in which the therapist needs to be fully present and compassionate with the patient. To be present and compassionate in the face of trauma and violence and pain, the therapist must be in a resourceful state, which is exactly what the patient must learn to do. So, the healthy therapeutic relationship provides a model that resonates with the patient.[5] Through this resonance the patient can begin to have the same type of relationship with himself or herself.

Finally, in the third phase of therapy, patients learn to reconnect with themselves and the world. This step is consistently foreshadowed within the therapeutic relationship in several manners. First, the therapist is attempting to connect with the trauma patient who has learned/chosen to disconnect for what he or she perceives as necessities of survival. Second, the therapist holds in his or her mind the awareness that there is nothing really wrong or damaged about the patient. The patient has only lost connection with his or her true self. Once the connection has been reestablished, suffering ends. Third and perhaps most importantly, the therapist knows that there is nothing really different between the patient and himself or herself. The therapist holds the awareness that we are already connected. It is just a matter of the patient waking up from the dream that we are not connected.

I will not be spending a great deal of time on the therapeutic relationship until the last chapter of this book. Let me say here in the beginning that problems within the therapeutic relationship will undermine all of the tools that will be discussed. For those readers who want to focus on this aspect first, I would recommend reading chapter 8, entitled "If You Meet the Tool on the Road, Leave It!" before reading the chapters on the various tools.

It may seem a bit odd to some, after having read these last few paragraphs, that most of this book is about tools. To this seeming paradox, I will offer the following metaphor. To be a virtuoso musician you still need to learn scales and many other techniques first. Only after you have mastered the scales and techniques can you improvise the music.

---

[5]It is not uncommon to refer to this process as *modeling*. Modeling is a concept of learning by watching. While I am sure this also happens, I am now more of the opinion that the process at work is one of resonance. An energetic morphic field (Sheldrake, 1981, 1989) is created in the relationship. This field has certain qualities or energetic aspects that we would label compassion, empathy, and so on. The strength of morphic fields increases with use. Little by little the energetic field of the patient's consciousness begins to become entrained to the healthier field contained within the therapeutic relationship. Eventually, the patient will begin to be able to sustain the same types of patterns toward himself or herself. It may seem to some that the distinction between modeling and resonance is not valuable. I mention it because it pertains to the fact that it is not the therapist's behavior that is modeled. It is the therapist's "connection" to which the patient resonates.

CHAPTER 3

The Tools Framework

"If the only thing you have is a hammer, everything starts to look like a nail."

The title of this book is *Tools for Transforming Trauma*. The use of the word *tools* goes beyond the fact that it forms alliteration. The actual use of the term came from my patients. I would ask people what was helpful about therapy and many of them literally said that I had taught them "tools to help solve my problems." They liked the fact that they had something specific that they could use to master various situations.

In fact, my experience of learning hypnosis paralleled my patients' experience. I was glad that I had the tool of hypnosis to deal with some of the difficult clinical situations that I found myself in over the years. Beyond having specific skills, having the tools gave me more confidence that I could handle the situation. The belief that I could handle a difficult situation became part of the SoC I brought to therapy, just as it became part of the SoC that my patients brought to the problems they had to negotiate. So there is an interaction effect between the specific skill or tool and the experience of the person using the tool.

The use of the term *tool* connotes several other things as well. Let's compare the terms *tool* and *technique*. First, technique connotes a highly specialized knowledge that perhaps not everyone can use. Tool is a more down-to-earth concept. Anyone can use a screwdriver. A tool has some flexibility around how it can be used. However, you would not want to use a saw to hammer a nail, even though it could be done.

The central tenet of the tools framework is that clinicians should have many different tools in their "black bag." By having different tools and

51

the knowledge about the appropriate situations in which they can be used and why they work, you will have more flexibility and more success. I want to underscore the importance of knowing the rationale behind the use of the tools. Without this, you will just be a technician only able to use the tool in a rigid fashion. When you understand the rationale behind the tools, you will be able to use feedback from the patient to modify your use of a tool. You won't be using tool X because Robert Schwarz told you to; you will be using it because you will have assessed the situation and come to the conclusion that tool X would be a good place to start.

The use of a tools framework necessitates a different type of assessment than one based on the DSM or other types of pathology classification schemes. The use of tools involves an assessment that begins with an evaluation of the end goal to be achieved. Let's return to the carpentry metaphor for a minute. In therapy workshops, there are always some people who ask, "Can I use such and such tool with a patient who has such and such type of trauma?" The answer is always the same: "It depends on what you want to achieve with this person. What goals do you and the patient have?" In other words, the assessment must include something more than a mere description of symptoms. It should include the goals of the patient and the therapist. The goals need to be articulated sufficiently well so that some specific tool or action becomes obvious. There must be some decryption about an alternative SoC and associated behavior that the patient needs to be directed towards.

Taking the time and asking the appropriate questions to help a patient move toward a description of a well-formed goal is, of course, an intervention or tool in itself. As stated in chapter 2, creating a well-formed goal brings focus to the therapy for both therapist and patient. Of course this does not always happen for a variety of reasons. My experience is that the degree to which a patient can construct a goal in a well-formed manner is highly correlated with the length and ease of the therapy.

☐ The TOTE Model

The acronym TOTE stands for test, operate, test, exit. It was first described by Premack (1976) and also by Dilts (1980). The essence of the model is that the behavior of an intelligent organism is goal motivated rather than stimulus–response motivated. Internal representations exist that allow the organism to evaluate its own behaviors as it moves towards a given goal. For our purposes here, we can state that human activity is goal directed and can be described as a series of more or less complicated TOTEs. A simple example is the action of hammering in a nail. There is a test performed visually or kinesthetically, "Is the nail flush with the wood?" There must be a representation of the desired goal stored in the brain. In this case it would be a picture of a nail's head flush with the plane of the wood's surface, or the feeling of the nail's head and the wood's surface being on the same plane. At first the answer to the test question is "No." Therefore, the operation of hitting the nail with the hammer is performed. The test, "Is the nail flush with the wood?" is performed again. If the nail is not flush, then perform the operation again. If the nail is flush, then "Exit" the TOTE for hammering the nail. In reality, there are actually multiple TOTEs going on that make sure the hammer is held straight and the strike is on the head of the nail.

Any of our tools can be broken down into TOTEs. For the most part, I have not formally done this. It would be far too cumbersome. However, the idea that I want to underscore is that the tools are goal motivated. Therapists must have some representation of the goals they want to achieve in order for the TOTEs within therapy to work well. The more precise the representation, the more exacting one's use of the tools can be. For selecting and designing tools, there is a search TOTE. The search TOTE is roughly as follows. An internal representation of the goal is selected. For instance, instead of a patient having a flashback, the goal can be that a patient will be able to remember a traumatic event as a picture in his or her mind, while feeling comfortable and resourceful. The operation would be to look at the various tool characteristics and ask, "Does this tool help a person achieve the selected goal?" If it does not, keep searching for the correct tool. If the outcome of the tool is the outcome desired for the person, then exit the search TOTE, and begin the implementation TOTE.

A second idea that I want to underscore here is the importance of seeing therapy as a series of goal-directed steps that need to be constantly monitored and changed as a result of feedback from the test aspect of the TOTEs. In other words, therapists must constantly assess how their interventions are helping the patient move toward their goals. In many cases this assessment is at a relatively microlevel of the moment-to-moment interaction between the patient and the therapist. In addition, the therapist wants to notice and reinforce small changes that take the patient toward the therapeutic goals.

Let's look at a common example from basic hypnosis. As part of a hypnotic induction, a hypnotist can suggest the development of arm levitation. In this case, there are at least two goals: the development of arm levitation itself, and the linking of the levitation to the experience of deepening trance. The hypnotist suggests that the hand will get lighter and begin to lift up. The hypnotist then searches for any sign of movement (test), for instance, a small twitch of the index finger. As soon as one is found, the hypnotist reinforces this movement (operate) by saying, "That's right! The finger is beginning to lift, and soon more fingers will lift."[1] Then another finger lifts and the therapist notices this small feedback and reinforces it to increase the patient's response. Noticing and reinforcing small changes leads to the eventual lifting of the hand (test and exit). In addition, once the goal of arm levitation is being approached, the hypnotist can then link the next goal of deepening the trance by saying something like, "As the hand gets higher and higher, you will go deeper and deeper into trance." The therapist would then look for signs of trance deepening and reinforce those as well. In this manner, both therapeutic goals are achieved.

☐ Consistently Achieved Goals Require the Use of Different Operations

Most authors of Ericksonian influence (Dolan, 1991; Gilligan; 1987; Lankton & Lankton, 1983; Zeig, 1985) have emphasized the need to individualize treatment. People have a great many similarities that make it possible to use similar ideas and tools in treatment. Nevertheless, the small and unique differences that each person has may require shifts in the treatment of each person. The entire mathematical realm of chaos theory is based on the concept that small differences in initial conditions can lead to far-reaching differences in outcome. In the TOTE model, we would say that in order to achieve a similar goal with different people or situations, it is necessary to have more than one operation. If in the process the nail becomes crooked, the operation must be changed somewhat. Instead of hammering directly up and down, the carpenter would hammer at different angles.

In the example of creating arm levitation in order to deepen trance, what happens if the arm does not levitate? There are several options. One option is to take this information as feedback about the subject. It may be that the subject has some problem with "feeling light." Perhaps they are depressed. This might require new goals or some adjustment in the treatment. It may be that the subject simply does not do this type of activity well. So now the hypnotist knows to not use this type of activity, at least early in treatment. A second option is to take this turn of events and find a way to utilize it (Erickson & Rossi, 1979; Erickson, Rossi, & Rossi, 1976; Lankton & Lankton, 1983; Zeig, 1985). For instance, if the eventual goal of treatment is to stop smoking, the hypnotist might say,

---

[1]Ericksonian hypnotists tend to learn to say "That's right" as an identification with Erickson.

Your arm has not lifted off your lap. It has stayed comfortably in your lap. Perhaps your unconscious mind has a good reason for this. Can you notice that the arm is getting comfortably heavier and heavier? As you go deeper into trance your arm is getting more and more relaxed, so it feels heavier and heavier so that it will *stay comfortably* in your lap *all by itself.* As you go deeper into trance, you will discover that it will be more and more difficult and awkward for that hand to move toward your face. It will feel much better to you for it to stay in your lap.

The implication of these suggestions is that the person will feel more comfortable with his hand heavy and relaxed rather than the hand automatically lifting toward the face with a cigarette in it.

The broader the goal, the more operations are necessary in order to complete that goal. One point of this book is to provide clinicians with many different tools so they have increased flexibility in treating people. This is essential in treating severely traumatized people, many of whom have highly idiosyncratic manners of coping. A second point that must be stressed is that even though the tools are described in some detail, there can and should be some variation in how those tools are used with any given person. The variations in how the tools are applied should be based on the ongoing feedback the clinician receives from the patient as the tools are being applied.

☐ Interventions as Assessment and Feedback

It should be mentioned again that an intervention could be as small as a question or even the strategic use of silence. It could also be a rather involved process. An intervention could be something that the therapist uses with a patient. Or, it could be something that the patient uses in his or her life. Assessment is an ongoing process throughout the therapy. The therapist and hopefully the patient are continually assessing whether they are moving toward their goals, whether they have arrived at their goals, and whether they need to change their goals. In either case, interventions provide valuable feedback to the therapist and to the patient about what helps and what does not help. In fact, one could argue that an intervention is not a well-formed intervention without the assessment of the feedback from the intervention.

When an intervention moves a patient in the desired direction one of the feedback messages according to the central tenet of solution-focused therapy (SFT) (de Shazer, 1985) is that the therapist and/or patient should do more of it. When patients and therapists fail to attend to what works they often stop doing things that are helpful and then problems arise or come back.

Effective therapy is often accomplished in a step-by-step manner. A common pattern of treatment is the elicitation of a resourceful state followed by associating that state to other internal resources followed by applying this new complex of resourceful states to social contexts. So in this pattern once the feedback tells the therapist that the resources have been established, this should trigger an assessment and goal planning of how to link that resource up so that it becomes available to a patient in appropriate contexts. In the example of Gina (page 59), once a reference experience for feeling angry and safe simultaneously was established, the follow-up intervention was to have her talk to the person with whom she was angry.

There is a saying in NLP: "There is no failure, only feedback." This attitude is useful for both patients and therapists. When interventions do not go well, then the feedback is that it is time to do something different (de Shazer, 1985). The assessment must be to figure out what to do differently. The feedback from the "failed" intervention may provide information about aspects of the patient's style of responding, needed adjustments in the initial formulation, and additional aspects of a problem not previously recognized. It may also reveal that the therapist has misunderstood the patient's goals or motivations.

One final piece of important feedback is that there may be a needed adjustment in how the therapist interacts with the patient. In many instances, the patient's understanding about the intent of an intervention is very different than the therapist's understanding. For example, despite some very good work and positive changes in Jeff's (a patient with DID) life, he began to have a sudden increase in flashbacks and difficulty concentrating, which was disrupting his life. The question was raised about the meaning of this feedback. Eventually, Jeff was able to discuss how he thought that I was favoring the angry alters over the cooperative alters. He further thought that my recent emphasis on the need for him to learn to accept the angry alters as aspects of himself meant that he had to integrate them immediately and that the cooperative side would be overwhelmed. This panicked many of his helpful alters. I agreed that I could see how he had gotten these ideas from the various statements I had made over the last few sessions, and how it made sense to me why he had become so afraid and did not want to do the next piece of work that was planned. We also worked on how his perception of my intentions was a projection of how he felt about his own system of alters.[2]

---

[2] I have several reasons for this type of response. When working with patients who have had their realities denied and violated, I believe it is crucial to help affirm a patient's abilities to perceive accurately. To do this, it is important to find the bits of truth in what might otherwise be a distortion. Therapists need to

Once this was discussed, Jeff calmed down considerably and most of the symptoms abated.

In the final analysis, when all else does not solve the problem, the therapist probably needs to intervene on his or her own approach to the patient.

☐ Interventions and Assessments as Agents of Change

The most obvious way to think about an intervention is that it is used to help bring about some type of change. The therapist or the patient uses the tool, and as a result of that usage the desired goal is reached. The specific tools that are described in this book are clearly meant to be agents of change.

Depending on your training, it may be less obvious that questions and other information-gathering tools are also agents of change. Erickson, Rossi, and Rossi (1976, 1979) described a type of indirect suggestion called "questions that focus awareness." Their point was that the very act of asking a question such as, "Do you feel your arm getting lighter?" changes the focus of the subject's attention first to their arm and then also to begin searching for sensations of lightness. In addition, the person would be unconsciously orienting to the idea of lightness in its many variations other than the arm.

So the very act of asking questions begins to orient our patients to certain types of experiences. The specific and consistent use of certain types of questions can be a powerful agent of change. Examples of these types of questions include the miracle and scaling questions in SFT (de Shazer, 1985, 1988). A given answer to the miracle question is not as important as the act of answering the question, because once the patient has answered the question, the patient and the therapist are now thinking along different lines than before the question was asked. Narrative questions (White & Epston, 1990) have a strong orienting component.

---

look at how their communication might be easily misperceived. Jeff had raised enough specific points that I could see how he got his "mis"-understanding. He had picked up on some very salient points. In the future, I would have to be more careful about how I presented these ideas. In addition, patients who have been raised in abusive families have had very little experience with people applying the skill of empathy. So they themselves have little experience of putting oneself in another's shoes and understanding what they experienced, while at the same time maintaining one's own sense of self. I wanted to model this type of interaction. Finally, I think it is helpful for therapists to practice the concept of "there is not failure, only feedback" as a model for the patient.

The questions focus the patient's attention to aspects of his or her sense of self in relation to problems and strengths in such a way as to create a very different kind of experienced reality. In fact, it is the artistic act of forming questions in a certain way and then linking them one after the other that allows the narrative therapist to help a patient create a new story line about his or her life.

Returning to our systemic orientation, we must keep in mind that the types of questions we ask influence the data we get, which further influences us. Furthermore, these same questions also orient the therapist to certain SoCs that may or may not be helpful to working with a given patient. The questioning and information-gathering approaches that are used to help patients and therapists cocreate well-formed treatment goals are excellent examples of the dual influence on the therapist and the patient. Questions that focus on the past and internal feeling states will lead to certain types of data, therapist theories, and concomitant interventions. Questions about future goals and current problems lead to different data sets, therapeutic formulations, and interventions.

Theoretical ideas in turn will influence the types of data sought. For instance, a patient was seen in an inpatient setting. Her symptom was that she was mutilating her face. The symptom had gotten worse after her therapist had used EMDR to uncover past trauma. While there was ample evidence of physical abuse in the past, the therapist believed that there was more undiscovered abuse. This led to the use of EMDR, which led to a decompensation without any further abuse being discovered. A close questioning of the patient's current life status revealed that she was currently being physically abused by her husband and had not reported this to anyone.

☐ Translating DSM Diagnoses into Action Plans for Change

It is possible to start with a description of the problem or a pathology assessment and then translate this into an end goal. The goal is to translate the assessment into an action plan for the therapy. For example, the diagnosis of BPD carries with it many connotations. Many people would say that it is not a useful diagnosis because it is so stultifying. But, if we look at the symptoms of BPD, we see some rather specific problems: the use of all or nothing thinking, for example. This automatically suggests a goal of being able to hold two opposing thoughts or feelings simultaneously, or being able to see the shades of gray. Now the question becomes, "What tool might achieve such an effect?" In other words, the clinician might ask, "What type of experience or transaction can I invite the patient to engage in that would produce the desired goal?" This could be something in the office either internally for the patient or interpersonally between the patient and the therapist or someone else in the room. Or it could happen outside the office.

Many dissociative patients can be described as having borderline features. One of those features is the all-or-nothing processing coupled with splitting that is used to create separate parts of self usually referred to as alters. An alter of a dissociative patient tends to feel only one emotion. If you ask a DID patient about the possibility of experiencing two feelings simultaneously, the response you are likely to get is one of disbelief or a look of "this does not compute." At a certain point in treatment, it might be a good idea for the patient to have a reference experience of this very alien concept of feeling two feelings at the same time.

With this goal in mind I have designed a tool that can often be useful. Does it automatically get a patient to accept with equanimity the natural flow and interplay of emotions? Of course not. The goal of this tool is to give a patient an experiential understanding that he or she can feel two emotions at once (i.e., fear and comfort or fear and relative safety). Why choose fear and comfort or safety? Because that combination of feelings is part of the SoC we normally experience when we are somewhat afraid but relatively calm. Without connection to some sense of safety or calmness or comfort, fear becomes wild panic. Panic is often the experience of parts that have been severely traumatized. It is not even a remote possibility that a person could feel somewhat afraid and also feel that she can have a small level of comfort in their body.

The tool is an imagery tool based on the NLP idea of collapsing anchors and the rules of perception in art. I use this tool with patients who have an all-or-nothing quality to their emotions. As soon as they begin to feel a little sadness or fear or anger, they go into it full force. Gina was diagnosed with DID. She also had many borderline features, including causing many splits among the staff of the in-patient unit she was on. Either she hated and feared someone or she felt safe and liked someone. For example, during a session where she was talking about how she had been betrayed by another staff member, Lisa, Gina stated that she now knew Lisa was "no good." Gina was asked whether she thought it was possible to be angry with that person for making a mistake and also feel the relatively safe feelings that she used to feel with that person. The response was a rather sarcastic, "Yeh, right." I explained to Gina that I understood she had no experiential basis for this concept, but it was an experience that many people actually have and take for granted. Did she want to try an experiment that might help her really learn that she could have two very different feelings simultaneously?

Gina agreed, and she was asked to close her eyes and imagine a picture that was symbolic of her current negative feelings toward this person and really feel those feelings. This was an easy task. Then she was asked to put those feelings aside and think of a picture that symbolized the previously positive feelings of Lisa and allow herself to vividly remember those feelings that she used to feel in the past. Once it was clear that she was feeling those feelings, she was asked to put that picture and feeling aside. Then we talked briefly about the idea of foreground and background in pictures or movies. For instance, the foreground is what is dominant and so on. She was then asked to pick one of the pictures and place a large version of it in the foreground of her imagination and then place a smaller version of the other picture in the background almost out of sight. Then she was instructed that in a few moments she would be asked to have the pictures move back and forth in her mind until they came to a stop at relatively the same size and level in her mind. She was warned that since they were linked to her feelings, she should expect to feel a strong swing in her feelings going back and forth, like a roller coaster.

Gina did in fact experience a roller coaster effect, which was evident by the looks on her face. After about 3 minutes she said that the pictures were level in her mind. She reported feeling very strange that she had both feelings simultaneously and she no longer saw the staff member in an all-or-nothing way. Actually, she was quite stunned by this "ah hah" experience. She reported that for the first time she understood the concept of being angry with someone and still having a relationship with him or her. We talked at length about this. In order to solidify the work and link it to the real world, Gina was asked to talk with the staff member. The talk went quite well. There was marked decrease in the amount of all-or-nothing responding for the remainder of her hospital stay. Months later she would still comment on this one experience. I have used this tool with very similar effects whenever I have needed to create a reference experience for a patient about non–all-or-nothing thinking. Let us look at this example as a blueprint for translating DSM diagnostic descriptions into action plans.

☐ An Algorithm for Translating DSM Diagnoses into Action Plans

1. Look at the description of problem behaviors of that diagnosis.
2. Describe the healthy alternative behaviors in behaviorally specific ways. The behaviors can include internal actions such as using positive self-talk or holding feeling states simultaneously.
3. Search for common occurring examples (reference experiences) of the healthy behavior or some aspect of the healthy behavior.

4. Search through tools or sequences that you know can facilitate the experiencing of step 3. If one exists, exit this TOTE and use that tool.
5a. If step 4 does not produce results, return to step 1 and deconstruct the behavior into the smaller action sequences. In other words, How does a person actually do the behavior? How would you do the behavior if you had to? In the above example, as I thought about the problem behavior of alternating all-or-nothing feeling (all good vs. all bad) and how to create the problem, I realized that when I had similar intense feelings, it was as if they were right in my face and I saw nothing else.
5b. Repeat steps 2 and 3 and 4 for the new description. The idea of holding two feelings at a moderate distance came to mind. Then the idea of art techniques came to mind. Finally the use of anchoring or associating the feelings to images and the back and forth movement of the images settling in the center came from a couple of NLP ideas. In addition, this fit with the utilization principle of using what Gina already knew how to do, namely, bringing one aspect of her experience really close while the other receded into the background. I simply asked her to keep the process moving and alternating.

Using this type of TOTE will allow a therapist to be technically eclectic, while having a grounding theoretical frame. The importance of generating healthy reference experiences cannot be understated. Part of the first phase of treatment is to build healthy experiences that can be used to create stable SoCs of safety. Gina is a good example. She simply did not have available to her an experience that she could reference for what it meant to feel angry with someone and not have all the "good stuff" vanish. How could she feel safe without this basic requirement? This does not mean that she has never had an experience where she felt two feelings at once. It does mean that the experience was never sufficiently privileged (White & Epston, 1990), so that it became a relevant part of the story of who she is and how she can solve problems with people.

☐ The Interaction Between Therapist Skill Base and Personal Response

There are two positions regarding skill base and personal development in the therapy world. One position is that the bottom line of therapy is determined by the personal development of the therapist. This position states that it is the relationship issues, the therapeutic alliance, and transference and countertransference issues that are most important. This position would emphasize the need for personal therapy for the therapist. The second stance is that therapist skill development is most important. Here skill-based supervision would be seen as more important than personal therapy.

The tools framework advocates for a middle position, where the two dimensions of personal evolution and skill development are in a dynamic interaction. I would like to suggest the following matrix. The dimensions of the matrix are therapist skill level and degree of therapist personal evolution. Therapist skill level includes tools of change, tools of observation, tools of empathy, and tools of self-reflection. The evolution of the therapist has a number of components, including the degree of unresolved personal issues, unchallenged societal or culturally based prejudices, and specific reactivity to some of the difficulties common to working with severe trauma. The variables that we are measuring are skill acquisition and skill use, dysfunctional SoCs in the therapist, and their impact on therapist behavior. There are several hypotheses: The first is that the acquisition and effective use of specific skills will be proportional to the degree of personal evolution at the time of skill learning or use. The second and third hypotheses are dialectically opposed. The second hypothesis is that the degree of technical skill of a therapist, at any given moment, will be inversely proportional to the negative influence of personal issues of the therapist. The third hypothesis is that the more a therapist has effective skills available for a given problem, the less likely it is that there will be interference from personal issues.

At either end of the continuum the outcome is fairly clear. If you have many problems, it will impede your ability to acquire and use skills. If you have many problems and poor skills, your therapy will not be very good. If you are highly evolved with many skills, your therapy will be highly effective. If you are highly evolved you will probably be able to acquire skills fairly easily.

Most of us are somewhere in the middle of the bell-shaped curve, having some needed evolutionary steps to take and having certain clinical tools. When you do not have the requisite skills to work with a particular problem, you are going to feel increased anxiety and decreased mastery. So there will be a TOTE that will search for some combination of SoCs that can solve the problem. If no other tool can be found, you will begin to search personal history SoCs in order to solve the problem of how to respond to the patient. To the extent that you have unresolved problems or anxiety-based responses or culturally limited responses to the patient's issues, these will begin to leak into therapy.

If you have learned specific tools that will resolve a given patient's problems, then there will be no increase in anxiety and no additional search routines that can lead into your problematic personal history. Therefore, counterreactions and/or countertransference issues will not arise or at least not control your responses to the patient. Instead you will apply the tool that will solve the problem. The patient will feel better. You will feel increased mastery rather than anxiety. The degree to which you have acquired specific tools that will effectively resolve a patient's problems will increase your resiliency against the negative effects of countertransference, at least with respect to that patient.

As therapists acquire skills they will tend to evolve on a more personal level. This is for several reasons. First, they will have a new skill so they will be more effective and more confident. Second, they are likely to start noticing finer levels of distinction that will make them want to learn new things. Third, they are likely to develop a keener awareness of where their personal problems do show up. This happens, because now when a problem or difficulty shows up in a situation where the tool ought to have been effective, the therapist cannot claim lack of competence in the skill. So he or she must begin to question some of the finer points, such as, "Was there something about myself in the way I tried to use this tool that got in the way?" Of course, the very act of questioning oneself is a specific type of tool, is it not? We will be discussing this in chapter 8.

☐ From Tools to Art

Many people have idolized Milton Erickson. I have also heard people say that he could not have been as good as all of the stories about him suggest. It was only his reputation that began to create a halo effect. There have also been numerous mentions of the idea that Ericksonians should "trust their unconscious." All of these comments or reactions from people seem to come out of some ignorance about Erickson that has an important bearing on the tools framework.

Erickson was like a musician who practiced scales for hours a day. He would write out a 30-page transcript of an induction and begin to gradually condense it until it got down to a few pages. Then he would sit in front of a mirror and recite the induction. Who among us is that dedicated? In teaching workshops, it has been abundantly evident that many attendees have a reluctance to actually practice techniques that are taught. Erickson admonished students to learn as many techniques as possible so that they could have the flexibility to individualize treatment (Zeig, 1985). You can only trust your unconscious once it has been properly trained. Just like you can only play improvisational jazz once you have learned a great deal about music.

The detailed descriptions of the tools in this book as well as the reasoning behind them are not meant to be rigid proscriptions of what is correct and true. They are simply specific descriptions to facilitate learn-ing. The reason to memorize or thoroughly learn a tool is to become unconsciously competent at it. So instead of focusing one's attention on remembering what is the next step, you can focus your attention on your patient and the interaction between you and the patient. In this way, a technique in the hands of a technician becomes a tool in the hands of an artist or craftsman. You can make subtle or not-so-subtle changes in your intervention based on the needs of the moment. In addition, you will be able to combine the tools in creative ways to achieve specific goals. Hopefully, you will be able to articulate your reasoning behind making those changes or combinations. In the final analysis, it is the self of the therapist that becomes the tool and the artist simulta-neously. In Figure 3.1 is a chart of most of the tools described in this book and the chapters in which they are discussed in more detail. Fur-thermore a summarized account is given of the impact of the tools and the approximate phase of treatment a therapist would utilize the tool. It is readily apparent that any given tool has more than one effect on a patient. Again these assessments should be taken as approximations rather than absolute truth. They are meant to help guide the therapist in being clear what he or she is trying to achieve with the patient, and which tool will be most beneficial for the task at hand.

	Stage of therapy	Chap.	Reduce affect	Improve cognitive processing	Improve grounding	Identify traumatic memories	Process traumatic memories	Boundaries	Increase self-efficacy	Increase resources	Increase positive self-Image	Decrease self destructive behaviors	Change beliefs
Safe Place	First	4	•		•			(•)		•			
Breathing	First	4	•		•				•				
Problems Solving Check List	First	4	•	•					•	•		•	
Rainy Day Letter	First	4	•							(•)	(•)		
Sub-Modalities	First, second	4	•	(•)	•					•			
Containment symbols	First	4	•		•		(•)	•				•	
54321	First	4	•		•								
Peripheral vision	First (second)	4	•	•	•		(•)	•	•				
Energy Bubble	First (second)	4	•	•	•			•	•	•			
End state re-training	First-second	4	•		•				(•)				
Somatic/affect bridge	Second (first or third)	5			(•)	••	•						(•)
Ideomotor questioning	Second	5				••	••						(•)
T RC	Second (first or third)	5	•	•	•		••						
Safe remembering	Second	5				•	•						
Hypnotic abreaction	Second	5				•	•		(•)				
Creating alternative memories	Second (third)	5					•		•	•	•		•
Yes and	Second third	5	•	•	•			(•)	•	•	••		
Thought field therapy	All	6	••	•			••	•			•		
Current problem as chance to correct the past	Second (first or third)	7		•					••		•		(•)
Cultivating resources (external)	Second-third (but the sooner the better)	7							••	••	•		

Figure 3.1. Chart for tools, their goals, approximate timing by phase of treatment, and location by chapter.

	Stage of therapy	Chap	Reduce affect	Improve cognitive processing	Improve grounding	Identify traumatic memories	Process traumatic memories	Boundaries	Increase self-efficacy	Increase resources	Increase positive self Image	Decrease self destructive behaviors	Change beliefs
Cultivating resources internal	third	7	(•)						••	••	••		
Self-image thinking	third	7		(•)					•	•	•	••	(•)
Questions to link resources	All	7	•	•	•				••	••	••		
Aligning percep. posit.	Third (second)	7	(•)	•				••	•	•	•		
Compare and contrast	Third (second)	7		•				(•)			•	•	••
Then & now	All	7		•	•			(•)	•		•		
Externalizing problems	All	7	•	•				•	•		•		
Letter to God	Third	7									•		•
Counter practices to self sabotage	All	8	•						•	••	•	•	(•)
Tools for therapist development													
Translating DSM Dx into action plans	First (All)	3											
Counter-transference question list	All	8											
Solution oriented decision tree	All	8											
Solution oriented check list	All	8											
Cultivating resources (external)	All	7							••	••	•		
Cultivating resources internal	All	7							••	••	••		

First = the primary phase in which the tool would be used.

(first) = secondary or optional phases in which the tool will be used.

• = This goal is a main target of the tool.

(•) = This goal is either a secondary effect of the tool or the tool may assist in furthering this goal.

•• = This goal is strongly influenced by this tool.

The therapist development tools were not categorized by the target goals used for patients with the exception of cultivating resources. We all need to cultivate our resources.

Figure 3.1. (*Continued*) Chart of tools, their goals, approximate timing by phase of treatment, and location by chapter.

CHAPTER 4

Tools for Safety, Ego Support, and Ego Growth

Trauma cannot be destroyed, but it can be dissolved in a sea of resourcefulness.

Someone once asked me, "How can you stand listening to all the trauma that people tell you about?" This is a common question. The question is actually more intuitive than it appears. What the person is usually asking is, "How can you be empathetic with someone who is telling such painful stories and not feel horrible?" I finally came up with an answer that I think actually explains how I can stand it (and probably how many therapists can "stand it"). The answer is that I have learned how to listen to someone's pain, resonate with it, and stay connected to enough of my own resources that I can contain and metabolize the pain. In addition, I have come to realize that every time I do this, my own resourcefulness grows a little stronger.

A metaphor I use with and explain to patients is that they need to strengthen their emotional muscles. It is just like a physical workout. You need to practice consistently. You increase the stress gradually. There should be some pain, but not too much. It does not hurt to have a personal trainer. A substantial part of the therapy for trauma victims, especially victims of childhood trauma, is for them to be able to acknowledge and feel their feelings while maintaining a connection to a positive sense of who they are. As stated in the first chapter, this aspect of treatment is mostly contained in the second phase of treatment. The tools in this chapter are especially useful in the first phase of treatment.

Patients must build up their emotional muscles so they can remain safe and stable. Patients must develop resourceful SoCs so that they can dissolve their trauma in a sea resourcefulness.

☐ Affect Modulation

A central feature of PTSD as well as dissociative disorders is a dysregulation of affect. In simple language, people cannot regulate the intensity of their feelings, nor can they engage in problem-solving behavior to manage their feelings. The result is that their symptoms, such as flashbacks, tend to intensify over time. In addition, many PTSD patients engage in self-harming behavior or trauma-seeking behavior as an attempt to regulate their feelings.

The dysregulation of affect is driven from multiple levels of the individual's mind and body. In cases of severe early childhood abuse, where the child is subjected to repeated abuses, the dysregulation of affect is supported by changes in the person's neurobiology (van der Kolk et al., 1984). Essentially, the individual's nervous system has an impaired ability to stabilize and decrease sympathetic arousal. Metaphorically speaking, this is similar to bad shock absorbers on a car. The car hits a bump, and instead of a brief lurch and then a stable ride, the car bounces and bounces and bounces for some time. Therefore, later in life when a mildly traumatic incident (e.g., getting yelled at by one's boss) happens to a survivor of childhood abuse; her nervous system remains more highly aroused than someone who was not abused as a child. She will be biologically driven to be more upset for a given event than if she had not been hurt as a child. So in current time, she actually experiences more trauma, which further stresses her system.

On a more psychological level, when someone is traumatized to the point that they develop PTSD, their ability to process incoming stimulation has been overwhelmed (Horowitz, 1986). Nathanson's (1994) elucidation of affect theory has described how too rapid and too intense stimulation of a child leads to the development of dysphoric affect.

In the development of PTSD, the overwhelming stimulation leads to intense dysphoric affect, and the intense dysphoric affect itself becomes a source of further stressful stimulation that overwhelms the system. This leads to even more negative affect, such that an amplification circuit is created (Peterson, Prout, & Schwarz, 1991). This loop of overwhelming stimulation leading to increased dysphoric affect, leading to failed cognitive mediation, leading to even more dysphoric affect occurs both at the time of the trauma and later on during intrusive phases of the PTSD cycle.

It usually does not stop there. Many child abuse survivors learn to take counterdependent stances, thinking they should be strong and self-reliant and not ask for help. This type of SoC and associated problem-solving strategies increase affective dysregulation rather than modulate affect. Most people who exhibit PTSD (regardless of the trauma) are at least as upset with themselves for being symptomatic as they are that the traumatic event happened. The more individuals embrace a counter-dependent stance, the more they tend to get angry with themselves for having symptoms. If it were someone else, they would be understanding and empathic, but they should be stronger. In my work with people who developed PTSD after car accidents, a belief that one should be strong and not have symptoms coupled with a reluctance to ask for help (whether or not previous abuse existed) was highly correlated with higher levels of symptom and longer courses of recovery.

The common theme at the psychological, interpersonal, and biological level is that the traumatized individual loses connections to natural resources that, if available, would help to regulate affect. One of the most important ego-strengthening functions of therapy with trauma victims is to increase their ability to modulate affect. People need to be able to soothe themselves and contain the negative affect, sensation, and imagery, and to stay connected to resourceful states of mind when under stress.

Self-Soothing and Self-Care

Many patients who have been abused or simply mistreated as children have not been taught how to reduce negative aversive affect without resorting to problematic behavior such as using drugs or alcohol, or self-mutilation. It is not that patients are masochistic. They simply have no language or experience about how to calm down. One of the central functions of these behaviors is to reduce negative affect (Briere, 1992). In plain language, people do these behaviors to not feel so bad.

It is not simply that these people were repeatedly beaten or sexually abused as children. The accounts of child rearing from such individuals suggest that they were never taught appropriate self-regulation strategies. These children were not taught how to put words on feelings. They were not comforted sufficiently. One patient described how her mother gave her a Valium at the age of 11 when she was upset because her dog died. If there was repeated incest in the house, when there was comfort it was often paired with sexual stimulation and pain, so that comfort itself becomes a conditioned stimulus towards increased arousal as opposed to decreased arousal. They certainly were not protected, so they were in a state of constant arousal and vigilance.

The situation is compounded by the relatively recent findings that early trauma actually changes the neurology of children so that as they grow up and even as adults they have a decreased neurological ability to decrease autonomic arousal (van der Kolk et al., 1984). So it becomes even more important for survivors of abuse to learn parasympathetic mediated activities to decrease their autonomic arousal.

Healthy self-soothing activities are a source of decreased arousal, pleasant sensations, and calming affect. Self-soothing activities should have some or all of these characteristics: slow, gentle, or rhythmical in speed or movement; soft in texture; tone, or hue; quiet in volume. They include imagistic meditative practices including having a safe place, using breath to calm down, using calming self-talk, accessing calming positive sensations including warm baths and showers, appropriate use of food such as a warm cup of tea or hot chocolate, listening to gentle calming sounds or music, yoga, stretching, holding or gently touching oneself, gently rocking, seeking out a friend or other support to say soothing things or do soothing actions and allowing those things or actions to comfort oneself, going for a calming walk. Of course, there are other activities.

Healthy self-care activities include all of the self-soothing activities, but they are not limited to the quieting types of responses in the self-soothing category. There is a class of self-care activities that lead to a sense of accomplishment, strength, and increased self-esteem. They include exercise, sports, dance, gardening, painting, playing music, grooming, and so on.

The Obvious Is Not So Obvious

In many instances the patient needs to be educated about the nature and importance of these activities. The more traumatized the individual was, or the more dysfunctional the individual, the less the therapist should take for granted about the person's capacity to self-soothe. In fact, the therapist should not even assume that the patient and the therapist speak the same language when it comes to the very concept of "taking care of yourself."

This point was driven home to me when a patient and I were talking about her need to take better care of herself. She noted that in fact she did a variety of things to make herself feel better. Unfortunately, they were all strategies of sympathetic activation and sensation seeking. These included skydiving, bungee jumping, listening to heavy metal music, and driving really fast. It never occurred to her when that when I was talking about self-soothing, I was talking about things such as relaxation, yoga, deep breaths, warm baths, working in the garden, and so on.

Facilitating Good Use of Breathing

Many times, when patients become agitated or go into flashbacks, their breathing becomes short and shallow or they hold their breath. Neither of these patterns of breathing leads to decreased arousal. In addition, these breathing patterns help keep the patient associated to the fear-based SoC. It is useful to get the patient to take slow, deep, easy breaths to help break the pattern of arousal. Instructing patients to take a deep breath sometimes is insufficiently successful.

One trick that I have found to be helpful is, instead of instructing patients to take a deep breath, I instruct them to blow all the air out of their lungs first. Unless the lungs are empty, one cannot take a very deep breath. This seems to be a task that patients are more able to do, perhaps because breathing out is more akin to getting rid of something, which they are trying to do anyway. In any event, once they breathe out all the air in their lungs, it is virtually impossible not to take a deep breath automatically. All the patient has to do is focus on half the task of breathing, namely, breathing out. The rest is automatic. Once the pattern has been established, the concepts of exhaling tension, stress, and upset and in-haling peacefulness, relaxation, and centeredness can be added.

The reader should take a few minutes and experiment with this. Breathe all the air out of your lungs. It is best if you do this slowly. Keep going past what is comfortable. Breathe every last drop of air out. You will discover how deep your inhalation will be without any effort. Allow the inhalation to continue until your lungs are full. Make sure to do this slowly to avoid hyperventilation. If you begin to become dizzy, you are hyperventilating. Slow way down. It should take you about 10 seconds to exhale and 5 seconds to inhale. Pause for at least 1 second at the end of the inhale and then exhale slowly again.

Creating a Safe Place

For patients, a safe place is a SoC that is relatively calm and peaceful. There is no fight or flight response. There are relatively low amounts of inner dialogue. What dialogue there is contains content and perspectives that support low arousal and centeredness. The body's nervous system needs to relax in order to facilitate healing. The experience of internal safety can be independent of what is happening outside of the person. A self-help protocol for patients to find a "safe place" should include a relaxation induction, followed by a very open-ended approach to devel-oping imagery to which the patient can associate in order to feel safe. One problem with fixed imagery, such as a description of going to the beach, is that if the person does not like the beach, the entire exercise is usually a waste of time. Therapists either need to find out ahead of time the types of imagery that might be soothing, or use an open-ended approach. Once patients can feel safe and comfortable, they can begin to practice acquiring that feeling in various contexts. This approach is called self-image thinking (Lankton & Lankton, 1983), which is fully described in chapter 7.

This is not the only approach to creating this type of SoC. Linehan (1983a, 1983b) described in detail the use of mindfulness training in the treatment of BPD. It turns out that BPD in adults is highly correlated with histories of childhood trauma (Herman & van der Kolk, 1987). When a person is in a mindful state, he or she can observe what is happening within and around himself or herself while remaining relatively calm.

The Problem-Solving List

I have used this approach mostly with parasuicidal patients. However, it can be used with any patient who has a poverty of healthy self-soothing and self-care responses and who engages in self-harm, such as self-cutting. Patients are told, "Everyone has a numbered list of things they can do when they are feeling bad or things go wrong. You do number 1 first, and if you do not feel better you do number 2, and so on. Probably everyone has suicide on their list somewhere."

The patient is then asked, "When things go wrong, where is suicide/self-harm on your list?" Invariably, the patient says suicide or self-harm is in the top five, usually the top three. The therapist then says something like, "No wonder you do it so often. It is so high up on your list. You have the additional problem that if your first few problem-solving strategies do not work, the problem becomes a life and death issue, so the problem feels even bigger."

The patient is then given the homework assignment of creating a list with the numbers 1–20 on it. The patient is to put suicide/self-harm at number 20. He or she is then to fill in the other 19 spaces with things they can do before they do the destructive behavior. The patient is encouraged to think of some things in the office. It is useful to coach the patient to think of very small things such as, take a bath, put flowers on the table, go for a walk, or call a friend. It should be noted that the goal of this approach is not to end the destructive behavior. It would probably be too big a step for the patient, and he or she would just fail. The real goal is to begin to teach the patient about healthy self-soothing activities. Once the patient learns the utility of these types of behavior the self-regulating aspects of the self-harming behavior become superfluous. It can be moved back to number 30. Eventually, it is moved off the list entirely.

"Rainy Day" Letters from the Self

A strategy for self-soothing that relatively healthy people use when they are having bad days is to activate memories about better days or to remember that they have gotten through this before, or that they are closer to future goals, or that they are loved and appreciated by certain people. People with substantial PTSD may have never learned this type of strategy or, when they are being overwhelmed by negative affect and negative cognitions, they simply cannot access the memories or cannot stabilize those memories in their consciousness long enough to soothe themselves.

It is not that they do not have the good soothing experiences. It is either that they have never learned to use them to self-soothe, or they cannot use them when they are in the middle of the "rainy day." Therefore, a simple strategy is that when patients are in a hopeful and resourceful state of mind, they should write themselves a letter or letters to be read when they are feeling bad (Dolan, 1991). The letter can contain suggestions of things to do to self-soothe, stories of good times, reminders of goals, and so on. It is important to note that the very act of writing the letter stabilizes and strengthens a self-soothing and positive SoC. It also strengthens the function of planning to care for oneself. The combined act of writing and reading the letter strengthens the function of an observing ego. Future letters can reference the fact that the patient has successfully used previous letters, thereby building a chain of association about having an increased capacity to step outside one's immediate feelings into a larger sense of oneself. Below is an example:

Dear Bob,

   Since you are reading this letter, I know that you are feeling bad. I just wanted to remind you how proud I am of you for remembering to read the letter. I remember how I read the earlier letter that I wrote to myself and how it helped me remember that people do care for me and that these feelings would pass. I remember that at first I did not believe that the feelings would pass and that I read the letter several times before I went out into the garden and weeded. I hope you realize that things have definitely gotten better since we have been writing these letters to ourselves. I remember one time not so long ago, that I/you did not even read the letter. We just knew what was in it and that was enough to make us feel better. . . .

Businesses create strategic plans to guide them, especially in times of trouble. There really is nothing different here. If a patient does not like the idea of a letter to the self, they might be willing to develop a specific plan and write that down in bullet format.

Submodalities to Reduce Affect

How does a person know that a certain thought or memory should cause an intense reaction? For that matter, how do any of us know that one experience should lead to intense affect and another experience to mild affect? Certainly there is some mechanism at a biological level, but this is not something that we can affect with precision. Surely, there must be some code at the level of SoC. Most clinicians are aware of the major perceptual modalities: visual, auditory, kinesthetic, gustatory, and olfactory. So a patient might know that it is time to freak out when he sees see a mental picture of Vietnam or hears the sounds of helicopter blades. But not every picture of Vietnam will elicit a flashback. Not every sound that is similar to helicopter blades elicits a reaction. There are usually finer levels of distinction called *submodalities* (Bandler & MacDonald, 1988). Submodalities refer to the different aspects of each of the major modalities. In the visual sphere, they include distance, size, color, sharpness, and location in space. In the auditory channel, they include volume, tone, pitch, timbre, pattern, and location in space.

Submodalities provide us with a great deal of information about our experience at a preconscious level. Consider the following question. Think about two values or beliefs that you have, one of major importance and one of minor importance (an example might be being honest as important and looking good as less important). How do you know that one of them is important and the other not important? Often, people will answer that one feels more important. The question here is how does your body know to generate this feeling? Usually one can realize that there is something in terms of the submodalities of each belief that informs the person. For many people the mental image representing the important belief is bigger or nearer or sharper or more vividly colored.

When it comes to trauma and affect modulation, working with submodalities can quickly and directly impact the person's experience. There are three indications for using this tool.

1. to demonstrate to the person that it is his or her brain or consciousness that mediates experience;

2. to demonstrate that patients can regain direct control over their experience. While the therapist can also make this explicit in the therapeutic conversation, it is the experiential impact that is most relevant.
3. to give the therapist fairly direct access to the patient's inner experience in a manner that will allow the therapist to help the patient modulate affect so the patient can feel better.

Of course these dimensions will tend to reinforce each other. Patients feel better so they have more control as well as a tool that helps them feel in control so they will feel better.

There are fairly predictable submodality changes described in Figure 4.1. As you look at the chart you will realize that these are things that come out of everyday life. They show up in our language and our actions. The reason we developed color IMAX movie theaters with surround sound is to feel more a part of the experience. If you want to lower the intensity of an experience, you do the opposite of an IMAX movie.

In language, in order to convey the idea of not being engulfed in a situation, we say things like "step back from the scene," "get perspective,"

Size: Bigger is usually stronger, more powerful more important. Smaller is associated with less powerful and less important. To reduce power and importance of an image, shrink size of an entire image; change the relative size of the client vs. some other person so that the client is equal or bigger than the other person

Distance: Closer is usually more immediate & intense. Further away is less immediate and intense. Move pictures or sounds further away to reduce affect.

Location: In front and to the right tends to be happening now or in future-in back & to the left tends to be the past. To put things in the past move them behind or to the left of the person as if fading away.

Color: Color is more affect. Black and white is less affect. Muted tones tend to mute intensity. People can have fun playing with different color palettes.

Associated/Disassociated: Associated means the person is in the experience, which will increase affect and intensity. This is the position of looking out of one's own eyes. Dis-associated means meta to the experience, which decreases affect & intensity. This position is watching oneself as if in a movie.

Tunnel Vision (TV)/Peripheral Vision (PV): TV is associated with loss of boundaries & increased intensity. PV is associated with good boundaries and having perspective and less intensity.

Loudness: Louder is stronger and more intense. Softer is the opposite.

Pitch/Tone: Much information is carried in voice tone. Low & deep tone usually means more intensity and power. High tone with squeaky pitch is less powerful. Change internal voices to sound as if they have inhaled helium to reduce their power and fearfulness.

Figure 4.1. Submodalities to increase and reduce affect.

"see the whole picture." We design IMAX movie theaters and use language such as the previous examples because that is how our consciousness operates. Of course, most people have also been conditioned to these constructs throughout life, so they experientially understand that if you make the picture further away, smaller, and black and white, the intensity of the experience will diminish.

Submodality work will change immediate experience very quickly. It is not necessarily meant to permanently change the person's internal world, especially patients with long-term multiple traumas. Generally, one does not just do submodality work by itself. Usually, it is used in conjunction with other tools to increase therapeutic leverage. One exception to this can be as an initial intervention in changing intrusive experiences to demonstrate to the person that change is possible.

I will often suggest to a patient who hears harsh internal voices (usually of a critical parent or perpetrator) to keep the words the same, but to change the tone of the voice so it sounds as if the person had inhaled helium. Invariably the person starts to laugh and experiences the voices as no longer so "all-powerful." This experience can then be used as a tool of self-management for the specific target areas worked on in therapy (e.g., the critical voice). We can also start to talk about the patient's experience with this person and reduce the cognitive distortions indicating that this person really is all-powerful. Furthermore, if the patient finds himself or herself unable to use this tool at home, it becomes feedback for us to look at what else is getting in the way.

Another example of using the approach without other interventions can be the emergency phone call. For instance, I was visiting a psychiatrist friend of mine, when a patient called him in the middle of a flashback. The psychiatrist asked me what to do. I suggested that he tell her to put the flashback on a wall like a movie screen, make it small, black and white, with scratchy sound. Then she could imagine putting it in a container until their next session. She was able to do this. She felt much better. We could continue our dinner. In this example, we added the symbolic imagery of a container.

It is up to the therapist to help the patient determine which of the submodalities will have the biggest effect. One patient with DID would have intense flashbacks of chanting and punishing voices that would cause tremendous panic and much age regression. She would act as if the experience was happening in the present. I initially accepted her reality by saying, "You hear the voices all around you. They are scaring you." Then the submodalities were altered. "Soon you will begin to hear the voices moving. It may be to the left side or the right side. Sooner or later they will begin to move behind you." Once the patient agreed that the voices were moving behind her. It was further suggested that, "As they continue to move behind you, they will begin to get softer and softer. The further they go behind you, the softer they get." These choices of alteration were not random. What does it mean to most of us when we hear sounds move behind us getting softer and softer? It means that the sound is fading into the past. Sure enough, the patient reported that she felt herself back in the present, even though this was never suggested directly.

It is crucial to understand that submodality work does not focus on changing the content of a patient's experience. In the previous example, I did not try to change what the voices said. Nor did I try to get rid of them. Most people fail at altering their consciousness because they attempt to deny or discount the content of their experience, which includes important information that some part of them wants them to know. If the therapist joins in this struggle, then the therapist will just become part of the failure. Submodality work allows the therapist and the patient to keep the information and at the same time change the experience of the information.

Submodality work allows for a great deal of creativity on the part of the therapist and the patient. It affords both parties the chance to directly alter experience in very small ways that can make a big difference. In the examples used so far, we have focused on auditory and visual channels. These tend to be the areas most often used (at least by me). But one can also work in the kinesthetic (touch) and olfactory and taste channels as well.

In the kinesthetic channel the submodalities include temperature, rough/smooth/soft, location in the body, pressure, sharp/dull, and pain/pleasure. Olfactory/taste channels include submodalities of sweet/sour, floral, salty, musty, spicy, and so on.

When working with submodalities the general rule of thumb is to notice the sensory description patients give you about their symptoms and then invite them to change the submodalities that appear to be most central to their description. For instance, a patient described a horrific scene of abuse in which she was forced to have oral sex after being anally raped. When she began to describe what was happening, she would believe it was happening at the moment and would become highly agitated. A strategy needed to be developed so that this event could become a memory rather than a flashback. In the description, she made a face of disgust and dis-smell (Nathanson, 1994). It was hypothesized that it was the smell/taste that was so affectively overwhelming. Therefore, she was hypnotized and suggestions were given for her to hallucinate a variety of smells such as oranges, lemons, roses, and honeysuckle. Suggestions were then given that when this memory ever came up in her mind she would smell something different. She was given the option to choose what that smell would be. She chose lime. After this intervention, she would stay present and describe the event as if it were in the past.

☐ Creating and Strengthening Boundaries

The concept of boundaries is often used in therapeutic and self-help contexts. The problem is that it is rarely defined. Boundary violations are central aspects of any abusive situation and most cases of trauma. A boundary is the line of distinction between any two separate things. The most basic distinction for people is between that which is me and that which is not me. Somewhat finer distinctions include that which I feel, think, believe versus that which someone else feels, thinks, or believes. Boundaries are semipermeable. They allow exchange of information across the threshold. Boundaries can be in one of three major states: fully functional, impaired, and nonexistent (see Figure 4.2).

In addition, boundaries can be impaired in one of two ways. The first is a nonfunctioning boundary, so that way too much information crosses the boundary and eventually there is no boundary. The second is an overfunctioning boundary so that it becomes insufficiently flexible and porous to the point that it is a solid "wall."

There are two common misconceptions (usually by patients) about boundaries. The first is the confusion between a boundary and a wall. Boundaries allow exchange of information across the threshold. Walls do not allow information to cross. The border between the United States and Mexico is a boundary. The Iron Curtain was a wall. Skin is a boundary. It allows a great deal of information to cross via the senses. People who have been tortured, raped, and victimized have literally had their boundaries penetrated.

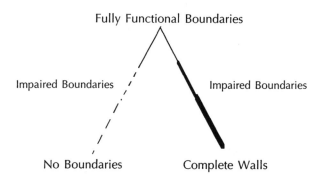

Figure 4.2. Functional and dysfunctional boundaries.

The natural reaction when one feels vulnerable and threatened is to want to strengthen those boundaries to the point of being a wall.[1] Clinically it is important to remember that people who have walls in place will increase their defensiveness if they feel vulnerable. Anyone with walls in place has impaired boundaries underneath. The correct therapeutic strategy with these people is to help them develop boundaries so they no longer need walls.

Boundaries Are Dynamic and Require Constant Upkeep

The second misconception is to think of boundaries as static things, as in, someone does not have good boundaries, but someone else creates or maintains good boundaries. Furthermore, one can have good boundaries at one point in time or in one context, relatively nonfunctional boundaries in a different context or point in time, and relatively strong walls in a third context or point in time. For those of us who were brought up in such a manner that we learned how to make boundaries fairly well most of the time, we rarely think about how we make them. It seems as if it is an innate thing we have, like our skin. Of course, this is an illusion.

There are at least three steps to good boundary maintenance. The first is the definition of the boundary; the second is the detection of possible boundary incursions by others or self; the third is the series of steps one can take if a boundary violation occurs. The three steps can be seen as part of the TOTE sequence. The definition of a boundary involves the storage of the test criterion (TC). The TC could be a picture of what I believe about who I am. The TC is built up and refined over time by a series of comparisons that mark out distinctions. For example, over time a child learns a series of distinctions about his body versus his parent's body. These eventually become encoded. As the child grows some elaboration occurs such as the boundary of "personal space" measured in terms of spatial distance between people. These distinctions have individual, familial, and even cultural dimensions (Hall, 1990). The second step of detection is carried out through a TOTE: Is this person at the appropriate distance? Then a third or action step is taken. If too far, move closer. If too close, step away, If really too close or person steps closer again, say, "Give me some space, man."

---

[1]This is exactly what happened with the Soviet Union and the Iron Curtain. The Russians had often been invaded. Since they felt vulnerable, they created a wall.

Boundaries Contain Internal States

Generally, people think of boundaries as membranes that stop intrusions from the outside. But, it is just as important to recognize that boundaries contain what is inside. In other words, boundaries contain internal states. One of the jobs of a therapist is to keep boundaried and contained any negative affective states that might leak out onto the patient. A more basic task of a boundary is to contain positive states. People with significant boundary problems do not know how to contain and maintain internal positive states. The positive affect and cognition seep out like water through a strainer.

Boundaries with Trauma, Abuse, and Neglect

In many regards any event that leads to a traumatic reaction is a boundary violation of one type or another. One could make the hypothesis that the degree and chronicity of the boundary violation would be a reasonable predictor of the development of PTSD. For instance, it has been pointed out that natural disasters do not lead to significant amounts of PTSD from an epidemiological point of view (Quarantelli, 1985), whereas violent crime in which the victim is in fear for his or her life has a high degree of PTSD as an outcome (Kilpatrick et al., 1989). The tornado destroys the boundary of your house, but it does not destroy your psychological boundaries. It is not personal. In violent crime, there is a personal attack.

Long-term childhood sexual abuse involves repeated boundary violations. The violations are not just during the sexualized acts of violence. They occur on a multitude of levels during everyday interaction in these dysfunctional families. In many cases, it is the neglect that contributes to boundary problems later in life. The neglect means that the child is not taught through modeling and interaction how to contain inner states of well-being. The child is not taught how to maintain an awareness of where his or her emotional boundaries exist, let alone learn the behavior that helps to maintain these boundaries.

Symbols of and Suggestions for Containment

One tool that has been used by many trauma therapists is a symbol for containment. The concept of containment is part of boundary making. The general idea is for the therapist and or the patient to pick a symbol of a container and then to put the dysphoric feeling in the container and seal it up for some prescribed amount of time or until certain conditions are in place. Symbols for containers include chests, bottles, boxes, caves, safes, bomb shelters, rooms, and so on.

The goal of this type of maneuver is not to get rid of the feelings. The patient is usually trying to get rid of the feelings, permanently. Of course, this is part of the problem. The use of symbols for containment has several goals. The first is to temporarily alleviate the intense affect that is often short-circuiting a person's cognitive abilities. Second, by teaching the patient that she can temporarily contain her own feelings, the patient experiences increased safety and some control and mastery. Third, by increasing safety and mastery, secondary feelings of helplessness and fear are reduced Fourth, it indirectly teaches the ideas that he has more resources than previously realized and that he can begin to activate these resources even when experiencing stress. In other words, it indirectly teaches the patient a different pattern for using the associative and dissociative processes. So instead of associating fully into an abreactive state while dissociating from current time and current resources, the patient learns that he can associate into a SoC that includes a powerful container that he can wrap around the intense affect.

There are four indications for using this tool:

1. when the goal is to help reground the patient because the patient is experiencing intense overwhelming affect or memories and appears to have no way to contain it;
2. when the goal is to decrease acting out because the patient is self-harming or acting out as a response to intense affect or memories;
3. when the goal is to prepare the patient for more intense work ahead of time by teaching this tool;
4. when the goal is to temporarily remove one affect or SoC to uncover an underlying affect or SoC. For instance, the patient uses one affect (usually in the anger/rage dimension) to deny and defend against pain and hurt.

In the first two situations the patient is often in a negative trance and may not be very resourceful. In these situations it is often better for the therapist to forgo the more democratic selection of container type. Instead the therapist can say:

Do you see that chest there in your mind? The one with the big heavy lid. (Usually the patient will answer "yes.") Good. I want you to open up the lid. Let me know when you have done that. . . . Now I want you to put those memories/feelings, etc. in the chest, so they will not overwhelm you right now. We will come back to them at a later time. Right now it is more important for you to feel grounded. Once all of those memories are in the chest close the lid.

There should be some sign of relief on the patient. The therapist needs to reinforce this. It is often helpful or even necessary to then give suggestions for relaxation and decreased arousal. In a crisis situation, once the patient has calmed down, it becomes especially important for the therapist to change the subject. You have just helped the patient put the intensely dysphoric experience in a container. If you or the patient starts talking about the problem immediately, it may break the seal on the container. It will also invite the patient to feel that he or she failed at containing the experience.

In using this tool the therapist needs to convey confidence that it will work. The best attitude for the therapist to have is presupposition that this will help. It is not so much that you say this out loud to the patient. It is more of an internal expectation. Just like you expect the sun to come up in the morning, the patient will get relief by putting the difficult experience in the container.

Before a therapist actively pursues traumatic material, it is important that the patient learn how to contain the feelings that arise, especially in the event that they cannot finish processing the material in one session (which is often the case). Usually, this goal is in the background of treatment. For example, when the patient called the psychiatrist in a crisis and both submodalities and containment imagery were used, the immediate goal was to help the patient calm down. There was an additional goal of helping the patient learn to contain and boundary dysphoric affect between sessions. In the event that the patient does not contain material well between sessions, this is feedback to the therapist that (a) the patient needs to learn these skills and (b) the amount of material covered in sessions should be reduced until the patient can contain the affect.

Some patients have had many experiences of being traumatized (e.g., dissociative disordered patients). It may be helpful to use a container that allows them to keep the traumatic experiences both contained and sorted. One good image of this is the image of safety deposit boxes in a vault. Each memory gets its own box. The boxes can be labeled. Different alters can have their own sections of the vault or they can have their own vault. The vault(s) can be closed and opened as needed. This imagery can be very useful in the second phase of treatment when more active work on traumatic memories is occurring. Events can be looked at and processed. Anything leftover and unprocessed gets put back in the box in the vault for later work.

Temporarily removing one affect or SoC to uncover an underlying affect or SoC is a somewhat different use of this tool. I have used this tool in one of two situations. First, either the patient or I make note of the fact that the patient is stuck in one SoC regarding some topic. Second, the patient has the sense that there is something underneath that he cannot access. Or, the patient has no sense that there is anything underneath at all, but I believe that there is something underneath. In this latter situation, the patient is feeling very unhappy about the unresourceful SoC in which he is stuck and believes that there is nothing more to him. I am looking for something resourceful "underneath" (as opposed to some trauma or other unresourceful SoC).

For example, one patient, Tony, reported always feeling cold and numb and empty. He despaired, because he believed that there was nothing else about him. Tony had been abused for many years. He would often become very angry and act out. Underneath the acting out was this experience of cold, empty numbness. He was asked to imagine the feeling of cold numbness being poured into a container. Tony imagined a tanker that usually carried liquid nitrogen. There was a pipeline from his body into the truck. After a few minutes he saw icicles forming on the pipe, but did not feel anything changing for him. Tony was worried that his fear that there was nothing else to him but anger and emptiness was true. He was told in a calm yet very expectant tone, "Just keep the lines open and flowing." After a few more minutes his body began to shake, without any feelings. Tony was uncharacteristically intrigued by this. In a few more minutes he began to cry. After a while, Tony recounted how he had often had to walk the streets and was often very cold and scared. He had repeatedly told himself in an autohypnotic fashion that he felt nothing. Nothing was going to hurt him. It is important to note that this was not a recovered memory. Tony had always remembered this. He just had never talked about it and never realized it had any significance in his life.

Tony was then given a choice of whether or not he wanted to keep the frozen material in the tanker or have it come back into him. It is important to give patients this choice for two reasons. First, it is respectful of their rights. Not being respectful of these rights can provoke a patient into resisting. Second, the patient just might want to get those feelings back. This can become a point of discussion in the therapy, but at the end of the day the therapist should accede to the patient's wishes. Third, in either case the patient is being asked to be the agent of his or her own experience. Even if the patient chooses to put the old feeling back, the patient has tacitly agreed that he or she could remove the feelings. Should the patient want to not have those feelings return, then it is an active decision that is much more powerful than if the patient had not chosen.

Tony did not want to keep the frozen feeling. So we had him disconnect the hose from himself and sent the truck away. We also decided that he needed to do something with the child or new frozen feelings could develop. So he imagined bringing that child in front of a warm fire, where Tony, the adult, could talk with him at length. Tony reported that he actually felt warm. He often returned to this image in his own life for months to come.

In certain circumstances, the patient can be asked to try new options for coping behavior while the negative affect is in temporary storage. For instance, a patient who habitually used anger as a defense was asked to imagine how she would handle the conflicts with her young daughter now that the anger was safely stored away. She reported that she felt hurt that her daughter did not listen to her when she tried to set rules. She could imagine explaining to her daughter that it hurt her feelings that she did not listen to her. She was setting these rules to help the daughter. If the daughter was unhappy they could talk about the daughter's feelings. This was new thinking for the patient. She still had work to do to put this new fantasy into action, but at least now she had some experiential map to guide her.

Stabilizing Here-and-Now Reality: Getting Grounded

Most of us do not attend to the fact that it actually takes a boundary to stabilize here-and-now reality from there-and-then reality. The only time it might even reach a level of awareness is if someone is very upset and does not feel grounded. Many years ago I remember learning a ridiculously easy technique to ground patients at the end of a session if they had been very upset. They were to look around the room and report all of the different colors they saw. For most people this worked pretty well. This approach worked because the patient's SoC included large elements of internal experiences about past and current realities were in the background. By having them alter their attention, their SoC was changed to bring the current time and immediate visual perceptions to the foreground, thereby forcing their previous awareness into the background. It also worked well because these patients were much more used to having current reality in the foreground of experience. People who have been traumatized often have more practice at having the past intrude into awareness. So they need more help at stabilizing a here-and-now SoC.

Dolan's 54321 Exercise

Dolan (1991) has described an elaboration on the notice-the-colors strategy that can be quite effective at returning someone to a here-and-now SoC.

This approach is used when a patient is upset and more in touch with experience from the past and the patient needs to feel more in touch with the immediate present in order to calm down.

Patients are asked to say out loud 5 things they see, then 5 things they hear, and then 5 sensations they feel. Then they are asked to repeat the process for 4 items in each modality, then 3 in each modality, until they get to 1 example of each modality. They stop when they become calm. If they are not calm by the time they get to 1, they can start over again. It is helpful for the therapist to model this technique. It is important to tell the patients that they can repeat items. For instance, at this moment of writing:

> I can see the keyboard, the screen, the grass outside of my window, the gray desk, pink slips of paper. I hear the computer, the typing of the keys, the computer, the clock ticking, sounds from the other room. I feel my seat against the chair, coldness in my hands, the feel of the keys as I touch them, coldness in my feet, my back against the chair.

This would then be repeated with four examples of each, and then three, and so on. The person could notice the same things or different things. As a person does this exercise and becomes very focused on the immediate present, it is not unusual to lose track of the number of items one has said in a given round. This is usually a sign of the approach working. This approach is a bit like a minimindfulness meditation where the person is being asked to be aware of what he is aware of. The major difference is that this approach is semistructured.

The Use of Peripheral Vision to Stabilize Boundaries

This tool is a specialized use of the submodality of peripheral vision. The indication for using this tool is that the patient dealing with an experience that involves at least one other person and the patient is feeling out of control or unresourceful. The patient might report being unable to think or just getting sucked into the situation. The goal is to help the patient "step back from the situation" in order to get a "wider perspective." These are the words we use in everyday language that reveal the submodality involved.

The tool is taught as follows:

1. Have patients review the problem situation in their mind to notice how much tunnel vision there is and/or the lack of peripheral vision (PV).
2. Have patients learn about PV by having them focus on a point in

front of them (e.g., a lamp in the office) and then holding their index fingers up in the air toward the periphery of their vision. They must be able to keep the lamp in focus as well as see their fingers. Have the patient practice to see how wide they can get their peripheral vision.

3. Have patients review the scene again, but this time consciously putting back the peripheral vision. The patient should feel much more resourceful and see more options.

4a. Patients can be instructed to do step 2 at home at nonstressful times as an awareness training exercise.

4b. Then when difficult situations arise they can consciously use the exercises they have been practicing.

If the patient is in the middle of some type of intrusive experience a therapist can still use this tool. It will be most helpful if the quality of the intrusive experience is one of being engulfed. The therapist will usually have to condense the approach to simple instructions and exhortations as the patient reports the experience. The use of PV can be added to any other imagistic tool such as the energy bubble (see below) or TRC (see chapter 5) to increase the degree of separation a patient feels. The use of PV will not magically create boundaries for all situations. It can be part of the process of active boundary maintenance that we all need to do.

The Energy Bubble or Shield

The energy bubble can be a powerful tool in a patient's arsenal of self-help skills. Essentially the goal is to help the patient create a semipermeable boundary that keeps the patient feeling secure inside and keeping negativity from others outside. The image that I use and almost always tell patients is the idea of the shield of the starship *Enterprise* that allows Captain Picard to stay so calm and reasonable.

There are a number of indications for using this tool:

1. When patients interact with other people (in specific situations or even generally) and they have an impaired ability to (a) fend off manipulations and other intrusive actions on the part of others, (b) stay present because of perceived (accurately or inaccurately) threats from others; (c) remain assertive because of perceived (accurately or inaccurately) threats from others; (d) differentiate between the current context and previous contexts.

2. Intimacy problems based on the overuse of walls.

The first set of indications is self-explanatory. The second indication may not make immediate sense. It was stated earlier that people who do walls have impaired boundaries. Phenomenologically, people who do walls appear to be more aggressive, distant, and out of touch with their feelings than people whose boundary impairment is one of underuse. The appropriate treatment for people who are walled off is to teach them appropriate boundaries. When this happens they naturally relax their walls. For instance, Amy was an abuse survivor who reported having repeated difficulties with her 6-year-old daughter, Rebecca. Rebecca would do age-appropriate crying and demanding and so on. Amy described how when her daughter acted in this way, it felt like she was being attacked. The sound of Rebecca's crying or whining would send Amy into a tailspin. Amy knew that the child was not at fault. However, Amy was becoming more and more angry with her child and more distant. Amy was becoming angry with herself, because how could she be such a cold, unloving mother (the beginning of a negative spiral)?

Amy was taught the energy bubble. She was a bit surprised at the use of this tool. She thought she should be warmer and more affectionate. This seemed to be a paradox. What she did not understand was that it was her difficulty differentiating from her child that necessitated her distancing. Several developments occurred. First, she had immediate relief from the effects of her child's negative affective states. Second, Amy then felt more able to be with her child *spontaneously*. The spontaneous change made Amy feel much better as a mother. Third, Amy was then able to become aware of how her unmet needs as a child were resonating with Rebecca's neediness. This was a discussion in therapy for some time. However, during that time Amy remained much more functional as a mother.

There are six steps in this tool:

1. Patient education about boundaries. Patients are taught the preceding discussion of boundaries at a level that fits with their cognitive skills.
2. The creation of a visual symbol of a boundary. Patients can choose from the metaphor of a bubble or a shield. Each has a slightly different connotation. The symbol must include the concepts of (a) a membrane that distinguishes self from other, and (b) semipermeability so that the person can still remain in contact and not be walled off. These are almost always achieved through the metaphor of the shield having a color(s) and being translucent so the person can see through the shield. Sometimes a sound to the shield is added (such as a hum or buzz).
3. Within the boundary the person must be able to contain feelings of safety and/or centeredness as well as physical comfort.

4. The ability to modulate the strength of the shield
5. Practice using the tool in different contexts with appropriate feedback to both the patient and the therapist that the tool is being helpful.
6. Suggestions for the automatic nature of the tool. Implicit in this step as well as the previous one is the building up of a self-concept that the patient can activate and effectively use boundaries.

A full transcript of the session follows.

I would like you to allow yourself to imagine that you are surrounded, as near to or as far away from you as is comfortable, by an energy bubble or an energy shield. As you begin to imagine this, I want you to recognize that this energy bubble can appear in a variety of manners. It may seem very much like the energy shield that surrounds the starship *Enterprise* in one of the *Star Trek* series or movies. It should be translucent. You should be able to see through it clearly. It might have a tint to it, like blue or green, gold or silver, yellow or white, or whatever color is meaningful for you. It could shimmer or sparkle. It might even have a kaleidoscope of colors. Some people hear the energy of the bubble or the shield. It can sound like a hum or a drone. The important thing is that you can be aware of its presence in some manner.

Now when the energy bubble is on, three things happen. The first is that whenever you breathe in, you feel yourself breathing in safety and centeredness. Just allow yourself to take a slow deep breath and breathe in safety and centeredness. With each breath you take you can feel yourself feeling safer and safer. The second thing that happens is that with every breath you breathe out, you breathe out comfort that stays inside the bubble and surrounds you, so that as you continue to breathe out, you find yourself surrounded by more and more comfort. And, as you breathe out more comfort, you will discover that it becomes easier to breathe in safety, and as you breathe in safety it is easier to breath out comfort. So, the safety and the comfort continue to build upon each other with every breath you take and every breath you exhale. And it is nice to discover that your own ability to breathe can contribute to your safety and comfort.

Now the third quality of the shield is this. The bubble acts as a filter against anything that is negative. Anything that is outside of the shield that is negative cannot get through the shield. It filters out visual negativity like scowls on the face or auditory negativity like critical tones of voice. So, for instance, if someone were yelling at you, you would hear their words but the anger and shaming aspect of that communication would just not get through. The look on their face would not frighten you. You would be feeling comfortable and safe, and the negativity would get filtered out. If we return to the idea of the shield around the starship *Enterprise*, it would be like another ship firing on the *Enterprise*, but the shield keeps everyone inside safe. And since everyone is safe, the captain can remain calm and think about the best course of action. The captain might even try to communicate with the aliens. The protection of the shield makes it possible to not be recruited into fear or violence. This is one of the important paradoxes of this bubble/shield system. Because you now have a boundary that keeps you separate from outside influences, you actually can be closer to other people. Since you are safe and can resist being recruited into fear or attack, you can feel free to be more curious about others and to communicate with others. Just like the starship *Enterprise*, the shield allows you to explore the strange new worlds of other people and to reach out and go where you have not gone before. So if someone were firing anger or guilt or some other type of manipulation at you, the shield would stop that negative energy, and of course you would be continuing to breathe in safety and to breathe out comfort. The result would be that you would know what the person is doing, but you could resist being recruited into fear or attack. You would remain calm, and from the calmness you could think about how to handle things in a manner that truly suited you.

Now as I have been talking, you may have noticed that the shield's intensity has varied a bit, because one does not always need to have full-intensity shields. If there was a scale from 0–10 where 0 is no shield and 10 is full shield, sometimes a level of 2 or 3 would be sufficient, though at other times you would need a level of 9 or 10.

Everyone has their own idea of how to turn something on to different levels of intensity. Imagine that you can see in your mind's eye a control knob or a series of buttons with the numbers 0–10 such that you could set your energy bubble to that setting. Practice turning its strength up and down. Notice that as you increase its strength, the colors may get more intense or iridescent or the hum may get louder or change in pitch. And as it gets lower, the reverse happens. Even at full power you can still hear through it and see through it. You can still stay connected if you choose. Or, you can resist being pulled into the influence of negative energy.

In order to help your unconscious mind use the bubble to increasing levels of effectiveness, I would like you to practice using this technique in your mind.[2] First I would like you to make a picture of yourself in a situation with someone else that is neutral. It could be like you are watching a movie or a reflection of yourself in the mirror. This should be a situation without stress for you. Some people see this very clearly; other people just get more of a sense of this without clear pictures. Either way is fine. Either way you'll be training your mind to use the tool of the energy bubble. Just like any other tool, it is important to practice. Just allow yourself to see a picture of you and the other person and watch yourself as you turn on the bubble. Notice what it looks like around you. Do you

---

[2]The following use of rehearsing is self-image thinking (Lankton & Lankton, 1983) described in chapter 7.

notice any changes in you? Do you see yourself breathing a little bit more relaxed? Are your face muscles more relaxed? Do you stand a little taller? Do you smile more? Or do you say different things to this person? Take a moment and notice whatever it is you notice. You can feel free to adjust the bubble strength to the level that feels most appropriate for this situation.

Now as you continue to see yourself with the shield, let this scene fade and allow a different scene to develop about a situation that in the past was just slightly difficult. This new scene should be something that in the past was only slightly difficult. And as that scene develops, allow the bubble to adjust to whatever intensity is most appropriate for your well-being.

Once again watch yourself with the energy shield on. What changes do you see? As you are watching yourself in that scene, make sure that you continue to breathe in safety and breathe out comfort, because you are inside your bubble watching yourself being inside a bubble. Since the you that you are watching has this tool now, it is probable that you will notice that you respond to that situation differently than you previously did. This is to be expected and desired. That is, the point of having a new tool is to help a person master situations that used to be difficult. Just allow yourself to watch yourself handling the situation in a better manner. Does it surprise you that you can do this? Does it please you?

Assuming that you have handled this well, take a minute and imagine that you are stepping into the picture so that you are not watching this anymore; you do not see you and the other person, you see the other person through the energy bubble. You are now living it with your new tool in place. Notice how good it feels? Make any adjustments to allow yourself to feel even more resourceful. Many people find it helpful to maintain their peripheral vision. It is like maintaining a wide-angle view so that the person you see is in focus but so are other things in focus.

When you are satisfied with this situation, step out of the picture and take a moment to reflect on what this different way of handling things might mean to you.

Once again let the scene fade and let another scene develop of a situation that in the past was more difficult than the previous one. Make sure that it is just a little more difficult. As you listen to this tape several times, you can keep increasing the difficulty. It is important to take things step by step to increase your proficiency with the tool of the bubble and shield. Since this scene is of a situation that used to be more difficult, you will probably notice that the energy shield is automatically at a higher setting.

Watch yourself inside the shield breathing in safety and breathing out comfort. Notice how the bubble shimmers and filters out the negativity. I had one patient whose bubble would turn slightly orange every time a sound wave from a negative word hit the shield. She told me that the bubble turned orange as it dissipated the negative energy. She also told me that she had never been very good at even realizing that people were being negative with her. She had thought that there was just something wrong with her whenever she started to feel bad. After she learned this tool, she discovered that she would be having a conversation with someone and all of a sudden she would become aware of the orange glow. Then she would quickly review what had just happened and, sure enough, the person with whom she was talking had just sent some negative energy her way. So not only did she have the protection from the negativity, but she also learned to discern when someone was being mean or critical or shaming.

So watch yourself in this scene and notice how you handle things differently based upon your ability to filter out the negativity and to maintain safety and comfort. Allow yourself to be aware of how you hold your body differently, how you breathe differently, what you say differently. Notice to what extent you prefer this manner of response to your previous response pattern.

Assuming that you have handled this well, take a minute and imagine that you are stepping into the picture so that you are not watching this anymore; you do not see you and the other person, you see the other person through the energy bubble. You are now living it with your new tool in place. Notice how good it feels? Make any adjustments to allow yourself to feel even more resourceful. Be aware of how you maintain that peripheral vision. Notice that you can keep the situation in perspective. Allow yourself to become aware of what difference these types of coping responses might mean for your sense of yourself.

Then step back out of this picture, and as you do that I would like you to recognize that you have been training your brain. Allow yourself to memorize these experiences. You do not know how you know 6+6 is 12, but at one point you probably memorized it. Just allow yourself to remember what you saw, what you heard, and how you felt as you have been practicing and allow your unconscious mind to memorize it.

You have been training your brain to respond automatically. Now you have had plenty of experience at having your brain respond automatically for your benefit. For instance, your eye blinks without you even thinking of it if a piece of dirt heads toward it. If you have an itch, you automatically scratch it; often times you do not even realize that you had the itch or that you scratched it. Sometimes, only after you scratched the itch do you realize that you automatically took care of yourself. Still other times, you notice that you are automatically scratching an itch, but you do so without any conscious effort. Still other times, you have an itch and you automatically follow the urge to scratch. So you have plenty of experience automatically responding to take care of yourself. And since you have been listening to this tape and practicing, you will be able to automatically respond to the earliest warning signal that you need your bubble. I do not know exactly how you will first respond in an automatic fashion. There really is no way for me to know. I do know that you can respond automatically to the earliest signal for the need for shields in a variety of manners.

It may be that your unconscious will be so fast that you will automatically put on the shield in response to the situation and you will not even realize that this has happened. And even though you handle the situation better, you will just take it for granted that that is the way it is supposed to be. For instance, one time a friend of mine had been doing some work like the work you are doing now while listening to this tape. We had been in a meeting prior to the work and we went to a meeting after the work. I was aware of the work she had done because it was during a training seminar. I watched her automatically do the thing that she had rehearsed doing. She was obviously different in the second situation than in the first one, but when I asked her if she had noticed anything different about herself, she looked at me like I was a bit nuts, and responded, "No." When I told her what I had witnessed, she remembered that in fact she had done all those things automatically without any awareness of it at all.

You may also discover that you may automatically snap on the bubble without any awareness, and only after it has happened will you realize, "Hey, I just snapped on the bubble and handled the situation." Or you might realize that it is happening automatically while it is happening without any conscious effort on your part. There may be times that you automatically realize that you need that bubble, and then you automatically use your conscious effort to turn it on. I do not know which of these things will happen to you. Quite probably it will be a combination of these things at different times. I do not know exactly how you will respond automatically. What I do know is that your brain will respond automatically to protect you. What I do know is that once a person has a tool that works, the brain naturally and automatically chooses to use it.

Creating Boundaries Through Externalizing, and Symbolizing

Many survivors of abuse have difficulty separating their sense of self or identity from the pain they feel. There is a class of interventions that they can use to begin to get some distance and separation from the pain. I have already mentioned the use of symbols of containers.

Putting the Pain Out of the Body and On the Paper

Variation 1: Drawing or painting the pain. It is not my goal here to describe the variety of art therapy techniques. The goal of this particular task is for patients to imagine the pain they feel flow through their hands out through their fingers and onto the page in any way they like. They are to think of this task literally. That is, they can see their pain outside of themselves. The person can do this once a day or as needed.

Variation 2: Writing their pain words. This is the exact same task, except patients write out everything that is bothering them in sentences.

The Write/Draw, Read, Burn Task

Again patients are to either write or draw the pain, imagining it leave the body on day 1. On day 2 they are to read or look over what they have produced and then destroy the letter or drawing. On day 3 they are to start the procedure all over again. It is perfectly fine if they repeat exactly what they produced before, or they may produce different material. It is also helpful if the patient ritualizes this task by using a set time and place, for a specific amount of time, and specific pad of paper and pen. Finally, they are instructed that if they start to think about the pain or the trauma or other dysphoric feelings or obsessive thoughts related to the trauma at any time other than the prescribed time, they should tell themselves that they will think about it at the prescribed time and not at the current moment. The patient and therapist can discuss how much time to set aside based on the amount of time the patient spends feeling pain and other dysphoric experiences. One hour is the maximum. If they are not able to stop themselves from thinking about the trauma during the day, then they probably need to increase the amount of time they are writing or to condense the task to write, read, and burn on each day.

This approach, first described by de Shazer (1985), has several benefits in addition to simply writing down the pain, most of them having to do with boundary maintenance. The first is that the reading/viewing of the production helps to create a boundary and distance between the viewer and the production. The patient can reflect on what is on the paper. In the same vein, the patient destroys the production, which further separates the patient from what was on the page. Second, the act of destroying the production connotes that it is possible to eliminate the effects of the abuse or trauma. Third, the requirement of waiting until the allotted time to do the task and not focusing on the traumatic material helps to teach the patient inner boundaries to SoCs. It follows the central idea of both/and approach. Many people have the intrusive experience and want to get rid of it totally (an either/or strategy). Since the person makes no space for the material, it comes out at all sorts of inopportune times. This approach creates time for the traumatic material and space for symptom-free functioning. Fourth, since the task does not necessarily work in one round, it connotes the idea of active boundary maintenance. It is something akin to taking out the garbage. You cannot avoid making garbage. You must take the garbage outside of the boundary of your house so that you do not stink up your house.

☐ End State Retraining

End state retraining is a tool that is useful for dysfunctional behavioral sequences whose underlying motivation is to help the person move from a relatively uncomfortable state to one of increased comfort. These behaviors can range from compulsive eating to self-cutting behaviors. For instance, many trauma patients will engage in self-injurious behavior such as cutting in order to alleviate inner tension and pain. When asked, an alter of a patient with DID reported that she cut her arms to get rid of the pain in her vagina (that was a kinesthetic flashback).

What the patient is usually not aware of is that the behavioral act such as cutting is the initiating step of a sequence of changes in state of consciousness that leads to the desired state. Essentially, the patient experiences a domino effect. Unfortunately, the patient believes that the most salient feature of the sequence is the initiating behavior. The patient wrongly concludes that the only way to get to this better state of consciousness is to keep doing the initiating behavior (e.g., cutting).

End state retraining merely takes advantage of the overlearned domino effect by skipping the initiating behavior and ensuring that the dominos continue to fall toward the desired end state. Once the clinician has determined that the behavior is being used to reach a relatively positive state (as opposed to self-punishment), the patient is asked to imagine the usual sequence of events, including the initiating behavior, but as soon as the patient imagines the initiating behavior, she is asked to report the very first thing that she notices that lets her know that something is happening. When she reports this, she is asked to focus on that development happening and to then report the next thing that she notices that develops that lets her know that she is heading to the desired state. The types of data that we want are the submodalities that she notices.

Here is a sequence used with one patient, C, who cut herself. This has often been done when the patient is in the middle of an intense desire to cut.

C: (With intense agitation) *I have to cut, I have to cut. Please let me cut.*

T: *When you cut, what happens?*

C: *I feel better. Please I have to cut.*

T: *I am going to help you learn to feel better without cutting. What you really want is to feel better, right?*

C: *Yes. I really need to cut myself.*

T: *I would like you to imagine a time that you cut yourself. As you imagine this, please tell me the very first thing, no matter how small, that you notice that lets you know it's beginning to work.*

C: *I see the blood.*

T: *OK, you see the blood. What is the very next thing that lets you know you are beginning to get some relief?*

C: (Slight decrease in agitation and pressure) *There is warmth developing in my arm.*

T: *That's right, you are beginning to feel warmth developing in your arm. As you feel the warmth developing in your arm, what is the next thing that you notice that tells you that it is working?*

C: *The warmth goes up my neck.* (Increasingly calm)

T: *Good, you are feeling the warmth go up your neck. What is the next thing that you notice that tells you that it is working?*

C: *Well, I stop hearing all of those voices. This is weird.*

T: *All right, you stop hearing those voices. Does this mean that there is quietness developing in your mind?*

C: *Yes, it is getting quiet.*

T: *So as your mind is getting quieter, what is the next thing that you notice that tells you that it is working?*

C: *I see a kind of orange glow. It is so peaceful.* (Patient is calm and relaxed)

T: *So what do you call this experience of the orange glow?*

C: *I don't know. It's just an orange glowing relaxed feeling.*

T: *An orange glowing relaxed feeling. Is that a good name for it?*

C: *Yeh. I really like it.*

T: *This orange glowing relaxed feeling: It is the state of mind that you really want, is it not? The cutting was only a way to get to this feeling. And now you know that you no longer need the cutting, because you can skip that step.*

C: *Yeh, I feel so relaxed.*

T: *So you can remember that the next time you think you want to get to this feeling by cutting, you can remember that you can get here in a much more direct route. You remember what we did here. How you imagined the blood and that immediately led to your arm getting warmth. And once you felt the warmth developing in your arm, you notice that the warmth goes up your neck. And as the warmth goes up your neck, in a weird way the voices go away and your mind gets quiet. And as your mind gets quiet the orange glow that is so peaceful and relaxed develops. And your mind and body can memorize that you can get that orange glowing relaxed feeling whenever you need it. In fact, while you are feeling it now, you can even just say the words "orange glowing relaxed feeling" over and over in your mind. So that just thinking the words will remind your body and mind of the sequence of steps that we did here, the warmth moving up your arm and then into your neck, and then the voices going away and your mind getting quieter, and then the warm orange glow that is so peaceful and relaxing.*

You used to think that cutting was the most important part. You did not know that there was another way you could get to the orange glowing feeling. Actually, it is a step-by-step path to the orange glowing feeling. First, you imagined seeing the blood. Just imagining it was enough for you to begin to feel the warmth in your arm. And then, as you notice the warmth developing in your arm, it moves up toward your neck. And then you realize that the voices stop and your mind is getting quieter and quieter. And finally you arrive at the orange glowing feeling. So, the next time a situation develops where you would have begun to have that old desire to cut, you will automatically realize that you have a better way to get to the orange glowing feeling. And you will be able to remember the steps automatically. The warmth in your arms, moving up your arm toward your neck, your mind getting quieter, and the orange glowing feeling. As you get better at it, even just thinking about the orange glowing feeling will begin to make it happen automatically.

It is important to note that the therapist repeats the each development in the present tense and then asks, "As it continues to develop, what do you notice happening next?" This language helps to keep the dominos falling. Below are the steps used in end state retraining.

1. Have the patient imagine initiating behavior.
2. Ask the patient to focus on the very first thing (step A) she is aware of that lets her know the behavior is beginning to work. Have her tell you what it is. You are looking for the modalities (visual, kinesthetic, and auditory) as well as the submodality sequences that lead to the end state.
3. Say to the person, "That's right . . . you *are* beginning to feel [step A]. As you are feeling [step A], what is the very next thing that you notice *is* beginning to happen [step B]?"
4. Repeat previous section for step B and then step C. There usually are no more than 3–4 steps.
5. Develop an anchor or cue for this end state with a word, image, or gesture.
6. When the end state is achieved, reframe for the patient that it is this end state that he most wants. The problematic behavior was only a means to the end. Now he has a better means so he can get this end state in this new manner. The patient can use the cue word, image, or anchor. Posthypnotic-style suggestions are given about how new behavior will replace the old behavior. In the example above, notice the use of verb tense. The cue for cutting is separated from the actual behavior. It is a cue that, in the past, would have started the "old" (not the current) behavior. An audiotape can also be made of this process.

Trouble-Shooting End State Retraining

Problem 1. It does not work consistently. The most likely reason for this is that you are actually dealing with different cutting behaviors that are meeting different needs and may be linked to different ego states or alters (Calof, 1995). For instance, cutting on the right wrist may be very different psychologically from cutting on the left forearm. One option would be to redo the process on the different behavior. If this does not work, it may be that this self-harming behavior does not meet the original criterion that the goal is to reach a more positive state. The goal may be one of self-punishment. In this case, you cannot use this tool.

Problem 2. The domino effect toward a positive state does not happen. One possibility is that the behavior is not an attempt to get to a more positive state, so the tool will not work. A second possibility is that the therapist has not used language that associates the patient into the SoC being described and then links that state to the next SoC. For example, the therapist should say, "And *as* you feel X, what is the next thing you *notice developing?*" The word "as" helps to associate the patient into the feeling of "X." The question, "What is the next thing that you notice developing?" presupposes that something is developing that comes after "X."

Problem 3. Despite having used the tool on a number of states and experiencing some improvement in self-harming behavior, the patient still harms himself or herself. This actually is not a problem, per se. It is a limitation of the tool. The tool will give the patient a toehold on the behavior. It will teach the patient that he or she does have the ability to have control. It will not change the patient's underlying dynamic motivations. These issues need to be dealt with in therapy. The patient needs to make a clear contracts with himself or herself about giving up self-harm as a way to cope with life. In order to do this, it is usually necessary to understand the underlying motivations of the behavior. Once the motivation has been ascertained, alternative approaches to addressing those motivations must be found. In addition, in the case of dissociative disorders, the patient needs to resolve any number of issue that leave him or her vulnerable to the need to harm the self. One patient became very attached to the following line of thinking. If the patient felt trapped and hopeless with the resulting need to harm herself, she would think that she must have made some previous step or choice (hours, days, or weeks ago) that led her down this path. She would then try to identify what that choice was. Even if she could not, being able to recognize that she did have the possibility of learning how to control her feelings was usually sufficient to obviate the need to cut.

☐ Summary

The goal of this chapter has been to provide tools that help increase the number of resourceful SoCs of the patient. This goal is of primary importance in the initial phase of treatment, where building stability and safety is a necessary prerequisite for future work. In working with people who have had multiple traumas, the issues of safety and stabilization will continue to be present throughout treatment. It is the premise of this book that, if given a forced choice to work only on building resources or only on focusing on trauma, the former is the more effective choice. Luckily we do not have to be restricted by such either/or thinking. Even though trauma cannot be destroyed, it can be dissolved in a sea of resourcefulness. I have found that as therapy proceeds, I have had to remind myself and patients to follow the solution-oriented credo of "doing more of what works" and to come back to these tools as needed. Certain tools, such as submodalities, will also be very useful in phase 2 of treatment. The reader can refer to Figure 3.1 to see how the different tools can be used for different goals and in different parts of treatment.

5

CHAPTER

Tools for Transforming Traumatic Memory

☐ PTSD as a Disorder of Memory

In many respects the psychological problems that result from trauma (i.e., PTSD and DID, DESNOS) are problems with memory. The core problem in PTSD consists of a failure to integrate upsetting experience into autobiographical memory (van der Kolk, McFarlane, & van der Hart, 1996). In reviewing clinical data as well as studies, van der Kolk (1989) described what has been observed since the time of Janet (1889). Memories of traumatic incidents are initially organized more on a somatosensory perceptual level rather than on an autobiographical and verbal level. He noted that this supports Piaget's (1962) theory that failure of verbal memory leads to the organization of memory on an iconic level. Piaget stated: "It is because there is no immediate accommodation that there is a complete dissociation of inner activity from the external world. As the external world is solely represented by images, it is assimilated without resistance (i.e. unattached to other memories) to the unconscious ego."

Traumatic events by their very nature overwhelm the person's ability to process the information (Horowitz, 1973, 1986). "The information" is not a lot of dry facts and figures. The information includes intense pain, shock, fear, horror, rage, conflicting desires, life-and-death stakes, evaluations of personal actions and reactions, and so on. In many cases basic cognitive assumptions are shattered (Janoff-Bulman, 1985, 1992).

The coping system fails. The usual motto of "united we stand, divided we fall" is rendered useless. So a new strategy comes into plan. "United we collapse, divided we survive." The person automatically begins to dissociate aspects of the experience into separate compartments of the mind. In computer terms it is like taking information and putting it into different buffers for later processing. The alternation between intrusion and numbing (Horowitz, 1973, 1986) is the result of TOTEs having to do with bringing the memory back out of buffer for processing alternating with TOTEs that put the memory back into buffer when too affectively overwhelming.

The intrusion of traumatic memory can take several problematic forms:

1. Flashbacks of the event in which the person feels as if he is reliving the event.
2. Flashbacks of the feelings or sensations of the event without the content. In this situation the person may feel angry or scared without knowing why. She may also have painful sensations where she was originally injured. She may or may not remember the connection to the trauma.
3. Compulsive reexposure to or reenactment of the trauma. This can include a variety of phenomena, including combat soldiers becoming mercenaries and sexually abused women becoming prostitutes (van der Kolk, McFarlane, & van der Hart, 1996).
4. Self-harm and self-mutilation. These behaviors are usually done by the person as an attempt to reduce tension and other negative feelings (Briere, 1992). Nevertheless, they also create new experiences of trauma.

In all of these cases, rarely does the person understand that his current difficulties are related to his memories of trauma, which are usually partially if not completely dissociated from awareness (van der Kolk, McFarlane, & van der Hart, 1996). It is of significant interest to note that flashbacks tend to be highly correlated with the lack of verbal memory. Once patients can talk about their experience, the sensory and emotional quality of the flashback tends to vanish. When there is still some aspect of the flashback present, it tends to indicate that the patient has left out of the narrative some other important piece of the experience. It does not necessarily mean that there are more horrific events buried in the patient's unconscious. It is far more likely that there is simply some important emotional meaning that has been left out of the description.

Avoiding and numbing of traumatic memory is less dramatic than the intrusive side of the disorder. However, it is far more central to the process of PTSD and the dissociative disorders than is often recognized. Peterson, Prout, and Schwarz (1991) suggested that avoidance can occur on four levels: avoidance of affect/feelings (numbing), avoidance of knowledge (amnesia), avoidance of behavior (phobic responses), and avoidance of communication about the event. At this point I would also add avoidance of disowned or dissociated aspects of self.

Virtually all of the addiction behaviors (including drugs and alcohol, self-harm, gambling, bulimia, and addictive eating) in which survivors of trauma engage can be viewed as attempts to anesthetize and avoid painful memories. They are almost always partially successful (at least in the short run) and are therefore under reinforcement contingencies. In fact, once an addict stops using, it often takes 1 to 2 years for the numbing effects of drugs and alcohol to wear off. At that time the painful memories of trauma begin to surface. Many addicts relapse at this point. By the time patients enters treatment, they are often unaware of the origins of their impulses to engage in these activities.

Decreasing avoidance is a major aspect of the treatment of trauma regardless of school of thought (Peterson, Prout, & Schwarz, 1991). Van der Kolk, van der Hart, and Marmer (1996) stated:

> The essence of treatment of traumatic memories can be described as follows: (1) overcoming the phobia of the dissociated sense of self associated with the trauma, as well as the fear and shame associated with thinking about the trauma; (2) overcoming the phobia of the dissociated traumatic memories, which must be uncovered and transformed from the intrusive re-experiencing of trauma-related feelings and sensations to a trauma related narrative within a personal stream of consciousness; and (3) overcoming the phobia of life itself which includes the fear of being re-victimized, and the feeling that the victim will be unable to take charge of his or her own destiny. (p. 321)

Internalization of trauma and memory refers to the longer lasting characterological changes and schemes that result from trauma. A few of the basic changes that tend to occur are:

1. Impairment of basic trust, which is very common, especially when the trauma is inflicted on a child by a caregiver (Briere, 1988; Burgess, Hartmann, & McCormick, 1987; McCann & Pearlman, 1990: Pynoos et al., 1987; van der Kolk, 1996b).
2. A distorted sense of the victim being responsible for the trauma(s) (Kluft, 1990b; McCann & Pearlman, 1990; van der Kolk, 1996)
3. Negative effects on identity (van der Kolk, 1996b) such as the belief that one is bad, undeserving, or worthless (McCann & Pearlman, 1990), or even evil (Salter, 1995).

When you interview patients and begin to deconstruct how they know to believe that they are evil or worthless, or that it is time to self-harm or take a drink, you will find that they are being driven by traumatic memories. Patients are often completely unaware that they are being driven by images from the past. For the person, this is simply the way it is. These memories may or may not include cognitive distortions. Discovering the distortions can often be the key to transforming the problematic behavior or belief. The reason that working with memory is so important is because (a) it is the key to how the patient knows how to continue to behave in the same maladaptive ways, and (b) it is the one thing that the patient avoids like the plague.

In the fiction book *A Wizard of Earthsea* by Ursula LeGuin (1991), there are two valuable lessons for trauma patients. The first is the concept that a magician is able to work magic and control nature and others by knowing the "true name" of things. Knowing the truth is a powerful method of transforming anything. The second lesson is learned by the hero of the book, who is forced to run away from "an evil" force that he unleashes. When the hero finally stops running away and faces his foe, he discovers that it is only himself, and since he knows its true name he can transform it and reintegrate it back into himself.

☐ Memory and Healing

As stated in chapter 1, formal memory work with trauma survivors does not begin until the second phase of treatment. The reason is that by definition the traumatic material contained in the memories is of such intensity that the patient must have sufficient levels of coping to process the material. The reason the patient developed a trauma-based disorder in the first place was that she could not process the traumatic material (Horowitz, 1986; van der kolk, 1996b).

Formal memory work can be classified into two main categories: (a) memory accessing or retrieval, and (b) memory processing. Memory accessing or retrieval involves the use of therapeutic processes that assist a person in gaining access to and awareness of experiences the patient does not remember well or at all. It should be pointed out that many patients do have memories for traumatic events. However, they often have dissociated various aspects of the complete experience. The BASK model suggests that the four main constituents of an experience are behavior, affect, sensation, and knowledge (Braun, 1988). Any one of these components can be dissociated to lower the intensity of a memory. One major component that is regularly not consciously available to patients is the affect and emotion that went along with an event. Some people know an event occurred, but they do not remember how significant it was for them. Still other people remember event A, yet they do not realize that event A is connected with symptom B. Memory retrieval procedures are used to uncover these important links. These are the processes that have come under attack by people suggesting that therapists are wittingly or unwittingly creating so-called false memories (Loftus & Ketchum, 1994; Yapko, 1994). I will address this concern later in this chapter.

Memory processing is used on memories that have always been remembered or memories that have recently been remembered and are now available for "processing." These memories are usually painful and disruptive to the patient. The effect of these memories is almost always the driving force behind flashbacks and intrusive experience. These memories are often the internal proofs or reasons behind the cognitive distortions and negative self-concepts of patients. These memories will to varying degrees dominate patients' sense of who they are and what life is about.

Memory processing involves the use of techniques that allow patients to process or work through the experience of what happened to them. There are roughly three phases of healing traumatic memories that are depicted in Figure 5.1.

In the first phase, the person is in a place of either having his resources overwhelmed with the traumatic memory or blocking the memory in an attempt to be more resourceful. This is equivalent to the alternating numbing and intrusive phases described by Horowitz (1973, 1986). In the second phase, both the memory and the resources are sufficiently present to effectively work on the traumatic material without being retraumatized. The therapeutic goal should be that the work results in the person being able to remember what happened without being overwhelmed by negative affect and while being able to stay connected to a resourceful representation of the self.

Finally, memory work segues into stage 3 work that involves reconnecting with self and others in a new manner so that the traumatic events of the past (i.e., memories) become a less and less dominant aspect of the person's ongoing life, while resourceful experiences become more and more the dominant aspects of life. The traumas of the past are in the background of life. They are not in the foreground. This will be discussed in chapter 7.

As discussed in chapter 3 it is very important to understand the goal of a given tool in order to know how to use it. So let us look more closely at the goal of healing traumatic memories. What exactly is a "healed traumatic memory"? Let us define a traumatic memory as any experience that makes you uncomfortable to think back on. In this definition, we are including "large T" traumas (e.g., being raped) and "small t" traumas (e.g., being teased at school by a bunch of children). Let us look

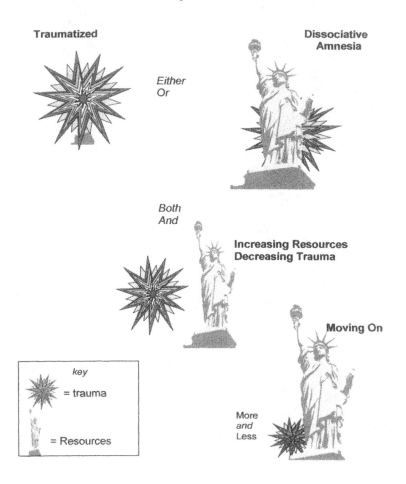

Figure 5.1. The process of working with memories: From "either/or" to "both/and" to "more and less."

at small t traumas to build up a reference experience for what a healed traumatic experience is like. We have all had them. When these events first happened, most people were very upset. As time passed, these events often became less and less important.

At some point in our life we look back at one of these events and several things occur:

1. We remember them with a fair amount of clarity.
2. We have absolutely no negative feelings as we remember the event. The event does not "loom large" in our personal sense of time and space.

3. We often have a small chuckle of compassion for ourselves because we see how this hurt us then, but now it no longer seems like a big deal.
4. We do not have significant cognitive distortions or negative beliefs such as self-blame or fearful views of the world.
5. We have little desire to spend a long time with this memory. It is simply a relatively unimportant event in the landscape of our life. It is as if we have gone into the museum of personal history[1] and had a nice visit with the memory. Then we leave the museum and go on with our life.

These are the qualities of a healed memory. An even more dramatic version of this is that when we visit the museum of personal history and visit the memory we have a great deal of compassion and empathy for ourselves in the past. We even have some level of appreciation for how this experience adds to the richness of our life. So when we leave the museum, our senses are sharpened, the colors of life are brighter, the scents are stronger, the melodies sweeter.

☐ Tools for Processing Memory in Phase 2 of Treatment

In this section I will be discussing specific tools for working with memories that are in conscious awareness. Unfortunately, most patients do not come to treatment with a list of specific memories that they want to detoxify. The only exception to this might be people who have had a single specific episode in their recent life. In these situations, therapy is often quite brief. At that point in time I would quickly move toward the tools of TRC (see later in this chapter) or thought field therapy (next chapter). For patients with more involved trauma histories, the situation is rarely this clean. In some instances a patient will describe a symptom such as feeling depressed. After talking about the situation the patient will reveal a specific memory that appears to be driving the depression. The patient may not have thought of this memory for years, nevertheless the memory was never dissociated or repressed.

In describing these approaches, I am assuming that sufficient assessment has been made that the patient is ready for this current round of memory work. I am also assuming that the patient has been properly prepared and agrees to doing the work. If the patient is expressing reluctance, resistance, or objections, that is a definite sign that more preparatory work needs to be done.

---

[1] I believe I came across this term from Robert Dilts.

One of the key components in preparing a patient is the concept of *dosing* (Horowitz, 1986). Patients need to be explicitly instructed that "more is not always better." If the work in therapy is on memory, many patients will wrongly conclude that if they want to get better quickly, they should do more work at home. If any type of journaling has been assigned, patients may think they should spend hours on the memories that came up in a session. The patient needs to be told not to overwhelm his or her system. *One hour a day of self-guided therapy work is the limit.*

Another important guideline in transforming memories is that the patient must bring more resources to the situation than she did the first time. (Ideally, she should bring sufficient resources to the endeavor that she is virtually guaranteed to be able to detoxify the memory.) Patients need to spend equal if not more time on strengthening their resources compared to dealing with past traumatic memories. Failure to adhere to this guideline risks retraumatizing the patient. The purpose of holding off memory work until phase 2 is to spend time helping patients build or rebuild their resourcefulness. It also allows time for the resource of the therapeutic relationship to develop.

One final and essential point before delving into working with memories is needed: Memories or events themselves have little importance by themselves. It is the meaning that we derive from these events that is important. It is how we use these events to construct our reality that is really important (see chapter 7).

Trauma Reassociative Conditioning

Trauma reassociative conditioning (TRC) can be one of the most powerful tools in the trauma therapist's tool bag. TRC is also known as visual/kinesthetic dissociation. I prefer the term trauma reassociative conditioning because I think it is a more accurate description of what the tool does. TRC allows the therapist to help a patient change his or her associative processes that relate to the trauma being "reconditioned." TRC helps the person stay associated to a resourceful present while remembering a traumatic past. In so doing, patients are allowed to create new meaning for themselves about those events.

Furthermore, it is an elegant tool because it allows a therapist to bring elements from each of the four aspects of successfully resolving trauma to bear on the problem at one time. These include:

1. regaining access to resources and being able to apply them in appropriate contexts;
2. maintaining appropriate boundaries;

3. honoring and valuing previously dissociated parts of the self;
4. learning to place the abuse in a larger context. Accessing and maintaining resources, therapeutic use of dissociation, the therapeutic relationship, submodalities,

TRC is particularly well designed, because it works on all three phases of trauma treatment at once. Its main use is in phase 2 of treatment, however, it can be used early on in treatment to help ground and stabilize a patient. The indications for using this approach are as follows:

1. TRC is a treatment of choice in discrete traumas, where the person is (a) still being overcome by intrusive experience, and (b) phobicly avoiding contexts to minimize intrusive experience.
2. As a secondary prevention measure soon after a trauma, to forestall the development of more intense intrusion/numbing cycles. In these contexts therapy can be very brief, often just a few sessions to achieve the target goal of resolving the intrusive experience.
3. To decrease or resolve flashbacks of specific trauma in cases of multiple traumas. In these contexts the intrusive experience of specific traumas may be quickly handled. However, dysfunctional beliefs, interpersonal coping strategies, and other chronic problems often need further treatment.
4. To experientially teach the concept of staying grounded in current time with resources while remembering a trauma instead of reliving the trauma. This strategy is used in the first phase of treatment in cases where the patient is collapsing into flashbacks all of the time.

TRC is an excellent example of the therapy that generates experience, rather than talking about some experience in the past. The therapy that comes from using TRC does not come from talking about the problem, so the therapist does not spend much time talking about the details of the content of the trauma with the patient. What is more important is that the therapist talk with the patient to make sure that the criteria needed for the appropriate use of TRC are present. Finding out about the details of the trauma can be done later if necessary.

If the patient needs to talk about the details of the traumatic event, then the therapist can listen empathically in order to help meet the patient's expectations and needs. If the therapist is more interested in doing an assessment, then details about the event can be recorded. These are in effect separate tools that most therapists have learned. They simply are not part of TRC.

Talking about the problem can have some negative consequences. The chief one is that the negative SoC may be reactivated, so that the patient once again is traumatized. This may inadvertently build up the belief that dealing with the trauma necessarily leads to collapsing into it. Many times in the inpatient setting I worked on, a patient was referred because he or she would collapse into the trauma. In situations where you know it is probable that a flashback will occur with little provocation, it is contraindicated to start asking about the trauma. Sometimes therapists and patients are stuck in the idea that therapy consists of talking about the trauma. The more they talk about the horror of the trauma the bigger and bigger this story looms in the patient's mind. Had TRC been used first, then the trajectory of the therapy could have been radically altered. After successful use of the procedure, the therapist and the patient may spend a lot of time talking about how much smaller the experience seems to be. The conversation can be about what differences can be in the patient's life now in terms of belief about self, actions to take, and so on.

In many ways abuse and trauma are like physical pain. Both have a tremendous capacity to capture attention. Both the therapist and patient can get sucked into the drama of trauma. It is not difficult to spend an entire session talking about the details, feeling, and reactions to a specific trauma. This is alright if in the next session, TRC is used. But often, there is another trauma or something else, and the reconditioning of the trauma keeps getting put off.

Step-By-Step Instructions for TRC and Commentary

1. *Educate the patient about the rationale for the procedure.* It is particularly important to make sure the patient understands that he is not supposed to feel the traumatic feelings as though he were back in the trauma, with the exception of the next step. He is to feel the resourceful feelings that you will be helping him to feel.

2. *Calibrate the trauma SoC.* Have the patient think of the traumatic experience. The patient needs to pick a discrete trauma that has a beginning and an end. Even if the person has had multiple traumas, each one has a beginning and an end. The beginning is just before the event began. The end is when the patient knew that this particular event was over and he was relatively safe (safe meaning that more of the trauma is not likely to occur for a period of time). **Explain to him that it will only be long enough so that you can see what they look like, if he starts to relive the trauma.** Then look for minimal cues of the trauma SoC. *As soon as you notice the smallest sign of trauma, have the patient stop thinking about it* and get out of the trauma

SoC. If necessary, have him get up, move around, change the subject. Talk about the weather.

There are many ways to detect SoC changes. The therapist can watch for changes in breathing. Usually the face gives away many clues, and there are changes in muscle tone, grimaces, and skin color. The important point is that the therapist discovers some nonverbal early warning sign that the patient is entering the traumatic SoC, so that later on, the therapist can stop that from happening.

3. *Elicit a description of a resourceful state* that the patient (a) would have needed to maintain, but lost due to the power of the original experience (this would have made it possible to metabolize the trauma); or (b) needs now so that dealing with the memory of the trauma would not be traumatic (i.e., delink the patient from his current resources).

This is the most important part of the TRC. You should give it the most attention. Most people try to get rid of their dysphoric symptoms. They avoid and run away. Rarely do they give much attention to the idea of staying with the negative thing, but making sure that they have enough resources to metabolize it. One cannot make a trauma go away. One can attempt to discount it, but that usually leads to further problems. As discussed in chapter 2 the effects of trauma are not just due to the damage from the wound itself. The effects of the trauma are equally (perhaps more than equally) caused by the cutting off of victims from their own resources. This step is the reconnection of people to their resources.

Resources used in this context tend to be described in one of two ways: feelings or complex evaluations. They include safety, strength, joy, feeling loved, knowing it is not my fault, knowing I will live/survive. It is important to recognize that whatever verbal description is given to the resource, it is a complex SoC with both affective and cognitive components. Luckily, we do not need to describe it fully, because patients know what they need, even if they cannot describe it fully.

This step is in itself a process of negotiation. It involves clinical acumen. A patient's first choice at a resource is often insufficient. It is up to the therapist to help make sure the patient has picked an adequate resource. I apply the following test(s):

1. When the patient describes the resource, does it seem to be something personally meaningful to her (rather than an abstract concept)? If it seems like an abstract concept, then I will ask questions to elicit a more "living resource." It is not the label for the resource that is important (e.g., changing the label from strength to courage); it is the underlying SoC attached to the label that is important. We are

trying to reconnect the person to *her* resources. It is the discussion itself that does this.

2. Is the described resource one that is in the direction of expecting too much of the self or overfunctioning or further numbing? If the answer is yes, I negotiate for another resource. For instance, a marine suggested a resource of believing that he was indestructible (see the accompanying video). This is clearly in the wrong direction. Another resource some patients have suggested is additional numbing.

3a. I attempt to associate into the resource. Does it feel OK from what I know about human nature in general, the patient in particular (i.e. her age, gender, personal history)? Does it feel strong enough?

4. In the ongoing discussion with the patient I am watching the non-verbal responses. I am looking for feedback that suggests we are beginning to access a SoC that would be resourceful for this problem. I am looking for congruence and increased energy. Clues include relaxing of face muscles, improved pallor, more relaxed breathing, and symmetry of body movements. The patient should become increasingly involved with the ideas we are discussing. The discussion will become compelling to the patient.

If these things are not happening, that is feedback to me that we are not heading in the correct direction. It should be clear from this detailed discussion that we are more in the realm of craft and art than science, at least as far as how a therapist does the process with someone.

At the end of this process, which can take up to 15 or 20 minutes (although 5 to 10 is often enough), the patient will have identified a resource by some label or name.

3b. *Elicit the resource SoC.* The next step is to have the patient think of a time he had this resource and imagine himself fully associated to that time so it is as if he is living it. Invite the patient to make it as vivid as possible. Ideally, it would be like a vivid positive flashback. Have the patient focus on what he sees, hears, and feels. Therapists who know hypnosis can use their training to help make the experience as vivid as possible.

Ask the patient to let you know when he is as fully involved in the experience as he can get. Then ask the patient to tell you what he calls this experience. He may use the same name as he originally used. Or, he may rename it. For instance a patient recently started off going for a resource she labeled "calm and strong." When she got to the experience itself, she called it "peaceful and serene."

3c. *Create anchors to stabilize the resource state.* Repeat the patient's label back to him in the same tone of voice that he used while the patient was in the positive experience. This creates an associative anchor or cue. Then tell the patient that you want him to create his own "positive button" to help bring back the state. Tell the patient to make a button using his hands. It could be a squeeze of the wrist, a fist, or an OK sign—whatever he would like to create. Make sure the patient is still strongly in the positive state. Have the patient make the positive button. You can also repeat the auditory label that he created. You have now created both auditory and kinesthetic anchors or associative cues that can be used to keep this resourceful SoC in place during the reconditioning phase of TRC.

5. *Have the patient establish a doubly dissociated point of view.* Specifically, have the patient imagine himself sitting in a movie theater. Why use a movie theater? It is an experience that most everyone has had many times. You can also use a television for children. It should *not* be a very good movie theater, other than very comfortable seats. It is a small screen and has poor sound. The person should imagine that he and you are sitting about two-thirds of the way back. It is fine if the person wants to include another significant helpful other or wants to sit further back. Ask the patient to tell you once he has this in mind. Then have the patient imagine himself floating up to the projection booth or off to the side even further back so that he can see you and him sitting together watching the blank screen. This double dissociation allows for a great deal of safety. It is also symbolic of creating an observing self that can see the patient in a therapeutic relationship with the therapist. You can also establish an anchor for this state by tapping on a table or snapping your fingers. (I have found, though, that this is usually unnecessary.)

6. *Recondition the SoCs linked to the trauma.* At this point the patient is now up in the projection booth watching himself sitting with you comfortably. He should also be feeling the resourceful state of mind both in the booth and in the chair. The goal is to hold these states constant while the patient reviews the trauma. The patient is instructed to keep the resource SoC constant while he watches the trauma from the beginning until he gets to the point after the traumatic event is over. The patient is told to use his "positive button" to strengthen the resource whenever he needs to. The patient can be told that he can watch the movie at a very fast speed if he wants. He can watch the movie more than once if he needs to. The suggestion is given that somehow the patient will know when he is finished. While the movie is running the therapist must reinforce the positive SoC with verbal suggestion. The therapist wants to keep the patient associated to the resource SoC, in the current year, to the current-aged self. To do this, the following language is used: "As you continue

up in the projection booth feeling [resource label] watching you and me sitting here feeling [resource label] in [current year] watching what the younger you went through back then, . . ."

While the patient watches the movie the therapist can suggest that he may notice something different that he had not realized before, or he may have a new perspective on what happened since he is reviewing this event in this new way. It can be helpful to underscore that this may be the first time that he has been able to acknowledge the trauma without being in it. This type of suggestion is an open-ended generative suggestion (Erickson & Rossi, 1976, 1979). If these suggestions are used, it is crucial that they be given with the intent that the "something different" is *not* to be about discovering a new and gorier aspect of the trauma. The intent is about the patient finding some cognitive understanding that will help him heal. The intent includes the assumptive belief that the patient already has the necessary knowledge internally to heal. It has been the inability to access that knowledge that has been the problem. In all of the times I have used this tool, I have never had a patient report that he now realized some additional piece of trauma that was more gory and horrible than what he thought. The "something different" is usually on the order of truly realizing how little, or scared, or blameless the person was.

It is imperative that the therapist keeps watching the patient for signs of trouble and not allow him to fall back into the traumatic feelings/experiences. If at any time the patient starts to develop the traumatic experience, reinforce the dissociation or resource anchor. If that does not work, use submodalities to reduce the affect by making the movie farther away or smaller or black and white. Sometimes it is enough to just remind the patient not to associate into the movie. If this does not work, stop the treatment. You will need to go back to the drawing boards. See the following section on trouble-shooting TRC.

7. *Revaluing the self.* When the patient finishes watching the old experience (He may need to watch more than one time; this is a matter of clinical acumen and the patient's own desires), release the dissociation cue and instruct the patient to float back to his body. Have the patient from the here and now resourceful position look at younger self at the end of the trauma. Have the patient walk down to the movie screen. Ask the patient to do one of the following things: either (a) step into the picture, (b) bring the younger self off the screen, or (c) just talk to the younger self on the screen. Instruct the patient to tell the younger self whatever "he needs for healing." In some cases the patient can be left completely on their own to say what they need to say to himself. It is often helpful to offer some

possible things to say. These can include (a) the patient is from the future and is living proof that the younger person survived, (b) that he made the best choice available to him at the time, (c) that the patient loves the younger self. These ideas should be offered in a tentative way. The patient should be given enough time and silence to do his own work. During this part of the treatment, the patient often has gentle tears of acceptance and love.

8. *Reintegration.* Once the patient is finished, have him bring the younger self off the screen and sit back down in the chair with the here-and-now self. Instruct the patient to imagine bringing the younger part inside the patient. The patient is then instructed to open his eyes and be fully present in the therapy room.

Once the patient is finished, there are several options that the therapist can take. The first is to test the work by having the patient think of the original old trauma and discover how much the affect and experience has changed. The goal is that the patient should look visibly more comfortable and should report feeling and thinking differently about the traumatic event. When asking the patient to do this it is important to make sure that the problem is appropriately put into the past. The therapist can say, "I would like you to think of the scene that *used to be* so problematic for you." Or, the therapist can say, "I'd like you to think of the *old* problem." It would be a mistake to say, " I'd like you to think of the problem that *gives* you so much trouble." This last sentence uses the present tense and is verbally reassociating the problem SoC to the present.

If the patient often had symptoms in certain contexts (e.g., every time he had to talk with his boss) an additional strategy would be to have the patient imagine a time in future where the old symptoms would have come up to see if the patient feels more comfortable. The patient should report that he feels a significant improvement over what he usually feels when he anticipates the context.

Troubleshooting the TRC Process

Problem 1. During the watching of the movie, the patient starts to lose his resourcefulness and collapses into the traumatic event.

1. Make sure that the therapist is using dissociative language that keeps the patient in the present and the trauma in the past, for instance, if the therapist says, *"Watch* the movie of the traumatic event *happening."* The use of the present tense "happening" could collapse the separation of the patient from what *"happened."* Make sure to

emphasize the difference between the resourceful patient in the current year and the younger self in the past.

2. Make sure that the patient's image of himself in the chair next to the therapist is an adult version of the self. In some cases patients have put a child version of themselves next to the therapist, which collapses the distinction between time and place.
3. Reinstruct the patient that you do not want him to feel what happened back then. Sometimes, patients just do not understand the instructions. This can happen if they have had previous therapy experience that emphasized catharsis.
4. Use submodalities to reduce intensity. Make the picture black and white, move it away, and/or make it smaller. Add peripheral vision.
5. Have the patient use his "positive button" to strengthen positive state. Increase the verbalization of the auditory label of the positive feeling as well as the dissociative language.
6. If all else fails, stop the process. Go back to the resource negotiation phase and pick a different resource and/or strengthen the resource by finding additional examples of it and pairing those examples to the same anchors. (In NLP, this is referred to as "stacking anchors.")

Problem 2. The patient starts to cry while watching the movie. Usually, this is not really a problem. If the patient is empathically crying *about* what happened to that younger person in the past, then the process is working well. Simply tell the patient that these empathic feelings are OK as long as they are the feelings of the adult self about what happened to the younger self (notice the continued use of the language that separates time and place) and make sure that he is still in contact with the resourceful SoC as well.

Problem 3. At step 7 the younger self is rejecting of the older self's help, or the patient can not tell the younger self that he or she loves the younger self. This type of problem occurs only with people who have had severe and ongoing childhood trauma. This problem has more to do with the patient's characterological issues or with his relationship with himself. These stances are usually complementary. The reason the younger self does not accept help is because the older self has a long history of being unloving and critical of the younger self. The reason the older self does not love the younger self usually has to do with huge amounts of shame and guilt about the actions of the younger self. It cannot be solved within the frame of the TRC itself. The therapist should take this as feedback and information about the patient's need to learn how to love and nurture himself and forgive himself. During the actual use of TRC, the therapist has several options. The first is to help the older self begin to recognize the constraints the younger self was under. So even if love is not possible, at this time, a beginning of understanding can be felt. A second option is to help the younger self be willing to *consider* accepting the help from the older self provided that the older self is willing to be more nurturing on an ongoing basis. A third option is to use a more formal redecision process (Goulding & Goulding, 1979). See Lankton and Lankton (1983) for an example of how to do this within an imagistic framework.

Problem 4. *No matter what the therapist does, the patient keeps collapsing into the trauma in a full revivification.* I have only seen this problem occur with people with significant dissociative disorders. It seems to be related to patients' conscious unwillingness to accept the reality and importance of what happened to them. They unconsciously feel compelled to relive the experience in order to feel its significance. The therapist has three options. The first is to leave the TRC model and use an abreactive model to help process the trauma (see Hammond, 1990, pp. 518–530 for details). The second is to back off attempting to process the trauma directly and to help the patient gain additional ability to regulate affect and/or reduce their use of denial, minimization, and avoidance before returning to this type of work. A third option might be to use a different model such as thought field therapy that might reduce the amount of affect.

Yes, And

Trauma-based thinking has a heavy reliance on "either/or" distinctions. This thinking pattern reaches its height in the splitting of a personality into separate and different parts (as in DID). The therapy of trauma is about helping patients move from an either/or perspective to a both/and perspective. Both/and thinking reaches its therapeutic and creative height when an individual can hold *seemingly* contradicting ideas together. An example would be to know that as a child a person was involved in abusing other children and the same person is deserving of forgiveness. Either/or thinking allows people, including some therapists, to split the world into the "bad" abusers and the "good" survivors. One problem with this dichotomy is that many victims of abuse have themselves acted abusively in some way.

In chapter 4, I discussed several tools that help patients modulate affect, such as creating images of containers or using an energy bubble. These tools tend to create SoCs that temporarily block out traumatic SoCs, because they are based on the idea that you cannot be in two SoCs at the same time. These tools are very useful in earlier phases of treatment, where the patient's resourcefulness or ego-strengths are less available.

In the middle phase of traumatic therapy where patients are actively working on processing and coming to terms with the traumatic events in their histories, the tool "yes, and" may be more useful. It can also be useful as part of the last phase of treatment. The goal of this tool is to help patients stay very much aware of trauma while they also stay very much aware of resourceful aspects of self. It is also a visual symbol for the concepts of the holistic self (see chapter 7). With patients with MPD/DID this tool would be useful when alters that usually block out dysphoric affect are learning to feel emotion or deal with trauma.

The tool itself is very simple. If a patient is experiencing something that is upsetting her at the moment, the patient is asked to take whatever it is that is traumatic and making her feel sad or scared and imagine it contained in a circle or picture (see Figure 5.2).

He is to visualize this somewhere in space around his body and connected to a picture of himself. The patient is instructed to not try and get rid of the picture or the feelings. The patient is then asked to imagine a series of resources or resourceful memories one by one. Each resource is put in a circle and also put around the person and connected to the

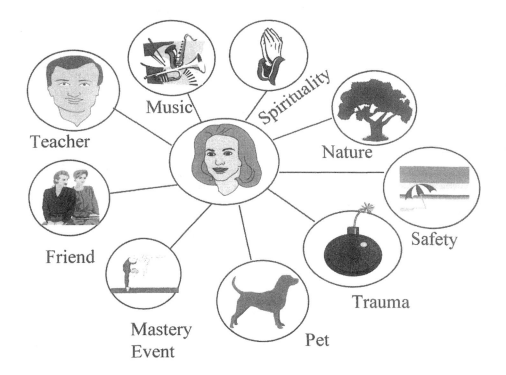

Figure 5.2. Yes, and—an inclusive tool to reconnect with resources.

person. These resources can be the good wishes and feelings of other people, especially mentors and friends, positive experiences, images of safety, and so on. The patient is instructed to only add to the imagery. Nothing is taken away. The therapist should see the patient becoming increasingly calm and centered with each additional resource.

As with all of the structured tools offered in this book, the therapist and patient can and should discuss the experience the patient has had. Particular attention should be made to directing the patient to his or her own awareness of how this new experience of the memory changes its impact on the patient's own sense of self. The therapist and the patient can discuss the content of the memory. A discussion about how the patient feels about the memory and himself or herself may be of use. "Yes, and" easily lends itself to a discussion in which the patient can become increasingly aware that he or she has more resources than previously realized. The patient can be complimented on his ability to stay fully present, relatively calm, and aware of the past. A discussion can ensue about how this change has implications for future developments for the patient.

The patient can then be instructed to use this tool at home as a coping skill when needed. In doing so, the patient will learn that he or she can be aware of whatever is painful at the same time that he or she is aware of positive things in life. The more patients can do this, the more they can move toward the traumatic events in their life in order to recover whatever was lost there. This tool merely concretizes what we normally do if we are successful at mastering a difficult experience. There is considerable room for customizing this tool for a given person.

People who have been severely abused simply have little experience in this type of coping strategy. Patients will have many reactions to this type of tool that can be grist for the therapeutic mill. The difference in this approach is that the grist will include a lot of discussion about how to cope with difficult life events as more of a whole person rather than focusing on simply being the victim of abuse or trauma.

One of the ways the therapist can know that this tool may be useful is that the patient is being flooded with memory or affect or sensation as if a part of the self is trying to get the person to process the information. Additionally, the patient may even report that he or she has tried to use a strategy of putting the material in a container without success. In working with dissociative patients, "yes, and" will be more useful as the parts are beginning to communicate more with each other. Once this starts happening, strategies that use therapeutic dissociation (i.e., containers) will run counter to the natural process of the system's attempt to heal. The patient needs to learn cognitive tools that support connection to awareness of multiple feelings within one alter or between several alters. An additional message of this type of tool is, "You are more than your bad memories." This message needs to be given in many different manners throughout treatment. One of the problems with older approaches was the message that the only way to get better was by abreacting all or most of your traumatic experiences. While dealing with the events that happened has its place in treatment, it is not the only aspect of treatment.

Abreactive Work

Abreaction is defined in the *Concise Oxford Dictionary* (1990) as the free expression and consequent release of a previously repressed emotion. Abreaction of past trauma has been a part of traditional approaches to psychotherapy and trauma treatment. Generally, it has not played a major role in Ericksonian and neo-Ericksonian approaches. Abreactive approaches generally involve the patient going back to a traumatic event and reexperiencing it, particularly the emotions involved. This is in contrast to TRC, where the goal is *not* to feel the feelings of the original event. Phillips and Frederick (1995) pointed out that abreaction is no longer seen as an end in itself. Instead, it is viewed as a vehicle that allows cognitive restructuring and mastery of traumatic material. The main criticism of this approach is that it can be retraumatizing and destabilizing for some patients. While one obvious choice may be to avoid this approach, sometimes this proves to be impractical or impossible (Kluft, 1990a).

There is a continuum of therapeutic work that is abreactive. On one end of the continuum is simply helping patients to focus their attention on an event in their lives that was traumatic (big T or small t). As discussed earlier, trauma patients (and many people in general) try to avoid talking about or feeling about these types of events. One of the main benefits of successful abreaction is that the person discovers that they do not have to avoid feelings. The simple act of telling "the story," especially if it has never been told, can bring tremendous relief. The not telling of the story or sometimes the secret story is like the proverbial elephant in the room that no one can mention. It simply requires increasing amounts of emotional, cognitive, and behavioral machinations to continue to avoid what is plainly there. Not telling leaves the person feeling cut off from self and others. The telling of the story with emotional vulnerability in the presence of a supportive other(s) and ideally a compassionate self helps to make the person feel whole (see chapter 7). A simple telling of the story may be accompanied by various amounts of emotion, depending on the patient. Moving along the continuum are various techniques in which the therapist asks the patient to focus his or her attention more closely on emotional aspects of an event to help increase the person's connection with his or her feelings. Dolan (1991) used a *safe remembering* approach that allows for connecting with feelings and connecting with resourceful SoCs. It shares similarities with the "Yes, and" approach and with TRC. In safe remembering, before a patient is encouraged to think back on a traumatic event, the patient is asked to gather associative anchors to the present and resourceful SoCs. These might include car keys, pictures, and so on. The patient is first instructed to focus on the positive associations to these cues. These links can be strengthened with hypnotic suggestions such as, "Every time you hold your car keys you can feel connected to the fact that this is the (current year) and to the awareness that you are now an adult with your own ability to drive. And as you are aware of these facts, you can feel an increased sense of safety and comfort no matter what else you are aware of." Once these links are fully established the patient can then hold, look at, or think about these positive anchors and allow himself or herself to think back to the traumatic events. The key to this approach is taking the time to build the positive associative anchors. As in both TRC and "yes, and" there is a demand characteristic to remember and have connections to positive feelings rather than to simply remember and relive the trauma.

At the other end of the continuum are hypnotically induced regressions and abreactions of traumatic events. Specific instructions on several of these procedures with different degrees of emotional intensity are given in the *Handbook of Hypnotic Suggestions and Metaphors* (Hammond, 1990, pp. 518–535). Along with the reliving of the feelings are usually suggestions that the traumatic feelings will no longer affect the patient or that the feelings will be transformed or metabolized. Built into the protocols is the opportunity to cognitively restructure the experiences. The use of these techniques requires specific training and supervision. In all of these approaches authors emphasize the need to manage the intensity of the affect so that the person does not become retraumatized.

Another issue associated with "abreactive work" is the question, "What is to be abreacted? One problem in the past was an almost exclusive focus on the traumatic events themselves. More current work now focuses on helping patients face the painful affect of letting go and loss. In fact, one can make the argument that it is often easier for people to obsess about traumatic events in their past than it is to face the loss of letting go of the wish for things to be different.

Submodality Work to Manage Affect During Memory Work

I have already discussed submodalities in chapter 4. Many of the alterations described in that section can be useful when patients are feeling overwhelmed by the affect of a memory. So I want to comment only on additional uses of submodalities during active memory work here. There are three situations that often respond well to this work. The goal here is to continue the memory work and control the intensity. A significant alternative may be to try and stop the work altogether, assess what the problem is, and then restart at a later time. The first situation is that the patient simply becomes overwhelmed with affect or moves into more of a flashback rather than a memory. This may occur in the middle of "planned" memory work[2] or it may happen that the patient simply begins to abreact. To reduce affect the therapist can instruct the patient to "put the memory on the wall over there like a movie. Make the picture small and black and white. Continue to tell me what you see that *happened* to that child/person back then." The therapist needs to use a fairly firm yet calm voice to connote a sense of safety and control. The reader may recognize that this is a highly condensed and simplified version of TRC.

A second situation is similar to the first. The main difference here is that even though the patient is not in a full abreaction, the patient communicates a strong sense of the memory feeling as if it were now, rather than in the past. Generally, the "memory" will be directly in front of the patient's face. The therapist can suggest to the patient to move the picture of the memory more and more to the patient's left. The left–right dimension is the submodality that is often associated with time. Moving a memory to the left will tend to make it feel like it is more in the past. Once the patient has some distance, he or she can review the memory with more equanimity.

The third situation has to do with the structure of the memory itself. In many instances the memory is coded in a highly distorted manner. One common (mis)coding for childhood abuse victims is that the perpetrator is seen as a relative giant compared to the child. Obviously, adults are bigger than children. However, the visual image that person has stored in memory is more of a code for how fearful the child felt rather than the physical reality at the time. When the image is seen again, it simply reevokes the intense fear. Suggesting to the patient to make the perpetrator smaller or the child bigger tends to help the patient have a more balanced perspective on the event. Another common problem has to do with the loss of boundaries and tunnel vision described in chapter 4. Suggesting that the patient to widen his or her visual field and look at

---

[2]By planned here, I am referring to the patient being asked to describe a memory without the benefit of a structure such as TRC or thought field therapy energy work.

what else is happening can also help the patient be more resourceful while dealing with the memory.

Creating Alternative Memories

In the movie *Back to the Future*, Marty McFly goes back in time and helps his father make one change at one moment in time (his father ends up standing up for himself and his wife-to-be, and knocking out the bad guy) and then everything becomes better for everyone in the future. This fantasy has a deep appeal to the unconscious mind. Many therapists suggest that understanding the past is not enough. Patients need to create a re-doing (Phillips & Frederick, 1995; Watkins, 1992) or a re-deciding (Goulding & Goulding, 1979) even if it is in fantasy. The goal is to create an alternative SoCs that supports more positive beliefs and schemas. It does not matter that it is not real. It matters that it is compelling and meaningful. After all, from a certain perspective all memory is narrative. These narratives inform our choices and actions day to day. It is important that the subject of the story be more resourceful. The goal is to give patients a different version of the narrative that they can refer to as they construct their lives.

The most common tool used to do this is imagery (with or without formal hypnosis), where a resourceful current self goes back and helps the unresourceful younger self. One alteration for dissociative patients is that specific current resourceful alters go back and help unresourceful alters. In this case it is important to spend considerable time making sure the appropriate alters are involved and alters that should not be involved are not.

The procedure is not unlike TRC. The main difference is that instead of watching the event on a screen, the patient goes back in time on a mission to help the younger self. This type of procedure is very flexible and can be done within formal hypnosis and ego state work (Watkins, 1992). It can be done simply as imagery. It can be done in a gestalt two-chair technique. It can be done standing up and walking along an imaginary timeline (Dilts, 1990; James & Woodsmall, 1988). In its most formal construction, the therapist needs to take time ahead of time to discuss with the patient what resources the younger self needed. Did the patient want to help the younger self be the one to actually do something different, such as fight back, say something, or leave? Or, does the patient want the older self to do the work of protecting the younger self, so that the older self fights back or takes the younger self out of the situation? Time needs to be taken to develop the resourceful SoC of the self who is going back in time. If resources are to be transferred to the younger self, it is often helpful to create an image or anchor of that resource. For example, Ann wanted to feel more powerful and strong. Once this SoC was retrieved and stabilized (as in TRC), an image of the sword of She-Ra (a cartoon character) was decided upon. This sword was then given to the 11-year-old Annie, who could feel the power and then yelled in a deep, powerful voice at her brother, who had physically and sexually abused her, that if he ever touched her again she would tell.

Once the resource has been developed, the person imagines going back in time. Generally the patient goes back in time to a point before the traumatic incident. The patient introduces the present self to the past self. The past self is told that the patient is from his future. He is here to help. Some rapport is established. A plan is decided upon. If resources are to be transferred to the younger self, this is practiced at least once. Then time is moved forward to the event in question and it is redone.

After a more masterful outcome to the event has been enacted, several additional steps can be taken to both solidify these changes into the usual SoC of the person as well as to link these changes to the future. In terms of stages of treatment, the following approaches are more in line with the reintegration themes of stage 3. Nevertheless, they flow seamlessly from the direct memory work itself. The first step is to have the different parts of self negotiate for continued mutual support. For instance, In the case of Ann she had been habitually scared and passive. She would not say what she wanted and needed, even to people who loved her. She often felt that her husband would take advantage of her. After the successful imagery work, the following "trialogue" took place:

Therapist: *First of all I want to congratulate the both of you on a job well done. Annie how did it feel to stand up for yourself?*

Annie: *It felt great and a little scary.*

Therapist: *Ann, how did it feel to help Annie?*

Ann: *It was really good to be able to do something that helped.*

Therapist: *I am glad that you mentioned that. In the future there are going to be many times when it will be important to state your needs and stand up for yourself. Most of these times won't even involve abuse. But, if you do not stand up for what you want and need you are likely to feel reminded of the old way things used to be with your brother. If you speak up for yourself it will feel like the way it is now or even better. I wonder if you, Annie, would be willing to continue to work with Ann over time to speak up. [Head nods "Yes."] Ann, would you be willing to work with Annie? [Head nods "Yes."] Annie, what do you need from Ann to continue this process into the future?*

Annie: *I need Ann to be there and to bring the sword of She-Ra. I need to be reassured that it is OK to speak up for myself.*

Therapist: *Ann, what do you need from Annie?*

Ann: *Well, I need Annie to let me know that there is something that she wants and that she is scared to speak up. Then I can help her be stronger. It is really important that she lets me know.*

Therapist: *Annie, are you able and willing to do what Ann asks so she can help you?*

Annie: *Yes.*

Therapist: *So Ann, if Annie does what you have asked, you will help her?*

Ann: *Absolutely.*

Therapist: *That is great. In a moment, I would like you to seal the deal on your pact by either a handshake or a hug or something of your own choosing. When you do this I would like you both to feel a very pleasant feeling that also makes you feel strong. I am not sure what you will notice. Many people feel something along the midline of their body. It may feel warm or strong. But it will be something that can be there whenever you work together. Okay, seal the deal now.*

The second step is to project these changes into the future. One approach is self-image thinking, which is described in chapter 7. Another approach is to have the person take the new skill that was just enacted "in the past" and imagine how their future time line would change based on this new agreement. For Ann, she imagined moving forward in time and stopped along the way at key moments where she had been passive and had not stood up for herself. She then imagined applying the new skill. She did this for several incidents (three to five is usually sufficient) between the past and current time and even projected this into the future. This can be done completely internally with only head nods letting the therapist know that all is okay. Or it can be done with a lot of dialoguing about what is happening and how that makes the person feel and think differently about herself.

Memory Work and Changes in Cognitions, Schemas, and Beliefs

As stated in chapter 1, PTSD as a disorder is created over a period of time through a cybernetic loop. The healing of PTSD is also created through a cybernetic loop. Up to this point, I have talked about the strong negative affect of the memories that drives patients. The other side of the equation is the meaning that people ascribe to their experiences. Traumas that occur late in life will be interpreted by a person according to existing beliefs and schemas. Early childhood trauma will be interpreted based on developmental level and existing schemas and will also create or color future beliefs. Many authors have described the cognitive distortions that are associated with trauma (Fine, 1990; McCann & Pearlman, 1990; Phillips & Frederick, 1995; Ross, 1995).

Traumatic memories and trauma-based beliefs are intertwined. However, it is not always clear if one or the other is the driving force. If you successfully process a memory, does an associated negative belief change? Or, if you change a belief, does an associated memory change? The answer seems to be that it depends on how global the belief is. Highly formal memory work such as TRC or thought field therapy (TFT) or EMDR will often lead to rather spontaneous change of belief about the meaning of the specific event. For instance, a patient felt that it was her fault that her child was hit and permanently crippled by a car. After processing the memory (with TFT), the patient reported that she no longer blamed herself for the event. This type of change sometimes happens with little or no direct mention or suggestion to change the interpretation.

McCann and Pearlman (1990) have described the importance of working with deeply held cognitive schemas in the areas of safety, self-esteem, trust, power, and intimacy. Working on a single traumatic memory about not feeling safe has a relatively low probability of changing the schema of not being safe in one shot. Generally, people will selectively focus on specific events, pieces of events, and interpretations of events to support what they already believe. Ross (1989) described the use of Socratic methods to begin to challenge a patient's cognitive schemas and how specific events in a patient's life support the schemas. McCann and Pearlman (1990) described a psychodynamic approach around these schemas that helps patients become aware of how the trauma(s) have disrupted their getting their needs met, how the schemas continue to prevent them from getting their needs met, and finally, how they can begin to discover new ways (changes in schema) to satisfy their needs.

Working with specific memories, while necessary, is not always sufficient to change limiting beliefs. However, successful memory[3] work automatically begins to have certain incremental effects on patients. First, many patients have never been able to talk about or review traumatic incidents without getting into highly overwhelmed states. The fact that a person now has had a mastery experience with a traumatic memory

---

[3]Successful memory work is defined here to mean either (a) being able to describe or review a memory without going into a flashback-like state, and/or (b) staying relatively comfortable and resourceful while reviewing the memory, and/or (c) at the end of the process returning to a resourceful state without untoward negative side effects.

decreases a sense of helplessness and victimization and increases self-esteem and self-efficacy. This event also becomes a new reference experience that increases the likelihood that he or she can do it again. Second, if a negative schema or belief is regularly supported by a patient with 10 reference memories, neutralizing this 1 memory weakens the belief. Or it may be better to say that it reduces the affective dysregulation around the belief so that the patient can have more psychological space to change the belief. A visual metaphor is that the traumatic memories are like screws that hold down the belief. The memory work loosens the screws so that the belief can be readjusted or changed. The therapist and patient may have to continue working with other memories.

It is not usually necessary or desirable to work on all 10 memories as the way to deal with the belief. At some point it is important to look at the belief itself and how the patient chooses to hang onto the belief and uses the memories to support the belief (see chapter 7). Looking back to Figure 1.1 in chapter 1, by working with both the affect associated with memories themselves and the cognitive beliefs, the therapist works both aspects of the deviation amplification circuit:cognitive processing and affective dysregulation.

In order to maximize the impact of a given piece of memory work on the patient's belief system, it is useful to follow up the memory work itself with questions or procedures that link the work to more helpful actions, beliefs, and schemas. The previous example with Ann and creating alternative memories gives two examples of this type of procedure. At this point, let me describe some less formalized interviewing approaches mostly taken from the narrative school of therapy (White & Epston, 1990). The therapist can engage the patient in questions about how other supportive people will respond to these changes. For instance, a line of questioning with Ann might be, Do you think your husband will appreciate you being more direct with him about your needs? How will this improve your relationship? Who else will be supportive of these changes? Were there people in your past who would have been cheering you on in your quest to be more assertive and stand up for yourself? What would you imagine them saying and doing every time you stood up and spoke up for yourself? A different line of questioning could focus on the patient's story about herself: Now that you have been able to imagine standing up and speaking up for yourself, what does this tell you about your ability to get your needs met? How does this development change your view of yourself? What types of actions do you think you are likely to do differently now? What do you think you will think about yourself when you act that way? Now that we have done this (memory) work, how does this change your view of what you went through as a child?

These questions can be easily adapted for DID patients: Now that these alters have worked together in resolving this memory, how does that change their understanding of each other? How does this change your perception of them? What do you think this development means for how you and they will interact in the future?

Moving from Victim of Others to Author of Creative Choices

Changing beliefs and longstanding schemas and ways of being in the world does not usually occur overnight. It takes time. Built into the approaches described in this chapter is the presupposition that people need to move from being passive victims of events to active authors of their own life stories. When a patient is asked to discuss what resources he or she needs to bring back to the younger self, the patient is being asked to take charge of his or her own needs. The patient is assuming responsibility for his or her own responses to past events as well as current life stories. Moving from passivity to self-efficacy needs to occur throughout therapy. It needs to be set up at the beginning of treatment. However, many patients do not really confront this issue until they get into the middle part of treatment. Therapists need to use tools that give patients felt reference experiences that tell them they can be the authors of their lives. When people have had long histories of trauma, it is usually necessary to work more specifically on their beliefs around the issues so that they feel free to actively choose to be authors. The work of remembering in phase 2 of treatment blends into the issues of integration and reconnection in phase 3. We will discuss this further in chapter 7.

☐ Memory Retrieval Approaches for Traumatic Memories

At the beginning of this chapter we discussed PTSD as a disorder of memory. In chapter 1 we reviewed how virtually all major authors in the field agree that retrieving and reconstructing memory into a verbal narrative is a crucial part of treatment (phase 2). The problem is that many PTSD and most dissociative patients do not have complete access to their memories in a manner that immediately allows for the construction of a verbal narrative. Furthermore, many of the symptoms of patients are actually disguised dissociative phenomena (Phillps & Frederick, 1995) related to unresolved traumas in the past (Cheek & Lecron, 1968; Rossi & Cheek, 1988). One cannot gain mastery over something one does not recall in an organized fashion. Hence the necessity to help patients retrieve and piece together memories. As discussed earlier, there has been considerable controversy created over this issue in the last 10 years (Calof, 1993a, b, 1994a, b, c; Loftus & Ketchum, 1994; Schwarz & Gilligan, 1995; Yapko, 1994). In this section I will discuss some of the clinical tools available to clinicians. In the following section I will discuss the controversy itself and its implication for practice.

In this section I will be discussing formal hypnotic approaches. Clinicians who want to use these approaches need to have formal training in hypnosis, and should be familiar with the guidelines (Hammond, 1995) and issues (Schwarz, 1995) involved with this type of work.

Preparing the Patient

A number of issues need to be discussed and worked through with patients when doing memory retrieval work. These are:

- The point of memory retrieval work is not to obsess about the past or to increase a sense of blame on others or self. It is to develop a sense of understanding and personal mastery over traumatic material that continues to significantly affect the patient.
- The measure of success of this work is not how many memories of trauma one remembers. The measure of success is the reduction of psychiatric symptoms as well as negative beliefs and unresourceful SoCs. Functioning in the day-to-day world should increase.
- Memories that are retrieved are not to be treated as the total and absolute truth. They need to be treated as personal truths. Memories of the past themselves are not the issue. It is the meaning derived from those memories and the actions informed by those meanings that are important.
- There should be some current, well-formed goal that the patient will move toward as a result of working on memories.
- Patients do not need to know or remember everything in order to get better.
- The reason that things are not going well now in current time may not necessarily have to do with some past trauma.
- Patient and therapist need to be willing to tolerate a significant amount of ambiguity along the way.
- Patients need to understand that the therapist cannot and will not use hypnosis or hypnotic techniques to "force" them to remember.

These issues may be discussed rather quickly or over a considerable period of time depending on the given situation. Therapists should always err on the side of caution in deciding whether or not a therapeutic under-standing and contract have been reached. In cases of dissociative disordered patients, therapists need to check to make sure that the entire system understands these issues. It is also important to clarify which alters are going to do the work and which ones are not, because it would be to destabilizing for that to remain unclear. With any patient, objections and concerns need to be thoroughly discussed before proceeding. Finally, thera-pists should be prepared to revisit these issues as therapy proceeds.

"Retrieved memories" in many instances are things that the patient already has some awareness of. Sometimes the person has simply not thought of the event for 20 years and did not "realize" its significance or connection to the problem at hand. In other cases, it is something the person truly had repressed or dissociated. In any case, once the memory is retrieved it needs to be "processed." This processing may be in one of the forms already described in this chapter, such as TRC. It may include correcting cognitive distortions or re-decisions. It may be that the memory will simply be more grist for the therapeutic mill. One advantage of a hypnotic approach is that if a patient can have a problem that is created in the unconscious, it can also be solved in the unconscious. In some cases, once a repressed traumatic experience has been identified (espe-cially an isolated trauma), its effects can be removed, not unlike remov-ing a splinter. A question often used in hypnosis is, "Now that we have uncovered this event and understand its meaning, can you be free of this problem or symptom?" (Rossi & Cheek, 1988). Sometimes the answer is "yes" and only some basic suggestive work remains to be done. If the answer is "no," more questions can be asked to ascertain what else needs to be done.

Affect/Somatic Bridge

This approach is most useful when patients describe feelings or sensa-tions for which they cannot account. This can include specific emotions or thoughts or specific sensations such as pressure in the chest, pain in a wrist, choking, and so on. The more specific or idiosyncratic the symp-tom and the more that it recurs, the more likely it is that this approach will be useful. The affect or somatic bridge developed by Wakins (1971) uses the central premise that the patient can use the symptom of a feel-ing or sensation as a bridge back to the origin of the experience. This approach can actually be done with or without formal hypnotic induc-tion. It is based on the premise that the feeling or sensation is some type of associative link between now and then. This is in fact very similar to the central principal used in EMDR (Shapiro, 1995).

As with all approaches, it is best to explain the goal of the approach to the patient and obtain permission. The second step is to have the patient associate back to a time when she had the feeling. In many cases this will not be necessary, because the patient will be feeling the feeling in the office. A sample script for the affect/Somatic bridge from that point on is as follows. A patient who had been sexually abused has a feeling of being choked.

> [Optional induction] . . . Focus your attention on the choking you feel around your neck. Allow it to be there. Let go of any attempt to make it less. We want to see this feeling as a communication from your body (or unconscious or another part of the mind). Even allow the signal to become clearer and stronger. Let it fill your awareness. . . .
>
> *Version A*: While your conscious mind is focusing on this feeling, your unconscious mind can be traveling back in time along this feeling to the source of it. Do not try to force yourself to remember. You simply make a request to your unconscious mind (to the part of you that is trying to communicate with you) to give you the original source of this feeling. It is like going to a bank teller and filling out a request to withdraw money. You do not demand it or rush it. You make the request and allow the teller time to process the request. Your unconscious mind is following the feeling back through time, younger and younger. You allow your unconscious mind to give you the gift of the first time you felt this feeling. It may not make sense to you at first. A memory or thought will simply come to your mind. When you become aware of something, let me know by allowing one of your fingers to lift up [ideomotor signaling; see next section].
>
> *Version B*: The feeling is becoming like a bridge through time and space that you can see in your mind. It might seem to you like a walking bridge or train tracks through the foggy mists of time. You are now traveling on that bridge further and further into the past. As you go back in time you are getting younger and younger. Even as you are getting younger, a part of your mind can stay connected to the safety of this office, the safety of the present. [This is a suggestion to facilitate safety and prevent too much regression. I sometimes leave out suggestions for getting younger and smaller altogether.] You might discover that the feeling gets stronger as you get closer to its source. You are going back to the first time you felt this feeling of choking in your throat. I am going to count back from 10 to 1. As I count, you will complete your journey by the time I get to 1. 10 . . . 9 . . . 8 . . . 7 . . . 6 . . . 5 . . . 4 . . . 3 . . . 2 . . . 1. Where are you now? What is happening?

Version A tends to be somewhat less intense affectively because Version B tends to put a person in a more associated position. Obviously, Version B is much more hypnotic. The structure in Version B is more useful for patients with less hypnotic talent. The patient and therapist can then discuss what is happening. What was trying to be communicated?

What is necessary for healing? The therapist needs to have no preconceived notions of what the symptom means or is a reference to. In the above case, the original feeling was *not* of being strangled or choked or forced to engage in oral sex. It came from an event at 5 years old when the patient was choking on something that she swallowed. Her mother then punished her. The patient did remember the event dimly and had never connected it to this sensation. This symptom first appeared when the patient was in over her head at work. The lesson the patient needed to learn was that sometimes you make mistakes and bite off more than you can chew (literally); and you need to be forgiving of yourself rather than punishing. The symptom stopped after this intervention.

Phillips and Frederick (1995) suggested that it is also beneficial to help patients retrieve positive memories. This approach parallels the contention throughout this book, namely the importance of noticing, eliciting, and elaborating resourceful ways of being in the world. Finding and strengthening positive memories in the past increases access to resources. It also creates a metasuggestion that memory work is not only about dealing with pain.

Ideomotor Questioning

Rossi and Cheek (1988) have described the theory and use of ideomotor signaling for accessing traumatic memories. Ideomotor signaling differs from conscious and volitional movement. The movements are minimal and perseverative. An everyday example of this type of movement is the small nodding people do when they are in agreement with a speaker. Ideomotor signaling involves asking questions to the "unconscious mind" of the hypnotized person that can be answered with "yes," "no," or "not ready to answer." These answers are usually assigned to a specific finger of one hand. Signaling does not necessarily need to be motoric. Signaling can be in form of internal pictures (for instance, seeing a version of the self signal "yes" or "no" with head nods). Following the utilization principle, the hypnotist seeks to find some type of specific communication that will provide for patient feedback.

The theory behind the approach is that traumatic memories become amnestic because they were encoded in a state-dependent form (i.e., a specific SoC). The SoC associated with the trauma is created and maintained at the biological level via neural modulation by neuropeptides (Rossi & Cheek, 1988). Rossi and Cheek (1988) hypothesized that ideomotor signaling is helpful because

> the relatively mild stress arousal that patients experience as they ideo-
> dynamically review their problems releases a pattern of information

substances (peptides and stress hormones) similar to that which originally encoded their problem in a state bound form. . . . [This] accesses the state bound amnesia that have blocked the patient's previous efforts at self-understanding. (p. 77)

Two possibilities derive from this hypothesis. First, actual conscious verbal recall is facilitated by taking this intermediate "ideomotor" approach. Second, actual conscious recall may not be necessary (or as necessary) to resolve the symptomatic problem. For instance, I have described in detail elsewhere (Schwarz, 1994) a variation on TRC that does not involve any conscious awareness of the trauma.

The permissiveness of the approach has two therapeutic aspects. The goal of memory retrieval becomes secondary to the process of activating these inner psychobiological processes of mind–body communication and healing in which the patient must engage to answer the question (Rossi & Cheek, 1988). Any response from the patient is utilized as feedback for the direction and pace of the therapy.

Second, ideomotor signaling facilitates therapeutic dissociation, which helps to deepen trance as well as to protect the patient from a fully associated recall (a revivified memory), which the patient is trying to avoid. Formal ideomotor signaling can be built into any approach, as can informal observation of the ideomotor signals or minimal cues communicated by the patient. Rossi and Cheek (1988) described two specific approaches: the retrospective approach and the progressive chronological approach. The retrospective approach, considered to be a safer technique, uses a "20 questions" style of asking questions. The questioning pattern is a clear example of the TOTE model. The general pattern of questions is as follows:

A Retrospective Approach to Ideomotor Questioning

Following a hypnotic induction and the establishment of "yes," "no," and "not-ready-to-answer" signals, the following steps are taken:

1. Accessing the problem
   (a) Is there a past trauma responsible for your symptoms? (If not, check for a group of events). If the answer is still "no," exit the entire procedure or segue into searching for other issues such as current conflicts, etc. (see Hammond & Cheek, 1988).
   (b) Did it occur before you were 30 years old? 20 years old? Etc.
   (c) Did it occur at home?/in Vietnam?/etc.
   (d) Allow your unconscious mind to review what is happening. When it knows what it is, your yes finger will lift. As it lifts, the memory

will come up and you will be able to talk about it. (If extra safety is desired, you can ask if it is OK for the conscious mind to know what it is.)

2. Therapeutic reframing
    (a) Is it alright to tell me about it? [The patient tells what happens, therapeutic suggestions and reframing are used as needed. Helping the patient to bring the more mature or adult understanding to the situation is helpful.][4]
    (b) Is there an earlier experience that might have set the stage or made you vulnerable to what you have just told me? [If "yes," proceed as in step 1 above.]

3. Ratifying therapeutic gains
    (a) Now that you know about this and have these new learnings (from the therapy in steps 2a and 2b), can you be well? [If the response is "no," more work needs to be done.]
    (b) Is there anything else we need to know before you can be free of this problem? [If the answer is "no," proceed to step 3c.] [If the answer is "yes," proceed to 3d.]
    (c) Let your unconscious mind give a "yes" signal when it is ready to give you a date of a completely satisfactory resolution of the problem into your conscious mind. [If a satisfactory response does not occur, more therapeutic work needs to be done.]
    (d) Ask the unconscious mind if it is willing to work on the problem over the week so more could be achieved in the following session(s). [Adapted from Rossi & Cheek, 1988, p. 29.]

In the progressive chronological approach, considered a more advanced approach, the patient is asked to go back to a time before the trauma occurs, then is taken forward in time to the point of the trauma, and then through the various stages of and reactions to the trauma. Throughout the process, ideomotor signaling is used. I have used this second approach in a modified form (Calof, 1994b) in helping to modify the degree of persecution that alters inflict on the rest of the system. These alters tend to be very angry because they were "born" to do very dirty jobs with no help, no preparation, no thanks, and in their minds no chance of ever getting clean again. These circumstances are explained to the patient. A cadre of helpful alters is decided upon who will go back and help this alter. A plan is created about how to help the alter, which includes preparation for what the alter must face, reframing that the deeds this alter must do are in order to protect the system, appreciation

---

[4]Depending on what is remembered, the therapist might segue into the process for resolving intrusive symptoms at this point.

for doing it, perhaps some additional resources if possible, and a promise that the alter can return later on in life, even though she or he has gotten his or her hands "very dirty." Ideomotor signals are used to regress the patient to just before the alter is "born or forced to do something horrible for the first time." A kind of time out is taken and the other alters help the new one with all of the above. Additional posthypnotic suggestions can be given that one day that part will be able to be in therapy and she or he will then be able to really talk about his or her concerns about what happened. In so doing, that part will be able to be re-united with the rest of the system she or he was born to protect. Obviously this is an example of both memory retrieval and memory processing work.[5]

Requests for Therapist Validation

One final problem that can occur in any memory work is that patients often ask for validation of their truth, while often they themselves have many doubts. While it is true that victims who have been silenced may need validation, some clinicians have assumed the role of external authority and "validator." It is important that patients learn to assume this function for their own personal histories. One intervention is to explore with patients how they could get direct corroboration of their suspicions or memories. Calof (1995) has suggested a number of alternatives to the therapist directly validating something as true when the therapist is in no position to know for sure if something is objectively true. The therapist should assume a complementary stance regarding the patient's uncertainty. This includes:

- Reflecting back the patient's doubt (e.g., "Your asking me whether I believe your memories makes me wonder if you are having a conflict in believing them yourself?").
- Confronting attempts to export the locus of authority (e.g., "I wonder if you want me to say it happened, so you won't have to admit it

---

[5]One could easily make the argument that this type of intervention is neither memory retrieval nor memory processing. Rather, it is therapeutic play rewriting. I have no argument with this as long as we agree with the narrative therapist that all experience is narrative and play-like. This rule applies to everyone. We would need to further agree that the difference between health and illness is the type of narrative we tell about ourselves. We would need to further agree that this type of analysis has little bearing on the issue of whether or not a given event actually happened.

yourself and so you can then take the other side and say it did not happen.").

- Focusing the patient on his or her own internal validation devices (e.g., "I would like you to do an experiment. There are two parts to it. Let yourself believe or say to yourself that your memories are false and be aware of your experience. Then let yourself believe or say to yourself that your memories are accurate. Notice your experience in both situations.").
- Accepting and aligning with the doubt and confusion having an underlying function, worthy of exploration (e.g., "I trust that deep inside there is probably a good reason not to be sure at this point. We should probably continue to focus on the meaning of the doubt as well as the troubling images that you keep having.").
- Focusing on the dynamics surrounding the surfacing of the memories.

Another approach is that the therapist can direct the patient to look at the possible advantages and disadvantages to remembering or resolving their doubts. This can often be done as a homework assignment, and then work with the issues that arise.

It can be difficult for both the patient and therapist to sit with the ambiguity of not knowing for sure. No one likes ambiguity and doubt. Perhaps this is the crux of the matter.

☐ Memory Distortion, Magnification, and Minimization: Clinical and Political Issues

In the last few years there has been an increasingly vigorous debate about the possibility that some people have incorrectly remembered that they were sexually abused. The stories have been in the magazines, on all of the major television news magazine shows, PBS, talk shows, and so on. The major bad guys in these stories are almost always therapists. The major advocates for this position have been the False Memory Syndrome Foundation and its scientific advisory board, including people like hypnotism researcher Martin Orne, memory researcher Elizabeth Loftus, and social psychologist Richard Ofshe to name a few.

The question on everyone's mind is, How can a person witness something horrible or be sadistically abused and not remember for 20 years, and then all of a sudden remember? How can a reasonable person believe that such a thing is possible?

This section has two goals. The first is to clarify the issues in the controversy. The second is to present clinicians with a number of guidelines that will help minimize the types of mistakes that could lead to the development of a magnified or distorted memory (i.e., a type II error or a false positive finding), to a magnified or distorted response to valid memories, or at least to the perception that one had acted with less than a reasonable level of care.

The question of whether or not memories of abuse can be "installed," made up, or severely distorted has significant scientific/clinical and sociopolitical ramifications. Clinicians do need to consider these issues. However, clinicians will be better served by recognizing that there are significant boundaries between the politics of this issue and the science of it.

Most experts who work with trauma have acknowledged the possibility that therapist-induced memory contamination can happen (e.g., Terr, 1994). The problem is that the advocates for the hypothesis that false memories are occurring at an epidemic rate do so without scientific foundation, despite their claims to the contrary. The term *false memory* is highly problematic. It is legalistic and argumentative. It defines the issue in terms of black and white thinking. From a clinical perspective, I prefer the terms *distortion of memory* or *magnification* and/or *minimization of memory*. This terminology includes issues of not just the memory itself, but responses to that memory. The fact is that it is not simply whether or not a memory is true. It is what we do with our memory that is the most relevant issue for adaptation or maladaptation. For example, some years back, there was a PBS television documentary that included the story of a woman who had a budding career as a professional singer. The story that was portrayed was that she gave her career up to go on a therapeutic odyssey to search for memories of the abuse that happened in her life. In the process she became more and more dysfunctional. Since this was portrayed on television, I have no idea as to how accurate this depiction was, so I am going to comment on the story. This is what I would call a magnification of the response to past trauma and traumatic memory. In my opinion, this type of treatment is not therapeutic. Whether or not the memories themselves are real is not really the issue. In the story this woman gave up a resourceful life for an unresourceful life. This outcome is antithetical to the nature of the approach being described in this book (as well as the consensus view of trauma treatment).

In order to really understand this issue, we need to separate the question of to what extent there is merit in the hypothesis of patients remembering largely or wholly untrue events of abuse and trauma from the question of what are the best practices for clinicians in helping clients understand their memories and creating meaning and action in their lives.

An Analysis of the Controversy[6]

The Incidence of Repressed and Recovered Memory

One of the central claims of the false memory position as advocated by people such as Yapko (1994), Loftus and Ketchum (1994), and Ofshe (1992) is that repressed memory is a relatively rare phenomenon. The logic follows that if people rarely forget traumatic incidents, then any recovered memory of forgotten trauma must be false. However, research suggests that memory loss for traumatic incidences is rather common. Loftus, Polonsky, and Fullilove (1994) found that trauma survivors have significant memory loss at an incident rate of 1 in 5 people. Herman and Schatzow (1987) found a 28% incidence rate of significant amnesia in a group of outpatient survivors. Briere and Conti (1993) found rates as high as 60%. Williams (1994) retrieved the hospital records of girls who were sexually abused. She then followed them up 17 years later. Thirty-eight percent did not remember being abused. In an as yet unpublished retrospective study using self-report measures, I found a 35% incidence rate for reported traumatic amnesia in a sample of inpatient survivors.

The Incidence of "False" or Distorted Memories

To date, there are only recirculated anecdotal reports of robust false memories of sexual abuse. There have been isolated legal cases where plaintiffs have successfully sued therapists claiming false memories were created. Nevertheless, no scientific study exists that documents the existence, let alone the widespread incidence of so-called "false memories" for sexual abuse that never happened. We simply do not know the incidence rate. On the other hand, even if the rate is 1%, this potentially represents a great deal of pain to the families involved.

Memory Distortion for Central Details Versus Peripheral Details

Most of the original work with memory distortion had to do with the testimony of eyewitnesses and the accuracy of their memories (Loftus,

---

[6]For those who want to review a well-researched review of the literature, I highly recommend the work of Jim Hopper, Ph.D. He has published his work on the web with many links and citations. Go to www.JMHopper.com

1975; McConkey & Sheehan, 1980). Another issue was whether or not memory could be altered due to social influences such as police questioning (Loftus & Zanni, 1975; McConkey, Labelle, Bibb, & Bryant, 1990). The outcome of this research was that the memories of witnesses were less reliable than had been previously thought. Furthermore, it was discovered that social influence could alter people's remembrances for events.

However, all of this experimental research (usually referred to as pseudomemory) focused on *small, peripheral* details, such as the color of a car or which direction the car was heading. The research showed that people did misremember these types of details. Nevertheless, this type of inaccuracy could be very important in a criminal case. There has never been a scientific study that has documented the installation of a pseudomemory for a central detail (e.g., a car accident happened when it did not really happen). It is simply not scientifically valid to use this type of research to support the hypothesis that people can be influenced to make up entire incidents of trauma or life histories of abuse.

Another limitation of this type of research is that it always focuses on innocuous and inconsequential details (such as whether a robber in a one-minute movie wore a scarf or not, or whether a phone was ringing). It is problematic, to say the least, to apply this research to the highly emotional and meaningful experiences that occur in incest or other types of childhood sexual abuse.

But, if one were to still insist that this type of research has some bearing on the recovered memory issue, I would submit that it actually supports a conclusion opposite to the one the false memory advocates propose. This research acts as a social-psychological paradigm for traumatic amnesia of childhood incest. Since relatively innocuous social pressure from incidental people in a subject's life can induce a meaningful false positive memory, then it is highly probably that continuous and/or intense social pressure (to deny and forget) with potentially dire social consequences from highly meaningful people (e.g., adult family members, respected clergy, etc.) could also cause false negative memories.

False Positives Versus False Negatives

In much of the mass market literature that is out now (e.g., Loftus & Ketchum, 1994; Yapko, 1994), there is a one-sided discussion about the false positive memories of abuse by the "survivors." The possibility of false negative memory in the accused is not even raised. Some of the experimental research found that it was easier to produce false negative pseudomemories than false positive ones (Lynn, Milano, & Weeks, 1991).

The crux of a false memory accusation is the parent or family member is saying that he or she did not do something that the child says that he or she did. There is no good reason to accept, a priori, the parents' story as the criterion measure of truth. Common sense and experience will tell us that some percentage of the accused are simply lying. But, it is highly probable that a significant percentage actually do not remember due to a variety of factors, including alcohol or drug intoxication at the time of the abuse, state-dependent memory, or denial or their own dissociative disorder.

Actual Memory Versus Report of Memory

It is absolutely crucial to understand that a verbal report of a memory is not the same thing as a memory. Murrey, Cross, and Whipple (1992) tried to determine if the demand characteristics of an experiment actually irrevocably altered the memory of a subject or simply changed what the subject reported as remembering. They have found that they could reduce the amount of pseudomemory by 50% by simply paying the subjects to give a truthful account. Schwarz (1995) described the distinction between memory and report of memory in a clinical situation in the following manner: A patient has an intrusive experience such as pain in her vagina as well as seeing her father's face. The person may then conclude (with or without the help of a therapist) that she must have been raped by her father. Even though she may report that she remembers Daddy raping her, it is not an accurate representation. She remembers the image/sensation combination and then adds the conclusion that she was raped. Then she verbally mislabels this as "I remember being raped" (see Terr, 1994, pp. 162–163). This distinction about verbal report versus actual memory does not mean that she was not raped by her father. This type of verbal mislabeling of complex experience happens all the time in contexts other than dissociated memories of abuse.

One approach that can help therapists clarify this problem is "deconstruction" (de Shazer, 1985). Essentially, the approach involves asking questions about the specific components of the construction, in this case the words "I remember Daddy raped me." For instance, the therapist can say something like, "I very much want to understand your actual experience. Could you tell me specifically what you see, hear, and feel in your memory that lets you know that your father raped you?" (Schwarz, 1995).

True/False Distinctions
Versus Degree of Distortion

It should not be surprising that the false memory position always uses the true/false dichotomy, since the position is often used in forensic settings or in legalistic arguments. In court, one is either guilty or not guilty of a specific charge. Everywhere else in life, there is much more room for shades of gray. Furthermore, in most of the anecdotal accounts in the false memory literature, one gets the picture of the all-good accused parents, Ward and June Cleaver, being victimized by their sick or brainwashed child. (It should not be lost on clinicians that this victim stance is a parallel process to the victim stance of many people who come to therapy as abuse victims. Victim stances are not adaptive for either side.)

It seems highly unlikely that a person who grew up in a healthy, loving, well-functioning family would erase their own happy personal history simply to comply with a therapist's suggestions or demand characteristics. The possibility is never raised that perhaps, in at least some cases, there is a middle truth. For example, the father did not physically rape his daughter as she charges but did commit a variety of sexual boundary violations, including masturbating to pornography in front of the daughter. Barrett (1994) has suggested using the approach of asking families to find the middle ground as a useful therapeutic stance with families who allege false memories.

Legal Versus Clinical Contexts

Finally, it is important to acknowledge that the therapy office and the courtroom have very different cultures. Therapists are explicitly not in the business of judging; courtrooms are exactly in the business of judging. As a therapist, I am not immediately interested in proving or disproving whether a memory is true or not. Therapy is a cooperative relationship, and we have time to sort the truth out. Court involves an adversarial relationship with limited time. It is inappropriate to apply the rules of evidence for court to therapy. It is also inappropriate to expect a court to accept the more lax criteria of evidence used in therapy.

I cannot think of a situation in which a therapist should actively advise a client to use the court to redress the injustice of his or her abuse. This type of action is fraught with perils. If for some reason a survivor chooses to go to court, then he or she has to play by the rules of that context.

Political Agendas Versus Clinical Concerns

The fact is that the scientific and clinical controversy about this subject is more in a state of not knowing than knowing. The clinical community has been very responsive to redressing some of the excesses over the past few years, as evidenced by the many clinical workshops (e.g., Barrett,

1994; Schwarz & Calof, 1994) and publications (e.g., Brown, Scheflin, & Hammond, 1998; Hammond et al., 1995). Nevertheless, clinicians should not be naive. There is a large-scale political agenda being waged to curtail or prevent therapists from working with client's traumatic memories that has little to do with addressing clinical mistakes. No matter how much we improve our clinical effectiveness and minimize type II errors, there is no reason to expect that this will appease a significant proportion of the people in the false memory camp, given the emotional and nonscientific basis for their beliefs and actions.

Clinical Issues

From a scientific or clinical point of view there are two types of errors we can make with respect to memory. In science experiments or even medical diagnostic terms, there are two types of outcome errors: type I errors or false negatives and type II errors or false positives. In a false negative, the doctor does not diagnose the cancer when it really is there or the experimenter does not find an effect even though it really exists. In type II errors the doctor diagnoses cancer when it is not there or the experimenter finds an effect that really does not exist. A so-called false memory or a significantly magnified memory is a type II error. Up to this point in time there is little evidence to suggest that patients remember trauma where there was happiness. However, there is clinical evidence to suggest that patients (with or without the help of therapists) can magnify memory of trauma in manners that are not therapeutic. This is still essentially a type II error. The concept of memory magnification as a type II error is an important clinical question that also resolves the issue of veracity. This is what I will address below.

I have stated from the outset that social reality is constructed. In an ongoing social interaction such as therapy, both parties have some level of involvement in how memory is constructed or how it is used in creating ongoing meaning or action in life. The relative influence of therapist and patient on that construction can be highly variable from context to context. Of course, therapists are not the only social factor in patients' social construction of their reality. Hopefully, therapists are an influence toward patients becoming "healthier" and more functional.[7]

As I pointed out in chapter 1, there is a cybernetic loop over time that leads to adaptation or maladaptation in PTSD. The question that we

---

[7]Of course, the terms *healthier* and *more functional* and the measures of these concepts are socially constructed as well.

must ask is, What are the patient and therapist variables that might influence this loop to increase the occurrence of type II errors?

Therapist Factors

Most therapists are motivated to help people. The question is, What are the therapist's presuppositions, assumptions and intentions about psychotherapy in general, and working with trauma in particular, that might cause him or her to become involved in a memory magnification loop? What are the presuppositions that could support therapist behaviors that would participate in memory magnification? Here are several possibilities:

- If someone has a "feeling" that she has been abused this means she absolutely must have been abused.
- If someone has been sexually abused this means that any psychiatric symptom or emotional problem stems from the abuse.
- The only way to get over sexual abuse is to recover every detail from the past (current life adjustment is not relevant).
- "Memories," dreams, and bodily senses of abuse are 100% correct and cannot be distorted.
- Hypnotic memories are more accurate than regular memories.
- Patients can never be swayed or manipulated by therapists into remembering or believing various things.
- When someone has the signs and symptoms associated with abuse histories and he says he does not remember, he must be in denial.

The following questions relate to one's intentions and beliefs about how to do therapy. It is self-evident which answers could support problematic therapist behavior.

- Does the therapist think he or she must recover memories to be a good trauma therapist?
- Does the therapist believe he or she must defend the "good" patient from the "bad" abuser?
- Does the therapist believe the patient must "always" do some certain thing in response to being abused (e.g., confront his/her offender)?
- Does the therapist place special emphasis on asking about abuse histories in all of his or her clients?

Below is a list of presuppositional stances that I believe help to undermine problematic therapist behavior. Whether one agrees or disagrees is less important than the reasoning behind the stances. The reader can ask, What are the presuppositional stances that I take, and how do they influence what I do?

Presuppositional Stances That Help Avoid Memory Magnification

- The demand characteristic of therapy should be for healing and for good functioning in the here and now.
- There are multiple reasons for symptoms (look for the most mundane and current in time first)
- There are multiple pathways to healing.
- Having access to resources is at least as important as working through trauma.
- Given sufficient support and access to resources, the client really does know what is best. Clients only need to remember what is necessary for healing. It is OK to not remember everything.
- All experience (including memory) is constructed. Facts do not drive people. It is meaning that drives people.
- Since indirect suggestions and presuppositions do influence people, as a therapist, (a) one should be aware of one's indirect communication, (b) one should be flexible in his or her presuppositional stance, (c) one should utilize suggestions that are healing (as measured by feedback from patient).
- Be willing to value not knowing, ambiguity, and confusion.

The other major sources of problematic therapist behaviors are countertransference issues. I suggest that virtually all of the coercive types of contamination come from this area. Coercive contamination refers to conscious attempts of the therapist to pressure clients about what they should do (e.g., they should take their abuser to court) or what the meaning of their experience is or is not (e.g., the fact that the person does not remember being abused means they are in denial).[8] In addition, many other therapeutic mistakes are products of countertransference issues. Here are a few of the more important possibilities.

Countertransference and Counterreactions That Can Support Memory Magnification and Response Magnification

- Need to be a savior, the only one who understands;
- therapist overinvolvement (e.g., becoming an advocate);
- therapist acting out or feelings of "normal" anger and rage at hearing abuse;

---

[8]These types of interventions are simply not advocated anywhere in the current mainstream literature about trauma treatment.

- therapist acting out or disowned feelings of client (via projective identification);
- therapist acting out needs of client by taking on a symmetrical role to
  client's role behavior;
- therapist acting out his or her own dynamics from past abuse (sexual,
  physical, or emotional), including anger and rage at one's own perpetrator, desire for revenge, projecting abuse-based images/beliefs/etc.
  onto clients, creating too much dependence based on his or her own
  wish for nurturance;
- fascination and enthrallment with dissociative pathology due to naiveté
  or narcissism;
- conscious or unconscious needs to choose frames of reference that
  keep clients sicker than necessary (e.g., in order to make more money
  or have a more stable practice, or to be needed.)

Patient Variables

If we assume that some patients do develop significantly distorted memories
in the direction of falsely believing they were abused, there would have
to be some motivation or reason why a patent would be willing to distort
and magnify his or her own memory in a direction that tends to only
cause a great deal of pain. When memory distortion is viewed as a continuum, the motivations listed below make a great deal of sense. It should
also be pointed out that in some cases patients maintain these stances in
spite of (not because of) therapist interventions.

Possible Motivations/Mechanisms for Clients to Magnify Traumatic Memories

- In memory work, the miscoding of covert abuse messages as overt acts;
- avoidance of pain and betrayal of family members by naming outside
  sources;
- "lesser" abuses not deemed significant enough or valid enough to justify feelings so "bigger" abuses are named;
- protection of the idealized family by naming an outside agency (e.g., a
  cult);
- with DID the multiplication of a single trauma by the separate memories of different alters (Calof, 1994);
- confabulation of real trauma with primary process material due to
  borderline psychosis;
- high suggestibility and/or strong need for compliance (Hammond et
  al., 1995), in a client who may have had substantial emotional trauma
  in his or her family.

Warning Flags That Reported Memories May Contain Significant Distortions

The following list of situations should be considered as warning flags for the clinician. These are clinical impressions and not based on empirical evidence. They are derived from the author's experience as well as The American Society for Clinical Hypnosis' guidelines on memory and hypnosis (Hammond et al., 1995). For instance, one patient said that she had a clear memory of being under 2 years old and her mother picking her up by her feet like a person would pick up a stick and bashing with her head into the corner of a countertop. The patient had no affect when she said this. She had no scar or trace of what was described as a blow that would most likely have bashed the skull in. This particular patient was also not interested in talking about more "garden variety" incidents of neglect and abuse. Another patient would go and pray and rock for about a half-hour and then come out of her room and state she had a new memory of abuse. She would do this repeatedly. In over hundreds of cases seen on an inpatient trauma unit, there were literally only a handful of such patients (less than 1%). It is important to note that if forced to take an "either/or" stance, therapists in this setting essentially did not believe these particular stories of these patients because their stories just did not make sense. It was in spite of the work of the staff that this behavior went on.

Nevertheless, there is no way a therapist can know for certain if a memory is true or not without independent evidence. These warning flags do not preclude the possibility that a memory is essentially correct. The warning flags are:

- The uncovered memory is of an event that occurred before the age of 3.
- The potential for litigation is raised or is already underway.
- The situation arises in the treatment of highly manipulative clients.
- The person was previously seen by an unlicensed therapist or lay hypnotist.
- The person insists on hypnosis immediately to uncover memories and is not willing to slow down and listen to potential problems with such a course of action.
- The person treats the memories with "la belle indifference" (as in a conversion disorder).
- A client prefers to talk about the more "gruesome" traumas (e.g., cult abuse at age 2) of very early childhood rather than the more "mundane" traumas of later childhood (father had sex with child at age 9 and/or mother beat child ages 9–11).

- The client talks about traumas with almost a sense of pride, as if it were a merit badge. (This is a subtle thing. It is likely that the therapist will respond to this with an uncomfortable or unsettled feeling.)
- The person reports a crystal clear memory of an incident from very early childhood and is not interested in having any doubts about it.

Treatment Strategies to Minimize Type II Errors

Before moving into specific treatment strategies, I want to underscore that it is my belief that the vast majority of clients' reported experiences of abuse are essentially accurate in their central details. There will never be a substitute for good listening from a therapist who can take the role of witness and help clients metabolize the trauma they have experienced. There are four possible situations that can develop with adult patients with issues of abuse. These are:

1. When clients know that they have been abused and that is their chief complaint.
2. When clients wonder if they were abused and ask to find out via hypnosis or some other process.
3. When clients come in with some other type of complaint and the therapist suspects abuse as the etiologic source of the complaint.
4. When neither therapist nor client focuses on abuse as a possibility, but memories or abuse-like experiences surface.

Therapists should be careful not to be wedded in a fundamentalist manner to a specific theory of causality or therapy that states that certain problems must necessarily be attributed to childhood sexual abuse. Therapists should also not assume that the only way for clients to get better is to remember the abuse and having a catharsis of the experience. One way to operationalize this concept is that a therapist should be able to generate at least one plausible alternative to the hypothesis that a given problem or symptom is due to a specific traumatic event in the past. It is the therapist's singular belief in any one therapeutic truth that has the potential ability to develop the clinical equivalent of the experimental demand characteristic (Orne, 1969).

For instance, a client was referred to me by a therapist because the client was not getting better. It was postulated that there seemed to be something in the client's past that might be causing this. The client described a situation with many sexually related problems that could easily lead to the suspicion of sexual abuse as a potential source of her difficulties. As part of the evaluation the client was asked about trauma and abuse. She denied physical or sexual abuse. Upon further inquiry she admitted that her first experience of intercourse was at 12 years old with her boyfriend. She felt she had to do this to keep her boyfriend. After this she became promiscuous and eventually ended up using drugs. The client had never really talked about this with her therapist. While it is possible that there was sexual abuse that the client did not remember, her issues of shame due to her sexual promiscuousness seemed to account for her problems.

When Clients Know They Have Been Abused

Sometimes patients come into treatment stating they have come because they are an adult child of an alcoholic or a survivor of sexual abuse or a passive-aggressive personality. The problem with complaints that are also diagnoses is that they do not necessarily lead the therapist or the client toward a desired end or goal. The chief danger here is unfocused, endless, or negative outcome therapy. The most important thing for the therapist to do is help the patient create well-formed goals (see chapter 2).

Another important area of questioning is an assessment of how the client has come to define sexual abuse as the problem. Has the client always known that he has been abused? How has this knowledge effected his development as a human being? If he were amnestic for a period of time, when did he remember? What were the circumstances? Did this happen as a result of a previous course of therapy? If so, what happened in that relationship? How did he come to define sexual abuse as the source of his current problem? Was it his formulation, a therapist's formulation, or someone else's?

A couple came in for marital problems, specifically, they had not had sex for 3 years. As part of the evaluation, they were asked if either had any history of abuse. They looked at each other for a minute. The man reported that the wife had been sexually abused. The wife did not see this as the source of her problem. She felt it was more the relationship. The husband labeled the abuse as the reason she was not having sex with him. What would you do in this situation?

One potential pitfall is endless searching in the past for explanations about why things aren't going better in the present. The worst-case scenario is that the client and/or the therapist begin to suspect that there must be more abuse than previously thought in order to explain why the client is not getting better. For example, Suzanne was seen in the hospital because she was mutilating herself in a dissociated state. The outpatient therapist thought that there must be more abuse in the past than the physical abuse that was known. It turned out that Suzanne was currently being physically abused by her husband. She had not revealed this. In my opinion it is unlikely that the patient in this example would have actually created a false memory. The most likely scenario was what was already happening: The therapy was going nowhere and the patient had destabilized.

If part of the assessment turns up that the client entered a previous therapy without memories of abuse, but uncovered them during the therapy, or the amount of abuse seems to multiply during the therapy, then a more careful approach is in order. This warning increases if the client's functioning deteriorates as more memories are recovered. This does not necessarily mean that the memories were untrue. It may mean that they were being magnified to too high a degree of importance in the patient's life. It is crucial to find out the respective roles of the therapist and client in constructing this reality. Changes in the perceived quality of the therapeutic relationship can be telling.

For example, Mary was seen in the hospital. She reported a history of abuse that she had always known about. Her therapy had been going poorly and she had been decompensating. Mary reported that the therapist had been of the opinion that since she was not getting better there must be more abuse in her past that she had repressed. Questioning revealed that they had not been working on the rather intense family conflicts that had been escalating due to Mary's changes from therapy. At one point, Mary had been reading about satanic ritual abuse in a magazine. She became "upset and anxious." When she reported this to her therapist, her therapist responded that this might mean that she had been ritually abused. When asked how she felt about this idea, Mary replied that it made her uneasy and that she felt that she lost a bond of trust with her therapist. Even though she felt fairly sure ritual abuse had not occurred, it was now difficult for her to get this idea out of her head as a possibility; why had she gotten so upset?

I told her that I did think there could be an alternative explanation for her reactions. She would have to decide for herself which explanation fit for her. Did she want to hear it? She agreed. She was asked if, while she was reading the story, she was imagining what it was like to be the victim, putting herself in that woman's shoes. She said that she had. It was then suggested that it would be rather normal to have the reactions she had, because if one just attempts to imagine being the recipient of ritual abuse, it is very upsetting and anxiety provoking. Over the next few days she reported thinking about this. She thought the new explanation fit her situation. She felt a great deal of relief. We worked on her family problems in relations to her known abuse history and the changes she was making.

When Clients Wonder If They Were Abused and Ask to Find Out

This is the area that may be at greatest risk for memory distortion and certainly increased exposure to that charge. The therapist needs to follow all of the guidelines of the previous section plus several additional considerations.

Perhaps the question that needs to be most answered by the client is, "How will learning whether or not you were abused help you in your current situation?" This line of inquiry will quickly lead back to the types of assessment raised in the previous section. Another line of questioning is, "What has even raised the question in your mind?"

One other crucial question is, "Suppose you find out that you were abused. What do you intend to do with that information?" If the answer is in the direction of acting out some type of punitive measure (e.g., cut off from the family or legal action), one would be advised to explore this fully before going any further. Obviously, if the client is already engaged in these actions, it is a serious warning flag.

There are a couple of other client reactions that serve as warning lights for me. The first is a relatively high level of insistence that this is the only way to proceed. The second is the client's need for me to do something immediately. The third is the client's need to know that some definite event occurred in the past. The insistence and need for immediacy has more than once been felt on the initial phone call. More than once the person on the other end of the line has refused to come in when he or she finds out that he or she will not be hypnotized at the first session.

If the therapist and client agree to use some type of specific protocol for retrieving memory, then the therapist needs to do several things. First, the client should be provided with the proper information for informed consent. The informed consent should at least include a potential limitation of rights to testify should the person become involved in a trial regarding his abuse or trauma memories; a discussion of the imperfections of memory, including memories recovered in hypnosis; discussion of the potential for psychological harm in using uncovering methods with people with fragile ego strength (Hammond et al., 1995). It may be advisable to codify this in an informed consent form. (See the ASCH guidelines for hypnosis and memory [Hammond et al., 1995] for a model form.) Second, the therapist needs to help set a neutral expectation with respect to remembering. Neutral in this context means that the clients understand that

- they may or may not recall something;
- if they do recall something, it may or may not be factually accurate;

- there are many potential sources of distortion (These include confabulation of two accurate facts to make an inaccurate remembrance,
a partial memory that becomes symbolically elaborated with fully symbolic
imagery that is interpreted as a real event.);
- if they do not remember something, there are alternative ways to
achieve their goals.

Therapists who do elect to use this approach should be well trained in
hypnosis as well as trauma work. It is important to go slow and respect
any "resistance." It is important not to entertain the option of "busting
through the defenses," which is tantamount to a rape of the unconscious. Clients will sometimes invite the therapist to go ahead and "bust
through the defenses." This opportunity should always be politely turned
down with appropriate education about how this would be a boundary
violation. If the person was in fact previously abused, the client has just
engaged in a request to reenact the trauma.

One approach that I particularly like is the use of ideomotor questioning (described earlier in this chapter; Cheek & Lecron, 1968; Rossi &
Cheek, 1988). The main reason I like this approach is that one can ask
the following two questions:

1. Does your unconscious mind think that there is something [or sexual
abuse] in your past that is responsible for you [current symptom]?
2. Does your unconscious mind think it would be useful for you to
know what this is?

These questions, if asked from a truly neutral place, offer the possibility that (a) there is not abuse in the person's past that is responsible for
the symptoms or (b) even if there is abuse, it would not be useful to
know it. There is an additional ambiance to this type of intervention. It
is the client who knows what is best for himself or herself at a deep level.
The therapist does not intrude his or her ideas or values. It is not unusual for clients to get "no" answers to either of these questions. In this
manner, the answer came from the client. When a "no" is received, the
client may become upset because of disconfirmed expectation. These
reactions can then be discussed and worked through. The search for
some bad event in the past can sometimes be the psychotherapeutic
equivalent of patients demanding from their medical doctors pain or
anxiety medication. A "no" coming from the "unconscious" allows the
therapist to say "no" and help the client look in alternative directions.

For instance, one client got the answer that there was one event of
sexual trauma and that was it. She did not believe that all of her problems could have come from this one event, which was nonviolent and

did not involve any sort of penetration or touching. What ensued was a course of treatment about what happened after the event. (Her father, the perpetrator, pulled away from his daughter. Apparently, it was an attempt to not let the abuse happen again.) The client never talked about this event. It was interweaved into a family script about not talking about feelings and staying distant, which was very much tied up with the client's chief complaint of marital and sexual problems.

Assuming one finally does do "memory retrieval" work using hypnosis or other imagery techniques, it is best to use a free recall method first, with the therapist just listening and occasionally saying "um hm" or "anything else?" After this is complete, the therapist could ask some follow-up questions. It is crucial that the questions not be leading and not con-tain any presuppositions. It would be wise in this day and age to make an audio- or videotape recording of this for the record. Any "memories" that are recovered need to be worked through as previously described.

When the Therapist Suspects Abuse as the Etiologic Source of the Complaint

This is the situation that is most criticized by false memory advocates (e.g. Yapko, 1994, Loftus & Ketchum, 1994). The archtypical example is that a client calls the therapist on the phone or comes in to a first session and complains of low self-esteem. Within a few minutes the therapist says something to the effect of, "I know what is wrong with you. You have probably been sexually abused!" Lets take the obvious problems first. Therapists should:

- never tell clients that the reason they have "x" problem is that they were sexually abused. It does not matter if you sugar coat it with words like "may."
- not imply the above by *arbitrarily* asking if they were sexually abused.
- not compound the above mistakes by insisting that patients are resisting or in denial when they insist they were not abused.

It does not matter, even if the therapist is sure that the client was abused. The way to get at the possibility of abuse is to take a thorough history. This includes a description of the complaint, current problems/stresses, and biographical information. Included in the biography can be questions about previous traumas including sexual abuse. The demeanor of this type of questioning should be compassionate and matter of fact, just like taking a sexual history. If the client does not endorse sexual abuse at that time, then the therapist has to work on the problem in some other manner. This does not mean that it may not come up later on.

When Neither Therapist nor Client Focuses on Abuse, but Memories Surface

In this situation no one has suspected abuse, but the client begins to have flashbacks or partial flashbacks (body memories) or other symptoms that are highly correlated with sexual abuse or other early childhood trauma. Another variant of the situation is the case of clients with previously known sexual abuse who develop new symptoms that point to additional trauma.

The central questions in this situation are, "Why now?" or "What current problem/dilemma is happening in the client's life that requires the activation of these memories/experiences in an attempt to solve a problem?" "What is going on in the treatment?" "What has changed in the person's life?" "What developmental milestone has been reached?" Even if it is objectively true that there was more abuse, it does not necessarily follow that the therapy should be about uncovering it. One of the biggest mistakes that I have seen in therapy with trauma survivors is doing too much uncovering work without enough safety and grounding in current time and social functioning.

One way to handle the eruption of more memories, especially in more dissociative clients, is to reverse the usual direction of causality. Instead of thinking that the trauma the client had in the past is causing the problem today (therefore solve the past and you will solve today), one can think that the client is having real problems in his or her current context (including the therapeutic relationship) that causes the activation of failed solution attempts encoded in the intrusive experience.

☐ Summary

Memory and its relationship to a personal narrative are at the heart of working with people who have been traumatized. In this chapter we have looked at tools that assist in eliciting and transforming the memories of past events as they impact on ongoing behavior and meaning making. They also impact the development of future actions and memories. Transforming traumatic memories is a central aspect of the middle phase of treatment. However, it is always in dynamic flux with maintaining sufficient safety and other resourceful states (phase 1 of treatment) as well as connecting the new transformations to aspects of self and others (phase 3 of treatment). Furthermore, it is also in dynamic relationship to the creation of future memories and meaning through the cultivation of resourceful ways of living (see chapter 7).

For instance, Trauma Reassociative Conditioning (TRC) is an excellent metaphor for effectively working with trauma utilizing all three phases of trauma treatment. TRC can be used during Phase 1 of treatment as a method for neutralizing flashbacks. Its greatest advantage is that the patient deals with the memory, but does not have to go into catharsis. Patients often have their first experience of remembering the trauma rather than reliving it. The goal here is to help the patient stabilize his or her ability for living in the present rather than reliving the past.

In phase two of treatment, TRC is used to help work through difficult memories and beliefs. While the goal is similar to phase 1, there is a difference. In phase 1, the therapist and patient do not actively look for symptomatic areas or problematic memories. You let sleeping dogs lie. TRC is only used when flash backs occur.

In phase 2 there is more of an active approach to going after problematic memories. TRC is one tool with which to process these problems. The goal is to help the patient increase his or her connection to devalued aspects of the self.

With respect to the issues surrounding memory distortion, the use of the principles and techniques described in this section cannot in and of themselves be used to prove the accuracy or inaccuracy of a memory. If it can be shown that a therapist has violated the principles described here it cannot be taken a priori that his or her patient's memories are therefore inaccurate. The most important thing for clinicians to do is to be aware of the issues involved. It should be evident to the reader that the vast majority of these comments and suggestions regarding minimizing memory distortion flow from the overall approach of emphasizing the development of resourcefulness as the central goal of treatment.

6

The Use of Thought Field Therapy in Treating Trauma

In chapter 5 we have discussed many ways to work with traumatic memories. Thought field therapy (TFT) provides another effective tool to transform the negativity of those memories. TFT works with the meridian system of the patient while the patient is focusing on the traumatic memory. As a result of the changes in the flow of meridian energy, the affect associated with the memory is neutralized. The memory rapidly becomes less traumatic.

☐ Embrace the Paradigm Shift (Weirdness)

TFT and other energy psychology approaches involve a paradigm shift.[1] When I teach TFT to professionals or to clients I tell them that what they

---

[1]At the time of this writing. The APA Committee on Continuing Education has specifically banned APA-approved providers from teaching TFT and other energy approaches. Such a banning is an unusual occurrence. Two reasons are given. The first is that there is little hard research to prove the effectiveness of these approaches. While this criticism is accurate, it has rarely been a reason to stop teaching trainings. Furthermore, many respected clinicians have vouched for its effectiveness in clinical approaches. The second reason given is that since it

are going to experience is weird. There is no way around this fact. So, the only advisable thing to do is acknowledge and even embrace this weirdness. For those not familiar with these techniques, just accept that this approach involves a paradigm shift. The thing to do is just keep an open and curious heart and mind. This approach has worked well with thousands of people.

In some ways TFT is more akin to physics and quantum mechanics than it is to psychology. Its reference to the term *field* is based on the idea that all matter is energy. In physics, "energy fields" are postulated to be the force that holds the energy of matter in a coherent form. Mathematically these fields are expressed by Faraday's field equations. A "thought field" is considered to be the energetic pattern that holds a thought or memory together in a coherent manner. Emotion is part of the thought and/or memory of an event. When you think about it, the idea of thoughts and emotions as energy makes perfect sense. After all, when you are upset, you can literally feel the energy. Thinking in terms of invisible energetic fields is truly a paradigm shift. The writings of Bohm (1980) on the implicate order of the universe and Sheldrake (1981, 1989) on morphic fields are simply startling and most definitely weird for those unaware of these ideas.

☐ A Brief History of TFT and Energy Therapy

The art of meridian-based therapy and acupuncture is at least two thousand years old. I have no doubt that more has been lost and forgotten in this tradition than we can ever imagine. The work we will be discussing has its roots in this tradition. The Chinese discovered that energy flows through the body in channels called *meridians*. These channels do not appear to correspond to known channels of the body in any consistent manner. The meridians are named after organs of the body. One of the functions of the meridians is to infuse these organs with energy so they will function properly. The meridians are thought to be channels that take Chi or Ki (life energy) and move it through the body. For instance,

---

uses meridians, it is not psychology. This argument is spurious. Psychologists use biofeedback. Brain waves and galvanic skin responses are not "psychology" either. So what are the real reasons? It is hard to know for sure. The last argument does demonstrate the degree of paradigm shift that energy psychology represents. Some very big claims were made originally for TFT that probably should not have been made. There are "fringe" elements doing other "energy work" (e.g., aura readings, etc.), which probably makes the APA nervous. Of course, today's fringe is often tomorrow's mainstream.

Chi enters the body at the lung meridian and then spreads through the other meridians.

In the mid 1960s, Chiropractor George Goodheart, Jr., developed applied kinesiology. He discovered that he could evaluate the body's functioning through a process of testing various muscles for relative strength. Goodheart worked with many different systems of the body, correlating their relative action on each other. Eventually, he came to the meridian system. He rediscovered what the Chinese had known: that you could determine which meridian(s) were involved in a problem by localizing a meridian and then testing a muscle to see if it were weak or strong. He also discovered that instead of using a needle to stimulate a meridian, he could use pressure or tapping.

One of Goodheart's students was psychiatrist John Diamond. Whereas Goodheart was more focused on physical problems, Diamond was more interested in emotional disorders. Diamond worked on correlating the meridians with various feeling states and emotional disorders. Diamond was particularly interested in the phenomena that when a patient would think about something distressing, he would test weak on muscle testing. If a patient thought of something positive, he would test strong. Diamond has spent a great deal of time and energy on elucidating the different positive and negative emotions associated with each meridian (Diamond, 1980a). For example, the stomach meridian is associated with disgust, deprivation, and disappointment on the negative poll and contentment and tranquility on the positive poll. As we shall see, the stomach meridian is one of the key treatment points with trauma.

In the early 1980s, the psychologist Roger Callahan took the 100-hour course in applied kinesiology. He began to experiment using tapping on meridian points to treat psychological problems. Eventually he was able to discover common patterns or algorithms that worked with a variety of people. Thought field therapy is the term coined by Dr. Callahan for the techniques that he developed. Dr. Callahan strongly believed in the idea that there is a specific sequence of meridian points for a given problem. Furthermore, these points must be stimulated in a specific order to remove the problem. One of his students, Gary Craig, did not find this to be true. He developed the emotional freedom technique (EFT), which uses a single algorithm that stimulates all of the energy points. Gallo has written a text on his method of assessment and treatment called *Energy Diagnostic and Treatment Methods* (EDXTM; Gallo, 1999, 2000). Gallo takes a middle position that singles out some specificity of meridians, but is not as concerned about order.

In any event, energy psychology is in its infancy, but there is a great deal of clinical experience that demonstrates the effectiveness of this method, especially with trauma.

☐ Mechanism of Therapeutic Action

The effectiveness of TFT provides additional construct validity to the importance of the affect regulation system as a major determinant of whether or not a person can metabolize the traumatic event (described in chapter one). A person overwhelmed with affect is not able to process the traumatic information. It is postulated that any intervention that assists the patient in modulating a person's affect while attempting to process the trauma assists in the resolution of traumatic symptoms. One study (van der Kolk and Ducey, 1994) found that patients who were having reduced symptomatology due to the use of medication had significant changes in responses to the Rorschach ink-blot test. The main difference was a shift from more Color-Form responses to more Form-Color responses. This shift suggests that the patient is in fact more able to modulate affect while cognitively processing the material rather than having the affect overwhelm the cognitive system.

Trauma reassociative conditioning (TRC) (described in Chapter 5) strategically prevents affective dysregulation by having the patient purposefully access resourceful SoCs while reviewing the trauma from a dissociated point of view. TFT appears to reduce affective dysregulation through another channel. It is postulated that the meridian system modulates the affect system and emotional responses of a person. It is not clear whether a disruption in the meridian system causes the affective dysregulation that leads to information overload, or whether information overload leads to high levels of affect that disrupts the energy system. It is most likely that there is a dynamic equilibrium between these systems (as described in chapter 1). In posttraumatic reactions this equilibrium is sufficiently disrupted so that it is not self-restoring.

In trauma the energy system becomes disrupted creating a "perturbation" or disruption in the thought fields associated with the traumatic memory. If you really think about it, there is no known specific causal mechanism for intense affect. In TFT it is postulated that the perturbation or distortion in the field associated with the memory generates the intense affect. The affect then impedes the informational processing system from working effectively. The continued cognitive overload increases the distortion that magnifies the affective overload. Finally, disruptions to the energy system of the body may influence other physical manifestations of the body, including neurotransmitters and other neuropeptides (the physical substances usually postulated as the cause of intense affect). TFT effects change by stimulating meridian points in a pattern that removes the distortion in the energy field associated with the event. When the energy system is corrected the individual can process the traumatic material while maintaining affective regulation. In fact, unlike EMDR, which often generates intense affect and catharsis, TFT trauma treatment is usually non cathartic. The patient quickly and almost inexplicably moves into a place where there is little emotional reaction to the events that happened. It is postulated that TFT works so rapidly because it is working on the energetic level. Since thoughts and feelings are more energy than they are matter, they change quickly. It is quite possible that there are also associated changes at the neurobiological level. The mind body connection does not need to be broken probably. In one study, scientists did find significant changes in cortical activity as measured by PET scan when different meridian points were stimulated with acupuncture (Cho et al., 1998).

When patients are asked to discuss the traumatic events after TFT treatment they often describe significantly beneficial shifts in their interpretations and beliefs about the traumatic events, especially in terms of negative self references. For example patients often spontaneously report feeling less critical about themselves. Patients who have felt angry about and abandoned over the death of a loved one spontaneously feel more connected to the deceased person. This occurs without any specific intervention of the therapist. Of course the therapist is then free to build upon and strengthen these changes. It is not clear how this change happens. It does appear to be similar to the kinds of changes seen with other interventions such as TRC. As found in the Rorchach/medication study, when patients affective-informational processing system is not overwhelmed with color/feeling, patients can transform the raw material of the traumatic experience into a form that supports positive meaning in their lives.

☐ TFT: A Noncathartic/ Non Retraumatizing Method

One of TFT's greatest benefits is that it appears to help resolve traumatic memories and symptoms without retraumatizing the person. It is essentially a nonabreactive method. There are three parts to a full treatment protocol in TFT. The first aspect of any approach is the sequence of meridian points used to treat the problem. The problem in the case of trauma is the negative emotional reactions to a traumatic event. These sequences are termed algorithms. The algorithms presented in this chapter were arrived at over many years of clinical experience. They have been shown to be highly effective (upwards of 85%) in treating trauma at a speed that is almost unbelievable (Figley & Carbonera, 1995). Within a matter of minutes most clients report dramatic drops in subjective units of distress (SUDs) as they think about the traumatic event.

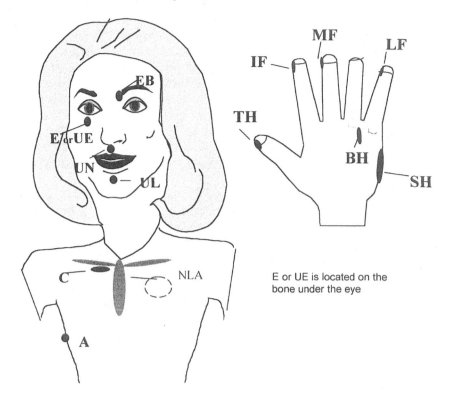

Figure 6.1. Thought field therapy treatment points.

The sequence of points is postulated to correspond to a "thought field." The points are depicted in Figure 6.1.

The Basic Trauma Protocol

1. The patient is asked to focus his attention on the trauma. (If the patient is in the middle of a flashback-type experience, this is already happening.)
2. The patient is asked to rate his distress on a scale of 0–10 (some people prefer 1–10), where 0 is no distress or upset at all and 10 is as much as possible.
3. The patient is instructed to tap the following meridian points about 10 times per point: the inside corner of the eyebrow (EB); under the eye on the bones of the eye socket directly under the pupil if the person looks straight ahead (UE); under the arm about 4 inches

below the armpit (where a woman's bra traverses the side of the chest; (A): under the collarbone at the point where the collarbone meets the sternum (C). This can be written as the formula EB → UE → A → C.

4. The patient is asked to report their current SUDs level. Generally it goes down by at least two points. If this is the case the treatment continues as follows. If the patient reports that the SUDs score has not moved or only gone down one point, go to step 9 and treat for psychological reversal.

5. The patient is then instructed to do what Callahan called the 9-gamut treatment. This procedure is thought to activate different parts of the brain. I use the metaphor that it helps to spread the treatment around the brain. The patient taps the back of his hand just behind the knuckle between the pinky and the ring finger in between the tendons (BH). While doing this all of the time, the patient performs the following tasks:
   Close the eyes
   Open the eyes
   Look down to the left (just the eyes, the head does not move)
   Look down to the right
   Roll the eyes 360 degrees in one direction (e.g., clockwise)
   Roll the eyes in the other direction (e.g., counterclockwise)
   Hum a tune for 5 seconds
   Count from 1 to 5 out loud
   Hum a tune for 5 seconds.

6. The patient is asked to re-rate the SUDs. If the SUDs continues to drop the patient is instructed to repeat the major sequence of EB → UE → A → C.

7. If the SUDs continues to drop and is not yet at a 1 or 0, the 9-gamut treatment is repeated followed by the major treatment again. If at any point the SUDs does not drop by at least 2 points (unless the person is already at a 4 or lower), go to step 9 and treat for psychological reversal.

8. Once the patient reports that she is at a 1 or 0, the last step is to have the patient continue to tap on the back of the hand while very slowly moving her eyes from the floor to the ceiling. At this point the treatment is essentially done. Patients report that they are no longer upset about the traumatic event. In many cases their thoughts and beliefs about the trauma spontaneously change. They tend to experience far less self-blame.

9. Treat for psychological reversal (PR; see following section).

10. Return to the point where treatment did not work and treat again. The SUDs should start dropping again. If the patient is not improving

you need to treat again for alternative PR. Then retreat the patient using the major sequence or 9-gamut.

Psychological Reversals and Blocks to Treatment

Perhaps one of the biggest potential breakthroughs of TFT is the understanding and treatment of psychological reversals (PRs). A PR is thought to be a polarity shift in the energy of a thought field. The result is a negativistic condition where one's motivation operates in a way that is directly opposite to the way one would expect (Callahan & Perry, 1991; Gallo, 1999). The phenomenon of psychological reversal has many implications for all types of therapy treatments for all types of problems. For our purposes at the present moment, it is related to blocks to the treatment working. Blocks to treatment can come in one of two places. The first place is at the beginning of treatment. After the first major treatment in the trauma algorithm (EB, UE, A, C), the client reports that there is no drop in SUDS. This is a strong indicator of one of two types of reversals. The first type of reversal is termed a "major or massive reversal." The appropriate treatment is that the client is asked to rub the neurolymphatic area (NLA) on the left side of their body while repeating the following affirmation three times: "I deeply and profoundly accept and forgive[2] myself with all my problems and limitations." The trauma algorithm is then reapplied. If the numbers start going down the reversal has been cleared. Proceed with the basic treatment. If the numbers do not go down, the patient probably has the second type of reversal, a

---

[2]Standard TFT has patients say "I accept myself." I have added "forgive " to the affirmation based on some of my own clinical work with colleague Dr. Kurt Ebert. In spiritual and energetic terms forgiveness has more healing power than acceptance. When you accept someone you are understanding of him or her, but not necessarily close. When you forgive someone you let him or her back into your heart. The mechanism of PR is not well understood. My position is that it is based on an unconscious lack of acceptance, lack of love or conditional love of some aspect of self. For instance, the person believes, "I am only lovable if I am not upset." Trauma is upsetting. The person becomes upset and then to that extent does not love the aspect of themselves that is upsetting. That aspect then becomes actually more upset. That aspect becomes "resistant" to getting better because it is based on the idea of its unlovability. Adding forgiveness increases the push to let go of resentment of the self. It also becomes diagnostic because some patients will resist the idea of forgiveness. An interesting piece of construct validity for the idea that forgiveness is a more powerful healing level is that many fewer people resist the affirmation of "I accept myself. . . ." A significant number of heavily abused clients will not say, " I forgive myself." These people are often heavily reversed and full of self-loathing. As part of the process, if the patient cannot say "forgive," then just have him say accept.

specific reversal, and is asked to rub the same spot while saying: "I deeply and profoundly accept and forgive myself even though I have this problem." The word "problem" can be replaced with the client's own words for the problem; for example, "even though I have been raped." Then redo the trauma algorithm once again. The numbers will almost always begin to go down.

The second place that PR shows up is in the middle of treatment. The SUDs have been dropping. Then all of a sudden they stop dropping. Callahan described this as a minireversal. It is as if there is a block to getting over the problem *completely*. As soon as the client reports that the SUDs has not dropped, the therapist has the client tap the side of his hand (SH) while saying the following affirmation three times, "I deeply and profoundly accept and forgive myself even though I STILL have SOME of this problem." Then restart the treatment on the section that did not lead to a drop in SUDs. For instance, the patient begins with SUDs of 9 the sequence of EB, UE, A, CB is tapped. The patient reports a SUDs of 6. Then the 9-gamut is applied and the patient reports a SUDs of 6. Apply the treatment for mini-PR and reapply the 9-gamut treatment. The numbers will then start to go down again.

If the numbers do not go down there are three other reversals the therapist can try that are relatively common with trauma patients. These reversals are called "criteria related reversals" (Gallo, 1999). The first is the patient taps SH and says three times, "I deeply and profoundly accept and forgive myself even if it is not safe to get over this problem (completely)." The word "completely" is added if the reversal is a minireversal. The second is the patient taps under the lower lip (UL) in the indentation before the chin starts. The patient says three times "I deeply and profoundly accept and forgive myself even if I do not deserve to get over this problem (completely)." The third reversal is treated by having the patient tap under the nose (UN) while saying, "I deeply and profoundly accept and forgive myself even if I never get over this problem (completely)." If the patient never started getting better and the other two reversal treatments did not work, these treatments may be helpful. In these cases the word "completely" is left out.

More Advanced Considerations

Anger and Guilt

When anger and guilt are present, additional points may need to be added to the basic algorithm. The little finger corresponds to the heart meridian that is often involved in anger problems. The index finger is on the large intestine meridian, which is often related to guilt feelings. The whole algorithm is then: EB → UE → A → C → LF → C → LIF → C, followed by the 9-gamut followed by the major treatment.

Clinically speaking, it only takes a few moments more to do the longer protocol. Therefore, it can save the patient extra rounds of treatment to do the whole thing all the time. In some cases treating with the basic protocol may bring no relief, even after all of the potential reversal are cleared. This may be because the main affect that was upsetting has to do with guilt or anger. Listening to the patient will often give clues to whether these additional points are needed. For instance, if the dominant affect is fear, and anger or self reproach are not part of the patient's comments, these additional points may not be necessary. If on the other hand there is a great deal of anger or guilt in the patient's comments, then these points are often helpful.

Complex PTSD or Multiple Traumas

In many cases the patient has had longstanding abuse or multiple traumatic incidents. In other cases the traumatic incident has many aspects to it. In these cases, it is often necessary to treat different aspects of the problem separately. Each traumatic incident or piece of the trauma must be treated. There are two ways to discover if this is necessary. The first is a useful clinical procedure no matter what the situation. After treating the patient for a trauma and the person reporting that he is calm, have the patient go over the traumatic incident slowly and in detail. The clinician can help the patient by feeding back to the patient details that were presented earlier. One of two things will happen. One possibility is that the patient will report that he or she does not feel distress. In this case the patient no longer needs treatment for this issue. In addition, the positive effect of the treatment has been reinforced by this procedure, because it demonstrates to the patient that a full exposure to the incident does not create distress.

The other possibility is that the patient will start to feel upset. In this case, the treatment is repeated on the aspect that is still upsetting. This phenomenon probably occurs because the aspect that the patient is now upset about was not well represented in the original thought field that the patient was thinking about when the first treatment was used. For example, Tammy was treated for a rape experience. She was able to get to a 0 relatively quickly. She was then asked to go over the incident again more slowly and in detail in her mind and say if she became even slightly upset. She reported that she did become upset when she remembered that her attacker had whispered in her ear, "You liked it didn't you!" She had not thought about this during the original treatment. She was asked to think about this and the complex trauma algorithm was used. After this was cleared, Tammy was asked to review the situation and include any other part of the experience that she had not considered. At this point, she burst into tears and talked about how upset she was thinking about being in the emergency room and feeling that she was not being treated very kindly. We then worked on this part of the experience. As we discussed in chapter 1, the recovery environment is a very important aspect of PTSD. It is very common to have patients traumatized by events in the emergency room or other similar places. This example also depicts how TFT is used within a therapeutic context that "works through" the traumatic material. In this incident both the affective dysregulation and cognitive processing side of the equation (from chapter 1) are being treated.

The second way that one discovers that more treatment is necessary is that the patient will continue to have flashbacks or other intrusive experiences in the real world. On closer inspection it is usually apparent that it is either a completely different incident or an untreated aspect of the treated incident. In either case, whatever is upsetting, the patient is treated. The therapist and patient can also discuss the meaning and function of these flashbacks.

It is not uncommon with complex cases to work with a patient on one problem. The patient feels better; then another problem pops up. The way to understand and explain this phenomenon (especially to the patient) is that the patient has had more than one traumatic event or aspect to the one trauma. The untreated part of the patient wants to feel better too. So, now that it knows that it can feel better it pops up and says, "Hey I am in pain, too. Please treat me."

Generalizing of Treatment Effect

It is quite common to treat one traumatic incident followed by relief from other similar problems. Usually there is some associative link between all of these events. Once one is treated, it is as if an energy wave is propagated through the associative link and all of the thought fields are corrected. Therefore, it is not necessary to treat every single trauma a patient has ever undergone. However, all of the abuse incidents are not all on the same associative chain. It may be necessary to treat all of the different chains.

Tuning into and Staying Tuned to the Thought Field

The patient is asked to think about the problem situation. This is referred to as tuning into the thought field or attunement (Gallo, 1999). The more vividly the patient can tune into the problem, the better treatment works. However, it is not necessary to "visualize." In fact, it is often better to tell the patient to "think about the problem so that it causes you the most distress" or "think about the problem so that it is like it is happening." This approach allows the patient to access the problem in whatever way works best (visual, auditory, kinesthetic). For instance, some people do not "visualize" well. Telling them to visualize will actually make it harder for them to tune in.

Once patients have attuned to the problem they tend to stay attuned to it. Even if they are not "thinking about it" during the procedure, they are usually attuned to the problem. It is not necessary or helpful to try to get patients to stay so deep in the trauma that the method becomes cathartic. When it is time to rate their discomfort, you ask, "Now tell me how much the event bothers you now." Or you can say, "Return to the original problem and tell me how much it bothers you." It is sometimes important to make it clear to the patient how much the event currently bothers him. Some people will give you a report of no change in SUDs because they are reporting a memory of how they felt at the time of the incident, even though they are much more comfortable now as they think about the experience.

The APEX Problem (or Cognitive Dissonance)

A common occurrence with this approach is that the patient will feel better but not attribute it to the treatment. Patients will say that you distracted them. Sometimes they will say they cannot think of the problem anymore. If you deconstruct this last statement, what you usually get is that the person cannot think about the trauma as if they are in the trauma, nor can they get the feeling of being traumatized. They sometimes are unable to get the vivid visual image that overwhelmed them previously. But if you asked them for what happened, they can tell you in a good verbal description. This fact sounds very much like the person has been able to move the traumatic memory from eidetic storage to long-term storage (a very desirable outcome).

For many people, it is just too outlandish that some silly tapping would have such a profound impact. So the patient does not believe it. This can be minimized by predicting it ahead of time. You tell the patient:

> After we have treated you, you are going to feel a lot better. In fact, you are going to feel so much better that it is not uncommon for people to not believe that tapping on these energy points could possibly be the reason. It is very common. So I just wanted to let you know that you may have some disbelief in a few minutes. It is just part of the weirdness that we were

talking about earlier. The important thing is that hopefully you will be feeling much better.

☐ When Treatment Does Not Work

The first thing to remember is that what I have described here is a highly condensed description of TFT. This treatment protocol will be helpful much of the time. I have presented it as one more tool for your treatment bag. Once you have tried it and found that (a) it is helpful and (b) it suits your style, you need to get more training. One of the reasons that you need more training is that there are other problems that sometimes block treatment from working. Some people simply have unusual thought field patterns.

Another problem that sometimes occurs is a layering effect. This is essentially the proverbial "peeling the onion" phenomenon. The first problem that you treated is no longer a problem. However, it is associated with a new layer of problem. If that new problem is not so much a "trauma problem," the trauma algorithm may not work. You can try to use an EFT protocol that is not content driven

The Basic EFT Protocol[3]

1. *Treat for major reversal*: Rub the sore spot while saying, "I deeply and profoundly accept and forgive myself with all my problems and limitations."
2. *Treat for specific reversal*: Rub the sore spot while saying, "I deeply and profoundly accept and forgive myself even though I have _____ [the problem]."
3. *Use the following algorithm*: EB → OE → UE → UN → LL → C → A → SH → LF → MF → IF → TH. At each point the patient should say "This problem or the actual description of the problem [e.g., fear of being raped]."
4. Follow by the 9-gamut
5. Repeat the algorithm.
6. Reassess the patient's SUDs.
7. *If not totally better, treat for reversal*: Rub the sore spot while saying, "I deeply and profoundly accept and forgive myself even though I still have some _____ [the problem]."

---

[3]For those who want to find out more about EFT, go to the EFT website www.Emofree.com.

8. *Repeat algorithm and 9-gamut followed by algorithm.* Continue until SUDs is 1 or 0.

9. If the quality of the problem changes then repeat the treatment using the new problem as the target. Make sure that you treat for reversal after each round. Treating for reversal is very important in this system. It is important that the patients try to accept and forgive themselves with some feeling.

☐ Integrating Energy Treatment Within a Broader Therapy Context

Just like any specific tool in treatment, these tools are to be used within a clinical relationship. There is a wide range of variability of how this will play out. In some cases treatment is very brief. The relationship is quickly established and limited in scope. For example, I sometimes see people soon after a trauma such as a rape or attack. In a single 75-minute session, the first 30 minutes of the session is used to take some history and establish rapport. The remaining time is spent explaining the process and then doing the process and then debriefing the patient. The patient may be seen for a follow-up session. In many cases this is the entire treatment.

On the other extreme, I have worked with dissociative clients who have had multiple therapists and multiple problems. Energy work may not come up for months. Even at that point, some patients have had significant issues to work through about the use of touch as part of the treatment (even if the touch is their own). In one DID case, after using TFT to work with a traumatic memory, the part that contained that memory spontaneously integrated. This caused a very large reaction in the rest of this patient's system. It took many months of treatment before the person was even ready to do further "energy work."

This type of approach, like many of the others in this book, is based on a relationship that includes active work on the part of the therapist. It is based on the premise that the real relationship with the therapist (as opposed to the transference relationship) is an important aspect of treatment. As discussed in chapters 5 and 8, it is also important that the therapist pay attention to his or her motivations and feelings for using this tool or any tool. It is important to pay attention to the patient's need for the therapist to just listen and be a witness versus the need to actively change anything.

Finally, I want to point out that you can use this approach in the event that you become traumatized by the stories of patients. This is an excellent method for cultivating a resourceful life for yourself. It will also give you a felt sense of how this treatment works.

How to Introduce TFT to Patients When You Are Still Learning

There are three basic guidelines for introducing new approaches. The first is to start with patients with whom you have some rapport and trust. By trust, I am referring to patients for whom you have a good sense of how they are responding to you and your interventions. In contrast, it would not be wise to try a brand new approach on a patient who is in crisis or with whom the therapeutic relationship is in crisis. The second guideline is to be honest. Tell the patient that this is something new that you have learned and that you think will be of help to them. You are just learning it. The third guideline is to give the patient the option to say "yes" or "no" to trying it. Most patients are happy that you are willing to try something new with them for their benefit. Create a guide sheet for yourself so that you do not have to worry if you are remembering it right. Occasionally look at the sheet. However, keep most of your attention on your patient. Make sure your patient knows that you are attending to his or her needs and try the procedure. If things do not work out well, accept full responsibility for the problem so the patient does not feel bad. Check and make sure that you and the patient have been following the instructions.

Conclusions

TFT and other energy therapies are powerful tools for trauma therapists and their clients. In addition to being effective in the office, patients can be given the treatment to take home and use if necessary.[4] While more research is necessary, TFT can help relieve suffering. As described here, TFT is most useful in phases 1 and 2 of treatment. In phase 1, TFT can be used to help stabilize the patient who is having flashbacks. The approach is particularly useful in this phase because of its noncathartic nature. Patients rapidly feel better without going deep into the traumatic memory. In phase 2 of treatment, TFT and energy work is obviously useful with working through traumatic material. There are other aspects to the approach to help patients diminish negative beliefs and increase positive

---

[4]Gallo & Vincenzi (2001) have written a self-help book using TFT.

beliefs (see Gallo, 2000, and Durlacher, 1994). In phase 3 of treatment, energy work can be useful in helping people overcome fear about connecting and reconnecting with aspects of their lives. Clinicians who want to use these approaches are urged to get additional training in these methods.

Tools for the Holistic Self

The question, "What is the self?" has interested philosophers for millennia. It is far beyond the scope of this book to describe the many views of self. Suffice it to say that in the late 20th century we must acknowledge that there is no one correct way of understanding the nature of the self. So we return to a variation of a theme that has run through this book: To which view of self do you want to associate? I choose to view the self as not being a singular undividable thing. The normal and healthy self can be viewed as having a type of multiplicity (Beahrs, 1982; Ross, 1992) or having parts or ego-states (Watkins, 1980) or multiple SoCs with different properties (Lankton, 1985).

The self is not a solid or static thing. It is dynamic and maintained by internal rules (Shor, 1959; Lankton, 1985: Erickson, 1980) or stories (White & Epston, 1990; deShazer, 1985,1988). The rules or stories are strongly influenced by current or past social context. Finally, these rules or stories have within them certain expectations about the future that work retroactively, influencing ongoing perception, meaning making, and action.

The "holistic self" is essentially a spiritual concept. It is important to note that it is only a concept and not a "thing." At best, it is a process of being that we move in and out of to greater or lesser extents throughout our lives. Spirituality can be thought of as increasing the connections between self and self, self and other, and self and "all that is" (usually referred to by the name God). The more interconnected one is at a given moment, the more that person will experience herself in sacred space. The holistic self is a somewhat more operationalized version of this spiritual idea. The goal of the process of the holistic self is to have internal rules or stories that allow a person to stay connected to different aspects of ongoing experience, especially in the face of trauma. In fact, it is the typical response of people to large or small t trauma to begin to disconnect from the rules of the holistic self. Returning to the rules of the holistic self is the path of recovery from trauma. These rules include:

1. *Maintain access to resources and be able to apply them to appropriate contexts*
   - This means having access to good feelings, relatively positive belief systems, and good self-images.
   - These are applied and maintained by supportive relationships to other people, satisfying life tasks, and so on.
2. *Maintain appropriate boundaries*
   - Internal between ego-states.
   - External with others.
3. *Honor and value previously dissociated parts of the self*
   - Be able to associate back into devalued and dissociated parts with resources.
   - Have empathy for the dissociated or injured parts of self.
   - Do and be in the present in manners that value and honor all parts.
4. *Learn to place the self in a larger context*
   - Identify social pressures and modulate their influence on the person so that the person can choose how to live life.
   - Learn to dissociate from the abused self and associate into a larger self.
   - Learn to shift attention from past to present and future.
   - Find learnings from the abuse or trauma.
5. *To know the "truth" or "that what is"*
   - Can acknowledge and accept painful feelings and actions.
   - Can acknowledge and accept positive feelings and actions.
   - Can create stories of understanding and forgiveness.

Let us look at Figure 7.1. The different arrows on the outer ring do not represent a sequential order. The various activities all interact with each other. The holistic self is a dynamic system. It is both a being and a doing. It must be continually replenished and recreated. The development of certain ways of being and acting will make it easier to stay connected to the holistic self. Many of these ways of doing are written in the arrows in the outside ring. The center of the diagram represents the importance of just being aware of ongoing experience. In terms of recovering from trauma and abuse, one specific action that a patient must take is to accept painful affect. It is also important to acknowledge that certain behaviors and beliefs that govern those behaviors are dysfunctional.

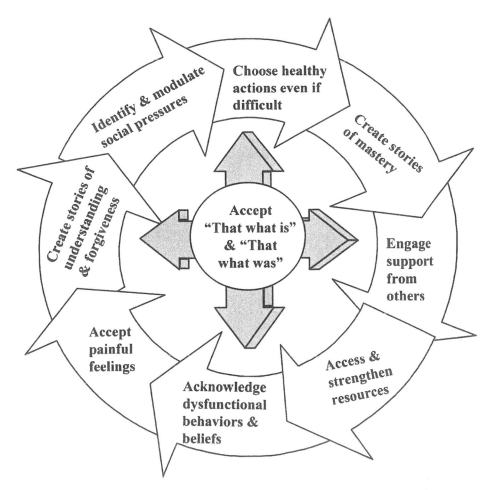

Figure 7.1. The process of the holistic self.

Let's explore these rules more fully. But before we do this, it is vitally important that the reader consider that these ideas apply to everyone equally. As therapists, we usually think in terms of applying them to patients. We must remember that they apply to us as well. In fact, most problems in therapy come from our inability to be sufficiently holistic with a given patient at given moments in the therapeutic process. We must also remember that patients live in social systems and these ideas apply to all of the people in those systems. As we widen our lens to look at cultural and societal factors in trauma and abuse, it becomes obvious that these concepts apply to the entire human population.

☐ Own and Value the Parts of the Self That Used to Be Disowned and Devalued

In terms of dealing with trauma and abuse there are four chief areas of the self that are disowned and devalued. These are feelings and experience, actions and stories, memory and awareness, agency and will.

☐ Feelings and Experiences

Fear, Pain, and Helplessness

Regardless of the type of trauma one undergoes, the experiences of fear, pain, and helplessness are often disowned or devalued due to their unpleasant and often overwhelming natures. These emotions usually lead to increased needs or wishes for nurturance. The desire to be taken care of (often referred to as dependency needs) is also commonly disowned and devalued. The reason this occurs is that the person who has been traumatized did not believe that anyone would be able to stay connected to him or her while he or she was expressing pain and asking for help. This belief may or may not be based on a realistic appraisal of the situation. One of the goals of family treatment is to help family members be able to stay connected to their own resourcefulness while listening to the traumatized person so the family members can stay connected to them. Again, the theme of staying connected to a sea of resources in order to stay connected to the trauma and yet detoxify the trauma reappears.

When patients refer to themselves as "weak" they are usually referring to one of these feelings or experiences. The emotion and experience of shame is interwoven throughout the devaluation process. In part it is shame about these feelings that drives the disowning of them. In part it is the experience of feeling shame itself that is disowned. Instead of simply being aware of the feeling, Nathanson (1994) has discussed the person's possible reactions as the "compass of shame." The person can withdraw, act out against others, or act against the self.

Power, Anger, and Rage

A second cluster of emotions and experiences includes power, anger, and rage. These feelings are most often devalued and denied when the trauma is related to childhood abuse. The denigration of these experiences is more common in women. This dynamic is very complex. At this point let us take a brief and incomplete look. The gender difference is largely cultural, having to do with the societal taboos against women expressing anger, whereas men are allowed to act out their anger. Abused men will be more likely to overvalue power, anger, and rage and devalue the helplessness, pain, and fear dimension. They will tend to choose to act out their shame over other dimensions of the compass of the shame (Nathanson, 1994). It should be noted that there are many men who devalue the experiences of anger and power. The people who devalue these experiences often associate anger and power with violence and rage due to social modeling in the family. The healthy expression of power and anger is often actively punished in abusive families. Appropriate assertiveness skills are rarely taught. Healthy expression of anger or power is conditioned to be an aversive experience. Power and violence are usually viewed as identical, because of the abusive experience. In fact, the very concept of power as a good thing is foreign to these survivors. They believe that if they become angry, they will become violent and rageful. Since they devalue power and anger, they are more likely to take positions in life that lead to victimization, which increases anger at some level. Eventually, the anger explodes into out-of-control rage. The episodes of rage acted out on the self or others prove to the person their original belief. So the cycle of devaluation is strengthened.

Sexual Feelings and Fantasies

One of the most difficult aspects of experience for some survivors of sexual abuse is their own sexual feelings and fantasies. Perhaps the most difficult issue is if, when the child was being sexually abused they were either sexually aroused or they wanted and desired the positive attention of their abuser. This can happen when the incest is nonviolent. According to Trepper and Barrett (1989), nonviolent incest is quite common. Even violent incest does not always start out this way. Victims of childhood abuse are completely unaware of the "grooming techniques" of pedophiles. Salter (1995) has documented detailed accounts of the methods these people use to befriend a child and gain trust before they sexually abuse the child.

Sexual arousal can happen even in a violent adult rape. One patient reported, with much shame, that she had actually begun to get aroused during a rape. When she was told that her reaction was not unusual, she expressed a great deal of relief. She had believed that there was something horribly wrong with her. Even a well-intentioned rape counselor can become part of a problem if the counselor inadvertently suggests to a patient to disown and devalue some aspect of the patient's experience.

My patient talked about how rape was a crime of violence and not sex, so how could she be such a deviant? In fact, it was the dominant story of the antirape movement, that said that rape is a crime of violence, not sexuality, that was part of her problem. In addition to the "natural" shame that these feelings engender, many abusers tell their young victims, "You really want it" and/or "You are making me do this to you." These thinking errors often get introjected in the patient's head (Salter, 1995) almost like a posthypnotic suggestion. When patients actually feel pleasure or arousal, they feel tremendous guilt and shame and usually resort to devaluing their bodies for betraying them or disowning their sexuality.

An associated problem is that therapists and other well-meaning people tend to create or reinforce the dissociative split between the "bad" perpetrator and the "good" victim. The usual goal is to help the patient not feel so bad about herself. The problem is that many times the world is not so clearly demarcated. In some cases victims have many positive feelings about their abusers. So if the abuser is bad and the patient loves the abuser, what does that make the patient? Furthermore, many victims have also engaged in some sort of perpetration or sexual or violent acting out behavior. Many times this information has never been provided to the helping professional or significant other. Once that person has labeled the official perpetrator as bad, the patient is not likely to ever reveal his or her own "badness." *Patients are highly sensitive to these comments because they resonate with beliefs that patients already have.*

☐ Actions and Stories

Meaning making and action are highly interdependent. The story a person tells about the meaning of a given situation will influence the behavior that person will engage in to deal with the situation. The type of action (including inaction) one takes in a given situation will influence the construction of the story of meaning that person creates. The causality loop is circular. While one can say that awareness and feelings in themselves are not good or bad, actions certainly can be judged as "good" or "bad" or having harmful or helpful consequences. The stories one tells about the meaning of various actions can also have real consequences for the patient or people with whom the patient interacts. The stories about the meaning of experiences and feelings can also have positive and negative consequences. Some meaning-making stories lead to more resourceful SoCs; others lead to less resourceful SoCs.

During traumatic situations, people are often forced to take some type of action, even if the action is one of nonaction. A soldier may leave his buddy on the battlefield and retreat, or kill an innocent civilian out of frustration. A hostage may break down and beg for his life. A sexual abuse survivor may begin to act out sexually with other children. All of these actions are likely to be perceived by the patient as less than desirable actions well after the trauma is over. In most cases, patients will devalue and disown aspects of themselves based on the actions that they took and more importantly the stories about the meaning of those actions.

The most common "story" that abuse and many trauma survivors tell to themselves is that they were to blame for the trauma or abuse occurring. It is important to distinguish behavioral self-blame from characterological self-blame (Janoff-Bulman, 1992). In behavioral self-blame a person is focusing on specific actions that were instrumental in causing the trauma to occur. The goal is to prevent the trauma from occurring again by avoiding the behavior. Instrumental self-blame is not pathological and can often be helpful (Janoff-Bulman, 1992). Characterological self-blame is a story about how the self of the person is at fault. Characterological self-blame is never helpful. Altering the story of characterological self-blame can be the most important link in transforming the negative effects of trauma (White & Epston, 1990; Shapiro, 1995).

When a patient presents with a single event of trauma occurring later in life, the devaluing process is often limited to the helplessness the patient felt as an immediate response to the trauma or in controlling symptoms. However, in ongoing traumatic situations such as child abuse or even war, there are often sequences of action, meaning making, and action over time that complicate matters considerably. For instance, sexually abused men and women who act out sexually after the abuse often tell themselves the following story: "The acting out proves that I wanted the abuse or it proves that I am bad."

In DID the host alter and others will have stories about how certain other alters are bad and should be gotten rid of, because they are angry or satanic, and so on. It may be that those parts engage in behaviors that must be stopped, such as self-harm or sexual acting out. However, it is the disowning and devaluing stories about those parts that are important factors in the behavior continuing. As we will see later, the dysfunctional behavior and meaning making often serve the defensive purpose of avoiding or containing overwhelming feelings and experiences. The therapeutic goal in the arena of feelings and experience is to accept, acknowledge and validate. In the arena of stories, the goal is to choose to discover or create meaning that is inclusive of the existence and even the importance of the aspect of self that "failed" to act appropriately or successfully (i.e., was helpless), as well as to create stories that support healthy behavior. In the arena of action, the goal is to choose healthy behavior that leads to increased satisfaction with life and increased elaboration of healthy stories about the self. We will discuss this issue further on in this chapter.

☐ Memory and Awareness and the Therapy of "That What Is"

The end goal of the therapy of "that what is" refers to helping people not disconnect from whatever is happening inside themselves or from what is happening to other people in their presence. Usually people disconnect from something that stimulates pain or fear or some other type of aversive or unacceptable experience. If current feelings, experiences, and meanings are overwhelming or unacceptable, the person will disconnect from the awareness of them in current time. People will often disconnect from the memory of prior feelings, experiences, meanings, and actions that were unacceptable or overwhelming. For our purposes here, memory is awareness of past awareness. Ideally, the holistic self is simply able to be aware of whatever is happening externally and internally on a moment-to-moment basis. This is essentially the same as the Buddhist perspective of mindfulness. In mindfulness, the self is able to be aware of its own stream of awareness and yet not be caught up in it, thereby transcending the self.

"That what is" also refers to the aspect of experience that is essential and irreducible (even if it has constructions layered on top of it). Even though some aspect of an experience is essential, it is not necessarily permanent. In terms of trauma or abuse, this could be many things, such as intense terror or rage, the awareness of an abuser's sadism, the experiences of helplessness or power, pain or pleasure, or the knowledge that one's parent will never love one in the way one wants to be loved. In PTSD, the traumatic incident overwhelms the person's ability to process the information and/or contain the affect. The person cannot be mindful of what is. So he or she attempts to avoid it or dissociate from it, devaluing the aspect of self that felt it or thought it. In this respect, the psychopathology of PTSD has to do with the person's inability to cope with what is and/or what was. Essentially, the practice of mindfulness creates a psychological container, a psychological fair witness that observes and contains whatever traumatic experience is occurring. In mindfulness, the goal is to be aware of whatever comes into one's awareness knowing full well it will change. Thomas Aquinas described this idea in an interesting manner in a reference to "sinful ideas." He said that sinful ideas were like birds that fly though your mind. They were unavoidable. You could not stop them from entering your mind, so do not even try. You can watch them fly through your mind. The important thing was to not make a nest for them. From this framework, the goal of therapy is to help the person become aware of what is or was, and also to know when to not make a nest for those experiences.

Earlier in this book I have discussed the importance of recognizing the constructed aspect of experience. The perspective being offered here is a countervailing one. Nevertheless, I would like to suggest that holding both views simultaneously is important and ultimately resolves the modern/postmodern dialectic. It is the denying, devaluing, and distancing of "that what is" that creates the construction of "that what is" as being an immutable "thing." When one treats "that what is" as an essential truth in the moment, it tends to change. This applies to victims of trauma as well as to therapists who treat victims of trauma.

In chapter 4 we discussed a variety of tools regarding affect tolerance. Many patients with chronic problems secondary to histories of trauma and abuse have long histories of acting out their emotions. They have little awareness of their painful feelings. As therapy is successful, patients begin to feel their feelings. The problem is that unless properly prepared, these patients will often decompensate, because they do not know how to understand what is happening to them. They think that therapy is supposed to make them feel better, not worse.

Andrea was a survivor of childhood sexual abuse by her father. She had a long history of avoiding what is and what was by using drugs and alcohol, overeating, and acting out sexually. Over several years she had made many gains in stabilizing her life in the here and now. After some rather successful work that had helped reduce her shame and self-blame about what happened to her she called from work in crisis. Andrea said that she was feeling awful. She did not understand why. After no specific problem could be found, she was asked whether she was feeling some of the angry feelings at her father that had been discussed in the previous session. She thought that maybe she was. She was then asked if she was trying not to feel upset by getting rid of the feelings. Andrea emphatically agreed with this assessment. She talked about how she was not using any of her acting out strategies, including eating. She had expected to not feel bad. It was suggested that she not try to shut her feelings down. They were normal and understandable. She should let herself feel them, knowing that they would come and go. She was asked to try this while on the phone and to report what her experience was. Andrea stated that she still felt angry, but somehow she was less anxious and less scared. She did not feel so badly about herself. She thought she could do this on her own. Not only did this help her manage her affect, but at the next session Andrea proceeded to describe a list of very shameful things she had done and had never told anyone.

☐ Be Connected to the Resources That Exist Internally and Externally

The term *resources* can mean many things. We can look at the term in a fairly large chunk, for instance, the resource of creating and maintaining boundaries. However, boundary maintenance can be broken into many smaller resources that can include awareness of proprioceptive stimuli, good breathing, positive self-talk, and staying associated to one's own perception.

A resource could be the willingness to fall down and get up again that every child feels in learning to walk. A resource can be the feeling of connection one has to one's family or to God. Most of us take most of our resources for granted.

Let us consider everyday life for a minute. How did someone figure out that a certain seed from a plant could be turned into what we call pepper? In fact, everything that we now have was discovered at some time in the past. Ancient herb gatherers and medicine men and women probably spent considerable time and energy looking for roots and plants that had special properties. They had to focus their attention on potential positive outcomes without knowing exactly what the positive outcome would be.

It is crucial for therapists to be on the look out for potential resources and resourceful states of consciousness. In addition, it is important to help patients begin to focus their attention in the search for their own resourcefulness. Finally, patients and therapists need to cultivate these resources. (This will be discussed more fully in a few pages.)

☐ Finding the Current Problem That Is Represented in the Return of the Past: Taking Healthy Action

Consider the following scenario. Rhonda, a patient with a diagnosis of MPD/DID and a reported history of ritual abuse, describes an increase of anxiety and agitation around holidays and especially certain ones, such as Christmas and Easter. One of her alters reports that the patient will be getting worse as Easter approaches because that is a time many rituals occurred. The particular concern is that there will be an increase in self-harming behavior and suicidality. As the holiday approaches, there is in fact an increase in flashbacks and agitation. These flashbacks occurred at night and were preventing her from getting adequate sleep. In one particular session, Rhonda reports that her mother called the night before pressuring her about dropping all of this "dealing in the past business." To make matters worse the mother cites one of the books out by reputable scientists about the myths of repressed memory. The patient discusses how her mother never took care of her or protected her from the abuse.

The goal of the therapist and Rhonda is for the patient to remain free of self-harming and suicidal behaviors during the holiday. The pressure is clearly increasing. What should be the approach at this point? Does the therapist work on the past abuse as the internal trigger for the current behavior? The premise in this approach is that when the patient works through the unresolved feelings of the past traumas linked to the holiday, the self-destructive behavior will stop. This is one way to work.

Let us look at it another way. What is the current time problem with holidays for Rhonda (and for many people)? The culture and the family states that one is supposed to spend quality, loving time with one's family. The sad fact is that for many people holidays are, at best, a time of high conflict, because of the need to deal with their families. Holidays are often a time where one's wishes for loving, supportive relationships are galvanized by the socially sanctioned myths of how holidays ought to be. The pain of letting go of the fantasy and acknowledging the reality can be very intense.

In the case of highly dysfunctional families, the matter becomes more complicated. A common characteristic of such families is the need to put on a good external show, while denying what is happening internally. In other words, the children in these families are not allowed to acknowledge what they see and hear and feel. If they attempt to comment on this or act on this, there are usually significant social sanctions, if not outright punishment. The child is supposed to act as if she is in a loving family. There is no problem. Therefore any thought or awareness that the child is not loved or supported must be the product of imagination or bad thinking or mental illness. In other words, there is a problem with the child. It is the child's fault. The only way out of this bind is through differentiating from the family and dealing with the grief that ensues.

The holidays, then, are very similar in nature to the abuse dynamics that create dissociative processes in the first place. The brain of the adult child when confronted with this situation searches for some similar circumstance to understand how to give this meaning. Then, based on that meaning, some type of action plan will form to deal with it. Between the extra affect laid down during the original holidays and the increased social pressure from the current holiday, the patient is likely to regress to tried and true methods for coping, namely increased use of dissociative strategies. Partial therapeutic progress can make matters worse in that the patient is caught between two worlds. Therapeutic progress usually includes some type of therapeutically based permission to acknowledge what one sees and hears and feels. Therefore, the patient is under the increased stress, because she is caught between the two worlds.

In the case of my patient, she had already decided to not spend this holiday with her family. The flashbacks she was experiencing had to do with incidents where she was punished if she disobeyed. Two of the important meanings that she took from these experiences were: (a) If there is a conflict, it is because she is bad. (b) Don't cry and acknowledge pain because that will increase the punishment. The third thing associated with these experiences (as well as many others) was (c) the hope that she would finally be loved by her abusive father if she could just get over how bad she was.

The flashbacks can be seen as phenomena of the patient trying to solve this problem. It can be construed as a recorded warning from the past, "Do not break the rules!" or it can be seen as an attempt to undo the past, "This is how you got into the bind in the first place—acknowledge it—do not succumb to it!" The old joke about the three umpires is apropos here. The first umpire says, "I call them as they are." The second umpire says, "I call them as I see them." The third umpire says, "They ain't nothing till I call them." It is up to the patient to make the meaning of the flashback by "calling them." It is up to the therapist to help open up the possibility for the patient to call them in a variety of ways.

So we can now see a current-time understanding for the return of this material.

1. Rhonda was being pressured into acting as if everything was fine, while denying her own reality.
2. There were social pressures being placed upon her to not break the rules.
3. If Rhonda goes ahead with her plan, she then faces the problem of giving up the wish that Mom and Dad will be there for her, because of their problems rather than because of her, which means that she will have to mourn.
4. There have been strong injunctions that this conflict is happening because she is bad and that she is not to cry or mourn.

This is exactly what was discussed. The patient spent a considerable amount of time crying comfortably in the session. She was asked which alternative was least onerous, the pain of mourning or the pain of living in the flashback. She thought the former was preferable. We also spent time reviewing how her current life situation was different than when she was a child. She had a job, her own money, her own car, friends, and so on. As part of a final step to help the patient take this work home with her, she was asked about the sequence of experience that led up to the flashback. She reported that as she drifted off to sleep, she would see a picture of her father's face with a look that he would use in public to express his disapproval. It would precede some sort of punishment later. She was then instructed to ask her inner alters to come up with some alternative to seeing her father's face as a way to understand how to cope with the conflict around holidays. She reported that the image of a bird in flight had come to mind. Some gentle suggestions were given that, when needed, this image would occur when she was falling asleep. She could fall into a deep restful sleep after seeing this image. We also talked about how she was going to spend her holiday in a healthy way rather than becoming symptomatic, such as spending time celebrating with her friends.

In order to use this approach the therapist needs to take the following general steps.

1. Believe that flashbacks and other symptoms can be understood from different vantage points.
2. Believe that one of those vantage points is that the symptom is an expression of a current dilemma.
3. Help the patient be open to or consider steps 1 and 2.
4. Ask the patient to think about what is currently going on that is related to the symptom.
5. Help the patient find an alternative meaning and/or action that they can take in the current time that will undermine the meaning or action they were forced to take because of the influence of the trauma.

The Difference Between Then and Now

Steps 4 and 5 can be taught to patients in a simple 4-step procedure developed by Dolan (1991) in which the patient asks 4 questions.

1. What is the theme/feeling embedded in "flashback/memory"?
2. What is the current problem that is similar to the "flashback/memory theme/feeling"?
3. How is now different than it was then? (What additional resources do you have?)
4. What can you do differently now based on the additional resources?

For instance, a patient, Mike, who had had a serious car crash and was feeling much better, began to have a resurgence of flashbacks about the accident every night. He identified the theme of the flashback as him doing something that he did not want to do. In the real situation he had increased the speed he was traveling because the friend he was taking to the airport was complaining that he was late. Mike then realized that at work he was succumbing to pressure to do a task for which he was not qualified. He felt it would end in a disaster. The major resources that he had that were different from the accident were awareness of the problem and time to think of an action plan. He decided he would refuse to work on the project, but would provide an alternative plan. His flashbacks stopped immediately.

Sally would often see her father in bed with her when she was having sex with her husband. She identified that the main theme of this intrusive experience was feeling out of control and dominated. In the current sexual experience with her husband, she recognized several similar issues. He preferred to leave the lights off, even though she had made a small request to leave them on. He often rushed to have intercourse even though she was not ready. She would sometimes have sex with him, even though he had not really spent much quality emotional time with her. Sally identified that her additional resources included being able to talk to her husband, who would listen if she really sat him down, as well as being more assertive, and having her own job, so that if the whole marriage foundered she could take care of herself instead of depending on her husband. She knew her husband wanted her to want to have sex. With this in mind, she scheduled an appointment to speak with him about all of this. She explained how the combination of his behavior plus her lack of response had reminded her of her childhood abuse. She knew that that was not fair to him or her. She negotiated for leaving the light on, much more foreplay, and either she would take responsibility for saying "no" to sex if she did not want it, or telling him that they had to spend more time just being together first so she could get in the mood. Her husband was relieved that she had talked with him. The intrusive visions vanished.

Cultivating Resourcefulness in Therapists and Patients

Einstein said that you couldn't solve a problem with the thinking that created the problem. Therapists and patients must ask questions and focus their attention toward the discovery or cocreation of resources. Unfortunately, therapy often becomes focused on what is wrong with the patient. In many cases this actually trains the person seeking help to believe that only discussions about problems are of any value. Therapists need to communicate that they are just as interested in what the patient does well or what makes the patient feel good. The severely traumatized person spends far too much energy on warding off traumatic memories, trauma based feelings and cognitions about the self and the world, so that there is little time and energy left for new and gratifying experiences (van der Kolk, McFarlane, & van der Hart, 1996). In order to truly transcend the effects of trauma, people need to actively and consistently engage in positive experiences that provide pleasure, mastery, and connection (Schwarz & Dolan, 1994; van der Kolk, McFarlane, & van der Hart, 1996).

People who have been abused and therapists who work with people who have been abused need to actively cultivate their resourcefulness both externally and internally. Therapist burnout and secondary traumatization are not the direct result of the toxicity of the trauma about which patients speak. They are the result of the traumatic dialogue disrupting the therapists' connections with their resourceful SoCs (exactly the same as for the survivors themselves). Trauma (like physical pain) has an uncanny ability to organize a person's attention and SoC. The most horrific story will not secondarily traumatize a therapist provided the therapist can use the tools of the holistic self and stay connected to their internal and external resources. Likewise the most horrifying abuse will not prevent a person from leading a good life provided he or she can cultivate a resourceful life.

I have used the word *cultivate* because of its connotation of an active, ongoing process. Resourcefulness is a practice of living. It includes internal practices such as knowing how to breathe. It includes external practices such as developing joyful hobbies. Both therapists and patients need to cultivate resourceful ways of being. So, I will not distinguish the two at this point unless some special comment is required.

Cultivating External Practices

I sometimes humorously refer to this aspect of therapy as "get a life therapy." People need to have more to their lives than talking about trauma or listening to people talk about trauma. The question one needs to answer is, "If you could choose one to three activities to do that bring you joy, peace, creativity, or some other highly desirable state of consciousness, what would you do?" Another good question is, "What do you do that helps bring you back to yourself?" (S. Gilligan, personal communication, 1996). There are so many possibilities. Several categories of things tend to come up a lot. These include:

Physical activity: Exercising, walking, biking, dancing, yoga, martial arts, gardening, and so on

Artistic activity: Playing or listening to music, painting, quilting, sculpting, dancing, acting, or writing

Fun activities: Going to movies or theater, reading (but not self-help books), playing cards

Community activities: Joining a group (not therapy), a church, or other spiritual practices

Growth or mastery activities: School, learning a foreign language, learning about computers, learning anything you do not already know (e.g., painting, acting, etc.)

It is clear that some of the activities could be placed in several categories. These activities are more than just fun. They create connections with other aspects of your self, with other people, with other ideas, and with other views of the world. Not only do you have connections to people and activities that will be supportive of you in real time (e.g., Thursday at 8:00 p.m. you have an art class that brings you joy). These connections become part of your internal world as well. So on Friday at noon, if you are dealing with something traumatic you can still feel connected to the joy you had on Thursday at 8:00 p.m. This does not mean that you are necessarily fully feeling a joyous feeling on Friday at 12:00 noon. You may be feeling sad, but a part of you can still be connected to the joy, so you do not have to run away from the sadness. You can deal with "that what is" and still feel connected to the feelings and memory of the day before.

Cultivating Internal Resourcefulness

Cultivating internal resourcefulness refers to the conscious steps that a person takes to increase their own ability to manage their SoCs in order to increase their ability to live a more effective and joyous life. There are a number of obvious and very helpful strategies. Once you have been able to successfully use the memory of a prior real-time experience to self-soothe at a difficult time (e.g., remembering the good feelings you had at 8:00 p.m. on Thursday when you are having a bad moment on Friday at noon) your ability to do it again increases. The ability will develop unconsciously. However, you can *cultivate* the entire sequence by reflecting on the entire process. You can notice that you did it and it worked. You can give yourself a compliment. You can imagine doing it again. You can imagine the outcome of doing it again. For example, since the birth of my son, Daniel, I have had many joyous moments with him. At the same time, I have heard many horrific stories about what has happened to my patients as children. I can remember a brief moment of time when I would look at my son and get images of what my patients told me. In this case, the trauma was leaking into my life. This was not a desirable outcome. So, I did several things. First, I took the time to build up my external resources by really savoring my joyous moments with Daniel. Second, when my patients told me horrific stories about their childhood, I would take very slow and deep breaths. I would allow myself to feel connected to the joy and connection I have with my son and his love for me and my love for him, and to the power of love in general. I found that even though I was investing a small amount of my self to connect with these resources, I was much more present in the room with my patient. I also found that I felt more resourceful and less traumatized. Third, I realized that this worked, and I felt good about it. Fourth, sometimes after I was finished having a peak experience with Daniel, I would take a moment and feel the good feelings in real time and imagine my self in the future with these feelings talking with patients. I would imagine myself in the chair connecting with the joyous moments in the past. This final step completes the circuit between the past looking to the future and the future looking back at the past looking toward the future.

Perhaps the most ubiquitous form of cultivating internal resources is the use of some type of meditative practice. This can include progressive muscular relaxation, self-hypnosis, mindfulness training, transcendental meditation, or yoga. I have noticed that patients who are highly successful at resolving their serious problems have usually embraced some form of meditative practice. It is really beyond the scope of this book to describe and instruct in these practices. However, I can describe a simple meditative practice described by Gray (1999). The person finds a comfortable position, closes his eyes, and uses the following mantra over and over: "Oh God my heart is open to you. Please come into my heart." The word *God* can be changed to universe, higher power, or any idea that connotes something bigger than the self. Interspersed with the mantra the person can focus on what they are thankful for, as well as what they would like in their life. This can include spiritual things such as more forgiveness and peace of mind, psychological things such as patience or calmness, or material things such as a better job. The person is to always and gently come back to the mantra. An additional aspect of this mediation is to have the fingers pointed up and kept apart as if they are antennae drawing in positive and loving energy from the universe. A person should do this once a day for 10–15 minutes.

There are many lovely aspects to this meditation. It cultivates the intention to connect with a higher power in a loving way. It cultivates the intention of being grateful. It cultivates the intention of whatever it is that the person is asking for.

Linking Resourceful SoCs

As one reconnects with devalued aspects of self, one regains access to the resources of that aspect of self. It is also important to strengthen and diversify connections between resources that are already available or becoming available. By diversify, I mean several things. First, the person can add additional contexts to which a resource can be applied. For instance, if a patient can be assertive at work, they learn to be assertive with more personal relationships. Or a person can learn to take deep breaths if they become scared. In *The Sexual Healing Journey* (Maltz, 1992), patients are helped to recover their sexuality by developing safety and comfort associated with touch and then linking those resources to more sexual and more intimate behaviors via increasingly difficult tasks.

Second, the person can interlock additional resources to a given problem context. If the problem context is being able to have sex with one's partner and feel safe and sexually aroused, a patient will need to know how to feel safe when her husband is sensually touching her. She then learns to feel safe and sexually aroused, perhaps via masturbation. Finally, these resources are linked together to create a solution state.

Third, once a person has developed or rediscovered a resourceful SoC, it is important to stabilize and strengthen that resource by linking it up with supporting associations, narratives, and relationships to the development of increased resourcefulness. For instance, Sarah had been severely abused. During a session she has an experience of not resisting a flashback. As a result, she cries softly and her body is relaxed without fidgeting. After some time, I draw her awareness to the level of comfort she is feeling even though she has faced a memory she has been avoiding. A discussion ensues in which Sarah recognizes the importance of this event as a reference experience for future times when she is tempted to fight a flashback. She spontaneously mentions how she was not defensive at work when being given some feedback. It worked out much better for her. She and I discuss how not being defensive is the interpersonal equivalent for the intrapersonal experience of allowing her feelings and memories to give her feedback. This discussion creates a narrative or verbal generalization about the importance of not being defensive in her relationship with herself and her relationship with others. She reports that in both events there was a special kind of internal quiet and calm that was similar, which was present as she spoke in the office. I suggest that she spend a few minutes being aware of that feeling and allowing her unconscious mind to memorize it and make whatever connections that would be helpful between the feeling, her process of recovery, and her day-to-day living a better life.

A DID patient develops a new image that supports that she is not a bad or evil person. This image is shared with all of the patient's alters. In addition, the patient discusses the implications of this knowledge in terms of her relationship with her abusive father and her employer and her friends.

There are a variety of tools that can be used to achieve these goals. In general the approach being advocated in this book is the importance of the therapist cultivating resources via the process of linking resourceful SoCs intrapersonally and interpersonally. The more dysfunctional the patient, the more the therapist must explicitly attend to this therapeutic function.

Self-Image Thinking

Lankton and Lankton (1983) have described a step-by-step approach to helping people retrieve or magnify positive states and then linking those states to new contexts. Self-image thinking was originally designed to be used as part of a hypnotic session. The tool has the following steps:

1. Have the patient imagine a time when they had the desired resource. The patient should imagine he is in the experience. Perceptually he should be looking out of his own eyes. He is associated to the experience. If the resourceful state of consciousness is what is currently happening, the patient should focus on his current sensory experience.
2. The patient creates a picture in his mind of himself having the resourceful SoC. In order to help stabilize and amplify the state, the patient should attend to physical features of the picture of himself. This is called the "central self-image."
2b. If the therapist is present, the therapist can feed back to the patient the actual changes the therapists sees in the patient's body (e.g., his face muscles are relaxed, his breathing is deep and regular, his lips are making a horizontal line).
3. The patient is asked to see a supportive other looking at him in this positive state. This transition step achieves several goals. First, it begins to help the patient visualize more complex images (i.e., several people in a scene). Second, since the other person is supportive, it mimics the developmental phase of others helping us get an image of ourselves. So it helps to link up our internal central self-image with internalized representations of supportive others. Third, future scenes will involve less supportive characters. Starting out successfully with an easier task increases the likelihood of success at a more difficult task.

4. The patient is asked to see three to four different future scenes unfold one at a time. The patient is asked to see himself deal with the situation with the resourceful SoC held constant. The patient will watch himself handle the situation differently. The patient is watching himself from a dissociated point of view. The first scene is not particularly stressful. The remaining scenes are increasingly stressful (at least they would have been in the past). Feedback from the patient is used to make sure that the patient is remaining resourceful and is successfully coping with the situation. This step links the resourceful SoCs to new contexts. The dissociated point of view will help the patient stay more objective and less emotional. Therapists, and even patients, can give positively oriented suggestions at this point about how the patient will be able to increasingly be able to actually do what he is imagining.

5. A further step is that the patient can be asked to step into or associate into one of the images from the future.[1] In doing so, the patient will have stronger feelings, so it is important that he is being successful. The patient can be asked how it feels and if there are any problems. This becomes an ecological check to make sure everything feels alright. If there are problems, this can be used to make adjustments. Assuming everything is fine, the patient can be asked to look back in time from where he is now (because he is in the future). The patient can be asked to reflect on how he got here. In particular, the patient can be asked to describe the hurdles or difficulties that he encountered and how he handled them so that he arrived in this successful place.

A condensed example of self-image thinking was what I did with my experiences with my son, Daniel. The resource was the good feelings in real time that I had with him. The central self-image was imagining my self in the future with these feelings talking with patients. I then associated into the image by imagining myself in the chair connecting with the joyous moments in the past.

☐ Solution-Oriented Questioning to Link Resources

Solution-oriented therapy (SOT) contains several sets of questions that also achieve the idea of linking up resourceful steps. The therapist will meticulously ask the patient about all the different small things that

---

[1]This procedure was originally designed by Erickson and referred to as pseudo-orientation in time (Erickson, 1980e).

need to occur in some linked fashion to get to a relatively small goal. SOT focuses on small goals for several reasons. One of them is the pre-supposition that if a small change occurs, it will increase the probability of some other change occurring. It is essentially a domino theory of change. The first of these sets follows the "miracle question." Once a person has identified what their goal is by answering the miracle question, the therapist asks questions that are designed to activate the person's attention to the links between the small steps that lead to resourceful solutions.

- What would be the first thing (smallest thing) that you would notice, that would let you know that a miracle has happened (that you are moving towards your goal)?
- Does that already happen in some small way now?
- What would need to happen for that to occur more often?
- What other things would you need to do for that to happen more often?

A second set of questions links up resources on an interpersonal dimension. These include: If those changes were happening, what would someone else (parents, friends, spouse, employer) notice about you? How would the changes that are happening to you affect them? (Or, if the focus was on the other person changing, the question could be, "How would the changes they were making affect you? How would the changes that you see in them lead even more toward you achieving your goal? As those events occurred, what else might change between you and them?"

For patients with dissociative disorders, the interpersonal questions are changed to interalter questions. For example, A DID patient named Marie had come to realize that her internal image of her self as being evil had changed (via another tool). The issue was making sure that this information was spread around her internal system. As different alters came out over the next few sessions, each was engaged in conversations about whether she had noticed this new information that Marie had discovered. For instance, here is a conversation between an alter named Amy (A) and the therapist (T).

T: *How did those changes affect Marie?*

A: *She is calmer. She is actually very shocked.*

T: *Are you shocked as well to discover that you all are not evil?*

A: *Absolutely. I had always thought I was evil inside.*

T: *So how does this change the way you and/or Marie interact in the system?*

A: *Well, I feel like I can listen better to what other parts have to say. Marie is definitely listening better.*

T: *How does listening better help the system's overall functioning?*

A: *Well, I think we are sleeping better. I do not know how that works, but I am glad it does. We both get less scared whenever memories come up, because we do not feel that they are proof that we are bad. Actually, we get just as scared, but instead of being alone with feeling that we are evil, we sort of talk to each other more and reassure each other.*

T: *So, the memories still scare you at first, but since you know that you are not evil, you can talk to each other and reassure each other so that after a while the fear gets considerably less.*

A: [Deep breath] *Yes.* [Becomes very still; this is usually associated with this patient being very centered and calm, as if there is no split for a moment.]

T: [After a long silence] *I imagine that you all are spreading this information around to different parts of the system.*

A: [Still very still] *Yeh, It's been quite an awakening. It's weird, though, how at times like this it gets so quiet inside. I really like it.*

Variations of this conversation occurred with many different parts throughout the patient's system.

Narrative Questions to Link a Resourceful Plotline

From a narrative therapy point of view, one of the goals of therapy is to create a literary plot that supports a more resourceful story about a patient's life (White & Epston, 1990). There is an assumption that there are all sorts of resourceful chunks of information that are not being used by the patient for one of several reasons; e.g., (a) they are isolated bits of information that do not fit the plot of the patient's narrative so they are disregarded; or (b) they do belong to an alternative plotline, but that plot is not the privileged plot, so it does not influence the patient's sense of self or his or her actions. From a narrative perspective, the therapist wants to link up isolated information and nondominant stories so that they become a bigger, more dominant plot in the patient's view of himself. One of the major differences between SOT and narrative is that narrative questioning will focus on the past to create an alternative plotline that supports a different future. Once some resourceful state or idea was established, a series of questions would ensue. In the following dialogue between a therapist and patient, the resource that has been established is that the patient had done a number of things to "resist" the impact of his father's physical and sexual abuse. Following the work of Wade (1996) this resisting was likened to a "resistance fighter" in a war. The patient, C, had accepted this reframe:

T: *Who in your life would not have been surprised to hear that you could act like a resistance fighter?*

C: *Well, I am not sure; I guess my grandfather might not have been surprised.*

T: *What things did he do or say in the past that supported your development as a resistance fighter, even if you did not realize it at the time?*

C: *That is a weird question. Well, my grandfather always said that I had a lot of spirit. He seemed to really like that about me. That always made me feel good. My father always said that I was stubborn and did not listen. He always used this as a reason to beat me. I always felt it was my fault somehow. I wish my grandfather had not died when I was so young. He would take me with him in to the garden and weed. He would talk about the importance of protecting the plants from the weeds. Most people I know hate weeding. To this day I always see weeding as a bit of an adventure, kind of like* Stars Wars—*the good plants against the forces of the weeds. Hmm, I never really thought about this exactly this way. Do you think he told me those things on purpose to help me?*

T: *What difference would it have made, if you knew back when you were being abused that your grandfather had seen that you could be a resistance fighter and that he was supporting that in you, maybe even growing that idea, so to speak, by his weeding stories?*

C: *Wow, I am not sure, but just thinking about it that way makes the whole thing feel different. Instead of it being my fault that I could not have been more cooperative, it feels like I was right in resisting.*

T: *Does thinking about it this way give you more support to act differently?*

C: *Well this has nothing to do with what my father did, but I think I am going to be a lot more assertive with my girlfriend. I usually do not fight back when she tries to manipulate me. I kind of know she is doing it, but I rarely feel the strength to say "no."*

T: *If you could consult with your internal sense of your grandfather, would that be of any help to you in supporting the changes you are making in your life?*

C: *That is so weird, that you asked that, because that is what I was kind of thinking about. I was thinking about a lot of the negativity in my life as weeds and sort of have this picture of my grandfather and I weeding. I can hear my grandfather talking to me about the importance of weeding if you want to have good vegetables. I just feel like I have to weed my life. And, this is really weird, but as I say that, I just get this sense of my grandfather smiling and being very proud of me.*

At this point a narrative therapist might continue asking questions about what that person might actually say and how that could be used in the future. A therapist comfortable with imagery or hypnosis could easily shift gears and have the patient imagine an actual conversation with this helpful other or doing the weeding of his life's negativity. Self-image thinking could be used to facilitate linking this new resourceful plotline from the past into the future.

As in solution-oriented questioning, narrative questioning with DID patients can take place between alters. In the example with Marie and Amy, other aspects of the conversation included the following:

C: *When I looked inside myself, that black ooze used to be there. Now it is gone. It is just amazing. What do you think about this black ooze not being there?*

T: *Well, to be honest with you, I was totally blown away by what you discovered. We have discussed how you were often told black was white. But that black ooze was never you; it belonged to your father. The amazing thing was that all that stuff you went through made you believe not only that the black ooze was not your father's, but that it was your real self. I mean, if you were going to write a piece of fiction, that would be an amazing story. The heroine is made to believe her father's sadism is her real self. Once that is accomplished, she is completely under his control, without ever doing anything again.*

C: [In deep thought] *You have such a different way of seeing things.* (Long silence) *It really is weird that I used to think that black stuff was who I was.*

T: *So, now that most of your parts know that the black ooze was not you at all, how does that change your image of who you are?*

A: *Well, part of the problem is that now, we do not know who we are as much. That is a good thing, because we used to think that we were evil, but now we have a lot of questions.*

T: *Do you think that being less sure that you are evil leads you to be more or less vulnerable to the mind games your father still tries to play on you?*

A: *It makes us less vulnerable, but we are still vulnerable.*

☐ Identify Social Pressures and Modulate Their Influence on the Person So That the Person Can Choose How to Live Life

The holistic self can decenter from itself and reflect upon the social influences that impact on one's life. In many ways this is akin to an observing ego. However, there are important distinctions. The use of the term *observing ego* is usually connected to psychodynamic treatment. The observations are usually aimed at internal impulses and their connection to feelings, thoughts, and immediate family members in the present and in the past. This is an important function. In addition to this function, it is also important to be able to identify and assess broader social and cultural influences. In the parlance of narrative therapy, the dominant story of a society or culture tends to marginalize and discount nondominant stories. One obvious example is the feminist critique on patriarchal culture. Not only is it important for women to be aware of how patriarchal society imposes ideas about women, it is also important for men to become aware of how the rules of patriarchy limit and influence their choices. A number of authors in narrative therapy (Jenkins, 1990; Pare & Tavano, 1996) have discussed in great detail how to work with men who act abusively to see that their beliefs and thinking and subsequent action are largely constrained by their embeddedness in certain patriarchal systems. The therapy is about helping these men identify these influences, which were totally unquestioned. Once identified, these influences can be challenged. The men can choose to think and act differently according to different social values. The therapy tool that is most useful to achieve these ends is called "externalizing problems," which will be discussed in the next section.

There are many less obvious influences that are quite relevant to working with trauma. There is a cultural denial about the existence and seriousness of severe abuse. For instance, the lack of a memorial for Vietnam veterans was a significant communication to many veterans of that war. Once the monument was built, a significant amount of healing took place. It is not an accident that there is not a national monument to survivors of childhood sexual abuse. Many victims of violent trauma are African American. Some of this has to do with the intersection of race and class; many Blacks are poor. But, what about the impact of all of the less obvious (to those of us who are White) traumas based on racism?

Even in the field of psychotherapy, there are significant social influences. The entire field of modern trauma treatment only began after the formal inclusion of PTSD in the DSM-III. Although, a great deal was known about trauma for years (Janet, 1919), it was the political influence of the rape movement, feminism, and Vietnam (where the men got traumatized) that made the difference. The current debate around so-called false memory syndrome is in fact largely a political and social disagreement that is couched in scientific terms. If it were really a scientific and clinical discussion, it would have a very different character. Even "old-fashioned" work around family-of-origin issues takes on a different spin when placed in a broader social context.

It is crucial that the reader understand that the label "the holistic self" is only a description of a way of thinking. It is not a thing. Furthermore, the approaches described in this chapter are by no means the only way to work towards these ends. In addition, that they appear in this section of the book reflects the way the author was thinking at the time of writing and his need for some structure to organize his ideas; not some a priori truth.

Identity, Identification, and the Locus of Perception

"I am weak." I am a victim." "I am evil." "It is my fault." These are all statements about identity.

There are several "tools" that can be used to influence a person's identity that come from different schools of treatment that share some interesting commonalties. These tools all act upon the meaning a person gives to the trauma or abuse in their life. In particular, they act on how the individual views herself and what she believes about herself because of the trauma or the effects of the trauma. From the perspective taken in this book, these approaches are very much linked up to the associative/dissociative process. I call this class of procedures "disowning in order to own." In other words, one needs to dissociate from some aspect of one's identity in order to associate into some other, more resourceful aspect of the self. After the therapeutic dissociation has been accomplished, the resourceful aspect of self helps, nurtures, and empathizes with the unresourceful aspect of self. Finally, the healthy aspect of self re-owns and revalues the hurt aspect of self so that the person feels whole again.

The metaphor of the "child within" (Whitfield, 1990) that was also popularized by Bradshaw (1992) is a good example of this approach. Bradshaw would talk about "big John" his adult self and "little John" his child within. Others would talk about "my inner child." It was the popularization of the idea that human being are not unitary beings, but rather we all have some degree of multiplicity (Beahrs, 1982) and we all have ego-states (Berne, 1972, 1977; Watkins & Watkins, 1997) that have some different ways of functioning. For the most part, this cutting up of the self was a new idea to the general culture.

The languaging used to speak about how "little Bob has a lot of hurt and rage that big Bob does not like to acknowledge" has a decidedly hypnotic effect. It is in the same pattern of a conscious/unconscious dissociative bind (Erickson, Rossi, & Rossi, 1976, 1979). It de-associates big Bob from little Bob. To be more specific, it allows big Bob to stay associated to his resources while dealing with little Bob, who is not associated to resources. Without the therapeutic dissociation, Bob would stay embedded in the nonresourceful state and be unable to acknowledge his behavior.

One of the main benefits of this approach, as used in the recovery movement, is that it helped the individual distance the self from the feeling of overwhelming shame. Without the distance, the shame would simply overwhelm the person and he or she would not be able to look at their behavior. Erickson (1980a) reported using exactly this type of intervention. He described several variations of this dissociation of identity. For instance, he often used this approach with children describing how it was understandable that the child of 6 had a certain problem, but that when the child turned 7, that old problem would not be present.

These approaches all impact on the locus of perception in terms of who is doing the perceiving and what is the object to be perceived. The main difference between the approaches has to do with where the line is drawn with respect to what will be dis-associated from the sense of self.

Externalizing Problems

A relatively new development in the world of psychotherapy has been the development of a narrative approach to therapy (Freedman & Coombs, 1996; White & Epston, 1990; Zimmerman & Dickerson, 1996).

The narrative approach suggests that the person is embedded in a social matrix that influences the person to come to believe that they themselves are the problem, instead of understanding that the problem comes from the requirements of the social context. This phenomenon reaches its height in severely abusive families. In these families, children are actively taught that they are the problem. Furthermore, there is little to no language or experience that provides a context for an alternative description.

One of the central tools of the narrative approach is the use of externalization. The central goal of this approach is to separate the experience of self from the experience of the problem. For example, instead of seeing oneself as bad and to blame for being abused, the patient is asked to look at how "self-blame" influences them. In other words, patients are invited to see the problem as separate from their identity. Once this is achieved, patients are then invited to see what has happened in their life to bring them under the influence of the problem and then what resources they have that they can bring to bear to fight off the influence of the problem. The steps of this approach are as follows:

1. Identify and name the problem.
2. Explore how the problem has influenced the patient up to this point.
3. Explore how the patient can influence the problem.
4. Explore the new outcomes that can occur as the patient influences the problem.

Tracy described how she felt that it was her fault that her father had abused her. In fact her father blamed her for being so sexy that he could not help himself. She was 10 years old at the time. The therapist names the problem: "So it seems that this blaming of yourself is a big part of the problem." Tracy responds that it is a big part of her depression and low self-esteem. Tracy and the therapist then elaborate how the "self-blame" influences her. One of the more salient points is that she gets angry with herself instead of her father. She also feels the need to keep doing more and more to make up for her "sin." She also describes how it is hard for her to feel good about her sexuality since she believed what her father said, that she turned him on. Another externalizing move is used by naming "her father's voice" as an ally of self-blame. Tracy and the therapist then discuss ways that she can influence the self-blame. What would take power away from the "self-blame" and "her father's voice"? For instance, Tracy states that she can remember that if it were anyone else she would blame the father rather than the child. A discussion ensues about how she will make sure to do this. Finally, Tracy and the therapist discuss how things might be different as she blames herself less. Another narrative move includes bringing other supportive characters into the new plot development. For instance, the therapist and Tracy discuss who would be supportive of this new development. She describes how a number of friends and family members would support this. She reports that her boyfriend would be supportive.

One cannot help but notice the structural similarities in the language pattern being used here and in the big John/little John approach. In both approaches there is de-associating language. What is different is the locus of attention that is being guided by the approach. In the big John/little John approach, there is a split between old and new (or young and current) selves; in the narrative approach the split is between the self and the problem (as well as social forces that have invited the person to buy into the problem). I think it is important to acknowledge that these approaches come from very different worldviews. Furthermore, they will probably lead the patient and the therapist into qualitatively different states of consciousness.

Aligning Perceptual Positions

Perceptual positions are an NLP concept that describes the perceptual basis that underlies the processes of identification and boundary making. It literally has to do with the locus of perception. Perceptual positions always take place in an interpersonal field of at least two people. There are three different positions: first, second, and third. These terms follow their use in grammar with reference to persons and pronouns. First position is the "I" position. In first position, one is looking out of one's own eyes, listening out of one's own ears, and feeling one's self in one's own body. In other words, in first position one is fully associated to oneself. Second position is the "you" or other position. In second position, one is looking out of the other's eyes, listening out of the other's ears, and feeling one's self in the other's body. In other words, in second position one is fully associated to the other person. This is the idea behind the saying, "Put yourself in someone else's shoes." Third position is an observer position. In third position one is fully associated to the position of an outside person. It is the position of a reporter.

The problem is that in many situations people are either not associated to the perceptual position that would be most useful for solving a problem, or they are in a mixed position. Furthermore, some people spend a great deal of time in only one position. For instance, there are people who spend inordinate amounts of time in second position. They are incredibly empathetic people, but they do not know their own needs. Other people can never get into second position; therefore, they have problems being empathetic. With reference to trauma, many survivors of childhood abuse have beliefs based on their abuser's ideas. In this language, they are in a mixed state between first and second position. The patient thinks, "I believe . . . ," when really this is an idea of their abuser.

When patients repeatedly act out abusively, they often are blocked from a first-position understanding of their own abuse, and in the midst of acting out, they are stuck in the second position of their own abuse. In other words, they have no perceptually based compassion for their own pain, and they have identified perceptually with their aggressor. For instance, Armand, a hospitalized patient, was having flashbacks of his own abuse. This was a man who had many urges to harm children. Armand would usually become very agitated and just say he was having a flashback. When he was asked to describe what he was seeing in the flashback, he stated, "I can see the hands and arms around my throat." When asked which was closer to his eyes, the arms or the hands, Armand said that the hands were farther away from him. He then talked about how he was looking down at himself. He was describing his abuse from the position of the abuser! It was no coincidence that his own impulse to choke children had the exact same perceptual quality. Armand had heard before that his impulses were acting out of his own abuse. But he had had only a dim, intellectualized understanding, at best, of the idea. When Armand got an experiential understanding, he truly began to understand what his acting out was about.

Most people are usually completely unaware of which position(s) they are in and therefore cannot move from one to the other. As agents of change, perceptual positions can give us a valuable tool.

Connirae Andreas was the original developer of the tool we call aligning perceptual positions. The rationale of the tool is that it can be used to clarify the locus of perception behind the thoughts and feelings a person is experiencing. It allows the person to own what belongs to her and acknowledge what belongs to the other, as well as see how the interaction between themselves and the other evolves over time. In learning this, the person's boundaries are strengthened considerably. This protocol can be used in a variety of situations with slight adjustments and differences in emphasis.

Aligning perceptual positions involves three things: (a) Recovering the use of one or several perceptual positions that are not used. (b) Clarifying the boundaries/distinctions between the different perceptual positions. (c) Increasing behavioral choice based on steps one and two.

Figure 7.2 reviews the benefits of recovering each of the perceptual positions. It is important to notice that there are differences when the

	FIRST	**SECOND**	**THIRD**
PRESENT	Needed resource for people who are emotionally numb, hyper care taking and other "co-dependent" behavior. Can be useful for therapists who become too empathetic with patients.	It is the needed resource for empathy with another person. Understanding of impact of acting out behavior. Necessary for treating perpetrators so they can understand what their victims feel. Cannot perpetrate or act out with good 2nd position available	Usually the most needed resource for survivors (at least as an intermediate step). Builds safety, and observing ego. Neutral ground least likely to be contaminated by beliefs of perpetrators or dysfunctional family members.
PAST	Recovering 1st position is necessary for treating perpetra-tors or survivors without compassion for themselves so they can understand what they felt as victims.	Useful in gaining understanding about perpetrators intentions and feelings. Clarify-ing perpetrators/ abusers/dysfunctional family members ideas from one's own beliefs.	Useful for gaining perspective in what has happened to them, and what the perpetrator(s) was really like.

Figure 7.2. The use of perceptual positions in past and present.

dimension of time is considered. For instance, recovery of first position usually has to do with helping a person become less numb to himself. Used in current-time context, this is often used to help create better understanding of one's own needs and wants and feelings. When the focus is in the past, the goal is often a better understanding of the pain and suffering the child had.

This tool can be varied greatly depending on the outcome one is trying to achieve. Therefore, the instructions given in Figure 7.3 need to be viewed as guidelines only. The reader should try to follow the logic underlying the steps.

In keeping with the theme of increasing resources before processing trauma, it is important to note that this tool is surprisingly effective at increasing a person's capacity for intimacy that has been impaired due to the overuse of dissociative walls. Ruth presented with the problem that she was having a difficult time with her daughter. Ruth stated that she was becoming very angry with her daughter without good reason. In fact, she was scared to death that she could not function as a mother and that she would become abusive, as her mother had been to her. Ruth's history of abuse led her to be emotionally cut off, with a very tough exterior. She had a very difficult time getting into first position. She would take a mixed first and third position. This was evidenced by her inability to really get into her own body and by her internal commenting about how she was a bad mother. In this situation it is best to start with third position as the first step. It became even clearer to Ruth that her daughter was just being a normal 5-year-old. The mother (Ruth) was getting inappropriately angry. In this third position, Ruth remained calm and detached about "the mother's" behavior. She was not self-critical. She was more curious. When she returned to first position and redid the scene again, Ruth found herself to be more patient with her daughter and more appreciative of her daughter's limitations as a child. More importantly, Ruth could actually get into first position now. She could truly be aware of her own body and her own point of view. Therefore, she also became aware of her own anxiety and agitation about her daughter's normal neediness.

When Ruth took second position with her daughter, she was shocked to find out how small she felt. She discovered that she became very scared when her mother would make certain faces and use certain tones of voice and that this made her want to cling more. In returning to third position, Ruth could really watch the entire interaction and see the pattern between Ruth and her daughter. She could also have insight that Ruth becomes upset because her daughter's neediness and desire for love and affection is something that Ruth deeply shares but almost never allows herself to feel. When Ruth finally returned to first position,

INSTRUCTIONS	COMMENTARY
1) Pick a scenario in which someone else is involved that has been problematic or seems to be related to the issue at hand Have three chairs (places to stand) in the shape of an Equilateral Triangle. Each chair is for 1 position.	Throughout the remainder of this approach, make sure the patient is in only one perceptual position at a time. Take as much time is needed to prevent contamination of each perceptual position.
2) Patient sits in 1st position chair. Lives the experience in 1st position. The patient is fully associated to being in his or her own body.	When the patient switches position, make sure to help them totally leave that position. Let them take a moment standing up. Coach them to leave that person in that chair.
3) Patient switches to 3rd position chair. Instruct patient to watch those two people over there go through the experience. Ask patient what he/she, in 3rd position, learned about him/her over there.	Suggest to the patient that they imagine that he is a reporter. Make sure to use appropriate language (e.g., if I am the patient in 3rd position my therapist should say what did you learn about what Bob did in that situation? What was he thinking?).
4) Have patient take knowledge back and sit in 1st person chair with knowledge (connection) from 3rd position and relive experience again. Ask how it is different.	The goal is that with the additional information and clarification of boundaries the patient's responses should naturally become more resourceful.
5) Move back to the 3rd position chair. Watch the patient go through the event with the new resource. Notice and talk about what is different.	This step is somewhat optional. It is used to strengthen the observing ego. It also gets the patient used to the process. It increases the safety of the patient. If the next step is being used to get into the head of the perpetrator, it is best to make sure the patient's first and third positions are really strong first.
6) Move to 2nd position chair. Go through the experience in 2nd position. Ask what experience is like (feelings, beliefs, etc.). This is usually the most difficult step. Before going through the experience. Take time to help the person really step in the shoes of the other by addressing the physicality of the person.	For instance if the patient is a woman and the other is her father you might say, "Look out of the eyes of Charlie. . . . Charlie you are 6 feet tall and have a deep voice. . . . Feel the muscles in your arms. . . . You see look down at Alicia over there, because she is only 5 feet tall. If the other person is an abuser, caution should be used. See the discussion below.
7) Move back to 3rd position chair. Watch experience again. Interview observer what s/he knows now that s/he has been in both positions.	This time, the patient has been in both people's shoes. Hopefully the patient can take a more systemic view at this point.
8) Sit back in first position, and relieve the experience with all of the knowledge gained from 2nd & 3rd position.	Significant shift in patient feelings and behavior should be evident if this protocol has been successful.
9) Move back to 3rd position chair and watch self with all their new knowledge and observe their new responses.	Optional step that allows for strengthened level of self-awareness about how the patient can be different in a positive way.

Figure 7.3. Instructions for aligning perceptual positions.

she could go through the scene and remain resourceful and empathically connected with her child. Her anxiety was much lower. In real life, the fights with her child stopped and her ability to mother effectively increased severalfold.

If the person involved is an abuser, the use of second position needs to be done with care. First, the therapist should be familiar with this tool. Second, the patient needs to be prepared. The main preparation is to help the patient understand the rationale for going into second position. The rationale is that the patient is already doing it in a mixed state. The patient is confusing the ideas of the abuser with her own ideas. The reason to take second position is to get clear what belongs to that person and what belongs to the patient. One of the things that can happen when people take second position with an abusive parent is that they sometimes become a lot clearer about what the parent is really upset about. For instance, one patient who had a mother who was verbally abusive really got that her mother was upset about her marriage. It was not the daughter's fault. If the abuser is a sadist, it may be very difficult for the patient to take this approach. Therapists should use a great deal of caution. If it is to be used, the patient should be completely stable and resourceful. If there is any doubt or question, this tool in this circumstance is probably not advised.

So when would a therapist want to use one approach versus the other? The first variable will be the frame of reference of the therapist. Some approaches do not fit well with a given therapist's general worldview or the assumptions they are using as part of the therapy. A second variable will be the specific goals that the therapist wants to achieve.

The use of externalization would be a logical choice if the patient's identity is thoroughly intertwined with the problem and the goal is to open up some psychological space between the patient and the problem. It is specifically designed to elicit alternative descriptions of the self in the patient's history. So, if the therapist wants to bring into the foreground of the patient's consciousness the various events and people in the patient's life that support a narrative that the patient is not to blame or that the patient is worthwhile, then the type of questioning and therapeutic stance in a narrative approach would be useful.

Another way to the use the idea of restorying is, after some positive change has occurred in the patient, to begin to weave this change into an alternative nonpathological narrative about the patient's life. The goal would be to link up this positive change with other positive events in order to make a coherent, meaningful, and compelling story. It would also be a logical choice if one wanted to focus on the issues of power and social influences.

In dealing with survivors of abuse, the one problem that tends to be cited as needing to be externalized is self-blame. White & Epston (1990) saw the internalization of self-blame as the main variable that keeps an individual dominated by abuse. As anyone that has worked with survivors of abuse will tell you, it is not very successful to just tell someone not to blame himself or herself.

To Be and to Act in the Present in Manners That Value All Parts

As we have talked about earlier, the past does not affect a person directly. It is one's memory of the past that has influence. As agents of change, we only care about the past if current behavior is problematic. While there are many approaches that one can use to attenuate the effects of one's memory of the past, there are also approaches that work directly on current behavior. The major advantage of working with present actions and awareness is that as soon as new behavior or new experience is created, it immediately makes new memories that begin to compete with old memories and behavioral patterns.

Over a lifetime, individuals develop a repertoire of coping strategies. When trauma occurs early in life, a person creates adaptations that invariably lead to the devaluation and/or dissociation of self. If in a given situation in the present, a person can be empathically connected to all different aspects of self and chart a course of action that takes into account the needs and values of those aspects of self, then the influence of past trauma has been minimized.

The main principle of this approach is to act your values. This simple principle is easier said than done. First, you have to know your values. Many people must learn to differentiate their own deep organic values from the "shoulds" and "oughts" learned in childhood. Second, you have to clarify any conflicts between different parts of the personality.

The fact of the matter is that if a person can be and act in a manner that values parts of the self, he or she does not need therapy of any sort. So this is a lofty ideal toward which we want to head. However, it is not an easy goal to attain. It can be useful to spend time using a combination of Socratic and solution-oriented questions to help a person begin to discern what their values are and how to act in accordance with them. A variation of the miracle question (de Shazer, 1983) that would be useful is: "Suppose you could create a value system or belief system that supported every part of you, what would that be?" What actions would you need to take to be in accordance with that system? When do you do that already, even a little bit?

As the patient begins to describe this system, the therapist can write it down. Eventually a document can be created for the patient that is like the constitution or the declaration of independence. This document can be used as a guidepost for future behavior.

Violence Begets Violence

This simple principle can be of immense help to trauma survivors. A patient did some work around her sex addiction issues using EMDR. She reported many experiences of which she was deeply ashamed, because of her sexual acting out behavior. By the end of the session she had calmed down considerably, but it was clear that she was not finished processing this information. She left the office grounded. That night she dissociated and hit her daughter. When she was next seen, we processed what had happened. There were many issues that appeared to converge to allow this to happen, including feelings of shame that came up during the EMDR. The common denominator of all of these pressures was that she had been violently berating herself. The patient was very ashamed of herself for hitting her child. She did not understand how she could have done this. It was insufficient for this patient to know that perhaps the feelings that came up from the memories were to blame. She had done this her daughter and wanted to be held accountable for her actions.

This became the major focus of the session. What happened that allowed her to hit her daughter? More importantly, she wanted to make sure that this never happened again. The bottom line was that she had been violent with herself in her berating of herself. Just like the alcoholic, a little bit of alcohol leads to more alcohol; anything else is just fooling around. Any form of violence that she engaged in opened the door for more violence. Violence against herself in terms of behavior or thinking was violence, and therefore left her vulnerable to hurting her daughter. This was something of an epiphany for her. She had never thought in terms of how her self-punishing and self-shaming inner dialogue was a form of mental violence. Dissociative patients often think that they can get better by getting rid of certain parts at worst or ignoring them at best. This type of thinking is essentially violent and certainly not loving or holistic. They need to understand that either they all get better or none of them will get better (R. P. Kluft, personal communication, 2000).

Challenging Dysfunctional Beliefs and Actions

In chapter 5 we reviewed methods to work with traumatic memory. We discussed how specific memories would be used to support cognitive schemas and beliefs. The working through of these phase 2 issues intermingles with the phase 3 work that we have been describing here. Inviting patients to look at their traumatic memories leads to challenges of their belief systems. Challenging patients to question their belief systems and create new ways of acting invites them to reconsider the meaning that they give to traumatic memories. If a patient is dealing with a limited number of traumas that occurred late in life, this dynamic may not be so involved. However, patients who grew up in severely dysfunctional families often do not even realize how distorted their schemas are.

Ross (1989, 1995) advocated focusing on the cognitive distortions of DID patients using a Socratic method to point out the distortions. One common example is to ask patients to consider if the exact same situation was occurring to someone else, would they have the same interpretation? The answer is invariably "no." The next question, then, is, "What makes you the one exception in the entire world?" At this point patients can begin to intellectually accept that perhaps there is a thinking distortion happening. In many cases simply labeling a thought process or a belief as a distortion is a revelation to patients. This does not mean that they are suddenly going to change their belief. Once a person begins to consider the possibility that what they are thinking is a distortion, it begins to open up some room for change.

So one tool is simply to let a person know in a nonjudgmental and noncritical fashion that the belief that they are to blame for someone else's actions is a distortion. This usually needs to be repeated many times. It may need to be explained by comparing the thought process to that of an egocentric 5-year-old child. Once a belief or cognition has been labeled a distortion, patients can be asked to explore how they know "the distortion" to be "true." One of the difficult things for therapists to do sometimes is to resist the desire to tell patients a "more healthy" cognition, such as, "It was not your fault." Many patients do need to hear that statement repeatedly. The problem is that when a therapist says this, it will tend to prevent the patient from exploring the underlying reasons he or she believes it was her fault. Therapy or support groups are ideal in this situation, because the fellow patients can be the ones who remind the person it was not their fault. When groups are not available, then individual therapists may have to play both roles. McCann and Pearlman (1990) described the common areas for distorted schema as including safety, trust, self-esteem, dependence/independence, and power. They focus on helping patients identify these themes, especially in relation to the normative needs that everyone has. In our parlance here, they help patients focus on the truth of "what was" with less judgment. They emphasize reteaching patients what normal needs are and normal ways to get them met. By changing these standards to which people measure themselves, their stories about themselves naturally change.

One of the outcomes of a pilot study (Schwarz & Dolan, 1995) with survivors who self-reported that they were far along in their recovery was a common strategy for improving their functioning at difficult choice points in their life that were dictated by their belief systems. The strategy was for the person to look at the choice point in which they found themselves. They would then imagine the two or three different paths that they could take from that point, and then they would compare and contrast which worked better for them.

There was one important nuance that these people recognized. They described the choices in terms of cost–benefit ratio. It was clearly recognized that one path was not all good and one path not all bad. Generally, it was a matter of choosing the least bad alternative. Many people who have been abused or traumatized think in black and white terms. They do not see any all-good alternatives, so they feel hopeless and helpless. The fact is that there are costs to any belief or action. There are also benefits. Patients almost always benefit when they are asked to reflect on the costs and benefits of a given train of action or a belief. Therapists need to help patients consider the differential effects of short-term and long-term cost–benefit analysis. In the study, subjects described the least bad alternative as difficult or hard choices that had better long-term benefits.

At some point, some patients will intellectually know that a belief is not functional for them. However, they cannot change it. This is almost always an issue of personal ecology (see chapter 3). At this point a number of options are available. One is asking the patient to look at the benefits of problem behavior or hanging on to a dysfunctional belief. It is best if this is not an intellectual discussion. To facilitate this, the therapist can use the "as if frame" described in chapter 2. The therapist can ask the patient to imagine that he or she took a pill that gives the countervailing healthy belief. Then the patient is asked to pay attention to his or her emotional reactions, objections, and so on. Another important area is to focus on how the person expects others would react to this change. One common issue is that if the person really let go of the belief, feelings of loss or helplessness, which are often tied to traumatic memories, flood in. One option is to simply be with the patient while he or she mourns. Another option is to treat the affect associated with these memories (e.g., with TFT, TRC, or EMDR).

Another option would be to focus on the blocked belief in a more open-ended fashion and see what comes up, such as using an EMDR protocol (Shapiro, 1995)[2] or affect bridge (see chapter 5). A different

---

[2]By now, readers may have noticed that I have mentioned EMDR many times and have not included it as one of the tools described in this book. The main reason for this is that it has been fully described elsewhere (Shapiro, 1995). It is a worthwhile approach. Even if a clinician never uses the actual technique, the thinking behind the technique can be quite valuable for those working with trauma.

approach would be to attempt to strengthen the opposing healthy belief using the meridian system (see Durlacher, 1994, and/or Gallo, 2000).

One final approach is one that subjects reported in our pilot study. This basic pattern can be used in several manners. The first is to ask patients to compare and contrast the effects of thinking different thoughts, such as, "It is my fault that I was abused" versus "I was not to blame for what happened, I was only a child." The patient can notice what impact thinking those thoughts has upon him or her. Usually what happens is that the patient becomes more agitated when focusing on the negative belief and less agitated when focusing on the positive belief.

Generally, it is best to start with the dysfunctional belief first (i.e., "It is my fault that I was abused"). There are several reasons: (a) the patient already believes this so there will be less resistance; (b) the patient is likely to have at least a mild increase in some dystonic symptom (sometimes patients can become highly agitated, so the therapist needs to be prepared), so he or she will want to leave this state and will be more able to entertain the healthier belief; (c) when the patient considers the healthier state, he or she will calm down. This reinforces this belief on an operant conditioning level. It is also preferable to end procedures in a positive state.

The second form of this pattern is to have the patient consider alternative paths in the future based on different beliefs or actions. The patient can then compare and contrast his or her reactions to the response of others and so on. This can be done in cognitive exercise frame or it can be done in a more guided imagery or hypnotic frame. In the hypnotic frame, the patient can be asked to imagine walking down a path to a fork in the road. Each path leads to one version of the future. The patient can then walk down each path. This is essentially the "ghost of Christmas yet to come" intervention. One other variation of this approach is that when the patient comes to the fork in the road, a figure walks down each of the alternatives paths toward the patient. The figure turns out to be the patient's future self. Each future self can take the patient into the particular future. Again, it is usually best to start with the dysfunctional belief first.

These approaches can stir up intense reactions. It is usually best for the therapist to intervene as little as possible in the content of the experience. The therapist should avoid telling the patient about how the belief is wrong or dysfunctional. The therapist should avoid calming the patient down during the dysfunctional sequence. It is the comparing and contrasting of the experiences themselves that effects the change. Once the comparing and contrasting are finished, the therapist can then ask the patient a variety of questions that will help the patient process the experience. Again, the therapist needs to stay neutral with respect to which belief is better. The questions can include:

- What was different about your experience with each path/belief?
- What were the pluses and minuses of each path/belief?
- Which path/belief gave you the most benefit for the least pain?
- Which path/belief did you prefer?
- What was it that you preferred about it?
- Which path/belief would help you in your recovery?
- Which path would the people who want the best for you want you to choose?
- Which path/belief would your perpetrator(s) want you to choose?
- Which path led to actions that you value?
- Which path was better for the majority of your parts?
- What was better about that path?

As the patient and therapist discuss these questions, more and more of the patient's sense of self or identity becomes separated from any given belief. Psychological space is created for the patient in which to consider which belief or action the patient wants to choose for himself or herself.

Acceptance and Forgiveness

The final phase of trauma treatment is about reconnection. As stated in chapter 1, reconnecting with resources starts in phase 1 of treatment. Cultivating resourcefulness is something that should also be emphasized throughout treatment. This entire chapter has been focused mostly on phase 3 aspects of recovery. The concept of the holistic self is essentially the goal of phase 3. The hallmark of the third phase of treatment is acceptance and forgiveness. All spiritual paths of healing lead to acceptance and forgiveness. This topic of spirituality actually requires its own book, so for now, we will discuss it only briefly.

If you are to value all of your parts, you must be understanding and forgiving of the parts of you that are upset, make mistakes, and are less than spiritually evolved. To the extent that you cannot follow the guidelines of the previous sentence, you need to be accepting and forgiving of yourself for this difficulty. In *A Course in Miracles* (Foundation for Inner Peace, 1975), there is a line that says: "There can be no suffering that fails to hide an unforgiving thought." It is crucial to understand that the benefit of forgiveness is always for the one who does the forgiving. Any benefit that accrues to the recipient of the forgiveness is a bonus. When we do not forgive, we are angry, resentful, fearful, hateful, and so on. These emotions are all low-energy emotions (Hawkins, 1995) that weaken us and hurt our own functioning (Diamond, 1980a; Hawkins, 1995). We feel these emotions and suffer. We are the ones who are stuck to the past events that have "injured us."

There are two levels of forgiveness and two foci of forgiveness. The first level of forgiveness is a letting go of negative feelings about and toward the "offending person." The second level of forgiveness is the making whole of the relationship with the offending person as if the hurt never took place. The first focus of forgiveness is the self. The second focus is the other.

In trauma work, acceptance and forgiveness of the self must usually come first. Most people who have PTSD from a specific event or long-standing trauma are not accepting or forgiving of their own feelings or actions or choices. When we are talking about forgiving the self, we are describing a relationship between our current self and out past self. In the case of DID, this would include the relationship between alters. There are a number of different aspects to forgiveness. First, the need for forgiveness implies that a mistake was made. The next issue is the recognition that mistakes are part of life. The next task is the understanding of the circumstances and limitations that made the mistake happen. To the extent that we do not accept and forgive our past selves, those aspects of us stay dissociated, unloved, and unhealed. If those aspects are not allowed to be loved and healed, then we are not loved and healed. For full healing to take place, we must reach a level of full forgiveness with ourselves, where we let all of us back into our own hearts.

The second focus of forgiveness has to do with forgiving someone else. The someone else can include a perpetrator, a parent who did not stop abuse from happening, God, and anyone else who has been involved in a person being hurt and/or not being saved or protected. The concept of forgiving an abuser or offender usually creates a great deal of havoc for a survivor of trauma. It is usually only late in the healing process that this step can even be entertained. The irony that most people do not realize is that without level 1 forgiveness (letting go of negative feelings), the survivor is more attached to the perpetrator than without forgiveness. A survivor needs to have enough psychological space to be able to acknowledge his or her own anger, hurt, and pain; to recognize that what was done to him or her was wrong and not his or her fault (or only partially his or her fault). The person needs to be able to let go of negative feelings in order to be able to turn his or her attention to the fact that there are sources of love and acceptance other than the perpetrator.

Since some perpetrators continue to be dangerous or hurtful, it may be necessary to not let that person back into one's heart. Unfortunately, most survivors of abuse or long-term trauma create beliefs about the "not OKness" of the world. Based on that belief they do not let people into their lives. Basically, they choose to not love others, nor to let others love them. In fact they actually draw more trauma to themselves in a somewhat mysterious fashion. So from this perspective, forgiving the other person means that the patient no longer uses the hurt and pain that resulted from the abuse to be a reason to close his or her heart from the rest of the world. Once a person reaches a level of forgiveness in which they release the resentment from being hurt, they are now in a position to let love from other people in their life again.

Forgiveness and God

People who have undergone abuse and trauma over long periods of time almost always have significant issues with God. God is essentially seen as a parent figure that is either abandoning or punishing. In either case, God certainly does not love the survivor. God is interpreted through the traumatized cognitive schema (Phillips & Frederick, 1995):

> Lack of safety: God did not protect me.
> Lack of trust: The universe is basically dangerous.
> Lack of intimacy: The inability to feel connected to a higher benevolent power.

Everyone make attributions about the nature of God, including survivors. The fact of the matter is that whatever characteristics we decide about the nature of God (including the belief that there is no God) is a reflection of our own level of consciousness (Hawkins, 1995). Hawkins (1995) referred to our perceptions about the nature of God as the God-view. It includes our ways of viewing God's intentions and actions. It also applies to our views of the intentions and actions of our parents and other authority figures. Finally, it is our own intentions and actions when we are in the position of authority, even if the authority is over ourselves. For example, the thought or belief of a survivor that she deserves to be punished for her actions emanates from her God-view. To put it another way, however we see God is a projection of our God-view. People who are upset with God because of the traumatic events in their lives need to forgive God, but not for God's sake. They need to do it for their own sake. It is not that God abandoned them. It is that in their hurt and pain, they abandoned God. It is not that God does not love them. It is that they do not love God. To put it another way, they need to forgive themselves for misunderstanding the nature of God.

Phillips and Frederick (1995) suggested that it is very important to initiate discussions about spirituality as part of the therapy process, often because patients will not bring up the topic themselves. I certainly concur that the topic is an important one. It is particularly germane during the third phase of therapy. However, my experience suggests that all therapists need to do is to listen for the theme of spirituality. Patients do bring up the topic all on their own. They may not say the words "spirituality" or "existential issue" or "God." But they do bring up the topic. It may be up to the therapist to help the patient put words on their concerns and to allow the patient to know that it is acceptable and desirable that they discuss their concern about God. In the therapeutic context, spirituality and forgiveness has to do with looking at our own choices in how we connect or disconnect from others and ourselves in the face of pain. Gilligan (1994) referred to this as the "courage to love." To put it another way, the therapist who is coming from a more psychospiritual perspective connects with the idea that there is absolutely nothing wrong with the patient, except that the patient does not know that there is nothing wrong with the patient. This is considered a universal law that applies equally to therapists. It is up to the therapist to help communicate this to the patient.[3]

The Illusion of Disconnection With "All That Is"

It is a spiritual axiom that God is all that is. This includes us. Therefore, any idea that we are not connected with God is an illusion. Any idea that we are not connected to each other is part of the same illusion. It is this illusion that causes us to suffer.[4] This suffering goes far beyond trauma patients. The illusion of separateness from the whole is clearly seen in DID.

> DID in individuals can be seen as a metaphor for the global dissociative multiplicity that is reaching a critical level of dysfunctionality. How much difference is there between one person splitting his or her personality into disowned parts that often attack each other, and the human species breaking off into different nation states, tribes and or classes and attacking and killing each other? Is there really any difference between a dissociative client cutting herself because in the short term it relieves tension, while in the long term it does harm, and corporations and governments allowing the poisoning of the eco-system for near-term profits or fear of being voted out of office? This is the same logic. It is the same psychosis. The mistaken belief is that one part can have dominion over another part without hurting the entire whole. I would further submit that the rise of dissociative disorders in the awareness of the mental health community and the culture

---

[3]For an excellent treatise on this subject readers are referred to the *Supplements to A Course in Miracles* (Foundation for Inner Peace, 1996).
[4]This is a position that is strongly advocated in *A Course in Miracles*.

in general reflects the planetary need for human being to heal the dissociative barriers between all of the different tribes and nation states, races and so on. We are reaching a point in population and technology that make this type of "either-or" functioning maladaptive for future survival of the planet. (Schwarz, 1998)

Connection With God as the Ultimate Resource

At the beginning of chapter 4, there is the line: *Trauma cannot be destroyed, but it can be dissolved in a sea of resourcefulness.* As I have also pointed out earlier, the problem with trauma is not just the direct impact of the trauma itself; it is the indirect impact of disconnecting a person from his or her resources that does the real damage. Anyone who has had a peak or transcendent experience knows that during those moments nothing can be upsetting or bothersome. While in the SoC of the peak experience, the pain of any past trauma is completely irrelevant. During these moments people feel one with the world. The world is seen as beautiful and good. According to Hawkins (1995), the level of consciousness of these states is one of love and/or joy. These states are very high on the spiritual developmental scale. Phillips and Frederick (1995) rightly pointed out that talking about "God" or exhorting people to get more spiritual is of little help. It is better to help people feel more connected to peak experiences (Maslow, 1970), moments of joy and love and connection. These are spiritual moments.

People have been educated about spirituality and God in very limited manners. It can be very helpful to provide alternative points of view. Generally, when I do this, I own it as my point of view, rather than any kind of "truth." Patients are then free to consider whether or not it works better for them. For instance, they can use the compare and contrast method of dealing with beliefs.

It is understandable that people cut off from God given their understanding of God as a bad parent (which is usually their understanding). The very language we use to discuss God is, in my opinion, problematic. God is almost always referred to in the usual manner of object or subject. It is very difficult not to think of God, at least in the back of your mind, as a kind of anthropomorphized superperson.

So I try to explain spirituality people in the following manner:

> The intention of spirituality is to connect with the creative and loving energy of the universe. The key word here is energy. God is not a thing or a guy with a beard or a woman with long flowing robes. If we do not feel connected to God, it is us who have done the cutting off. I find it helpful to

think of God as a certain kind of energy field that exists throughout the universe. Think of God as a kind of radio station with the call letters WGOD broadcasting love and understanding 24/7/365. The problem is that we do not usually tune in. We are listening to WFEAR or WMAD, WSHM (shame), etc. So it is up to us to tune in. Peak experiences, like those perfect moments at a sunset, are so wonderful because at those times we are tuned in to WGOD. If we tuned in all the time we would walk around feeling those feelings all the time. All healthy spiritual practices are about how to take more responsibility for tuning in. We need to look at how our thoughts, actions, and choices tune us in to either the WGOD (or WLOVE) or some less joyful station.

The point of the third phase of trauma treatment is to help people to choose to reconnect with life. In our unpublished study of 20 highly recovered survivors, each person had a sense of personal agency regarding taking direction and control in one's life toward positive and meaningful experiences. Almost everyone made references to taking time to connect with nature as a source of feeling connected to something larger than oneself. Cultivating a resourceful life, described earlier, is a spiritual practice.

At a minimum, therapists need to be on the lookout for these types of experiences in the patient's life. When found, they need to be focused on and expanded upon in terms of meaning for the patient, as potential plotline development in the story of the person's life, and as meaningful exceptions to the disconnection with the world and God. These types of reference experiences can be used to help people develop a sense of personal agency about choosing a more resourceful life (read as a life full of more resources).

Tools for Connection With God

Since we are already connected to God, it is generally more appropriate to help remove the blocks that people put up to perceiving the connection. In many cases this is not a formal tool. Rather it is opening up space for people to discuss their upset feelings about God and their sense of separateness. Not being able to talk about these feelings is a parallel process to not being able to talk about trauma or abuse. A more formal structure to accomplish this task is a feeling letter to God.

Feeling Letter to God

Gray (1992) has described in detail a specific letter-writing technique that helps couples resolve negative feelings toward each other and renew their connection to each other (see Gray, 1992, pp. 208–237). This technique can also be adapted to dealing with the same issues with God (J. Gray, personal communication, 1998) and can be done in the office out loud verbally. The letter is in three parts.

Part I is a letter from the person to God in which the person expresses the four healing emotions, anger, sadness, fear, and regret, or sorrow, along with his or her wants, needs, and wishes. The patient can talk about his or her feelings about God, himself/herself, or about a specific traumatic incident or traumatic period of life that the patient wants to tell God about. Gray emphasized the need to go through all of the emotions in order for healing to occur. The metaphor I use is a cylinder lock like the one on brief cases. A person needs to turn all of the different cylinders in order for the lock to open. Just focusing on one cylinder will never open the lock.

Needless to say, it may be very difficult for a trauma patient to tell God how angry he or she is with him or how scared he or she is of God. It is usually necessary to explain to the patient to think of God as the ultimate therapist. God can handle anything the patient has to say and remain loving and benevolent. The procedure may also stir up a great deal of emotion (which is actually the goal). The therapist can help the patient by providing the following sentence stems

> I feel angry that . . .
> I don't like . . .
> I wish . . .
> I feel sad that . . .
> I wanted . . .
> I expect. . .
> I feel scared that
> I do not want . . .
> I need . . .
> I feel sorry that (or because or when) . . .
> I want . . .
> I hope . . .

If this is being done verbally out loud, the therapist can deepen the experience by repeatedly asking, "What else makes you angry/did you want/scared you?" It is important to understand that this first part of the protocol is not the main healing part of the tool. It is the set-up for the healing. It is the next two parts that are crucial for healing.

Part II is a letter from God back to the patient. It is a letter that the patient would want God to say. The letter should express the love and understanding response that the patient wants to hear. In other words, the patient is asked to take responsibility to connect at least in fantasy with a more evolved God-view (Hawkins, 1995). To put it another way, this procedure begins to update and modify the previously negative schema of God. To put it yet another way, this procedure undermines the victim position and elevates a sense of agency.

The letter should refer to the first letter and use phrases such as

> Thank you for . . .
> I understand . . .
> I am sorry . . .
> Please forgive me for . . .
> You did not deserve . . .
> You deserve . . .
> I want . . .
> You will be able to . . .
> From now on I will . . .

Again, there can be many repetitions of a given initial sentence stem. If this is being done verbally in the office, there are a few choices. One is for the patient to use a gestalt two-chair technique and switch chairs when in the God position. The other approach is to have the therapist play the role of God and say the things that patients want to hear while the patient is instructed to soak it in as if it were from God. Each has advantages and disadvantages. Different therapists may or may not be comfortable taking the role of God.

In the final part of the letter, the patient writes back to God and expresses forgiveness or at least appreciation. The point here is just as expressed in the radio broadcast metaphor. The patient needs to let the signal in. This part of the ritual concretizes the letting in of the love from God. The letter can contain sentence stems such as

> Thank you for . . .
> I understand . . .
> I realize that . . .
> I forgive . . .
> I am grateful for . . .
> I trust that . . .
> Right now in my life, I am in the process of . . .

This type of process is often highly cathartic. However, it is not the same type of catharsis as dealing with a traumatic memory. There is usually a great sense of movement and openness. Certainly one or several sessions can be spent on processing the experience. Patients should never be forced to do this process until they are ready. They may need to do it more than once.

Creating and Nurturing Peak Experiences

Another spiritual axiom, as well as hypnotic approach, is that whatever you focus your attention on, you will increase. Therefore, it is beneficial to help patients notice and focus their attention on peak or near-peak experiences. Therapists can ask questions about when patients have felt especially joyful, peaceful, content, relaxed, or at one with the world. Imagery or hypnosis can be used to strengthen the connection to these states of consciousness. For instance, a Vietnam vet with PTSD described that he had been walking in the woods and "just felt connected to everything." He was told:

> Close your eyes and allow yourself to go back to that experience. Be back in the woods. See the different colors on the leaves. Hear the rustling of the leaves in the wind. Smell the scent of the moisture. Your conscious mind can remember the scene while your unconscious mind remembers the feeling that you just feel connected to everything. [This type of verbal patter continued until the patient signaled that he was really feeling the feeling]. Allow yourself to let this feeling sink into every cell of your body. You deserve this connection that actually is always there even though you have not always noticed it. You can begin to notice this type of experience more and more. Whenever you are walking in nature you can more easily feel connected to it. Your unconscious mind can begin to notice this connection in all sorts of other places as well. Perhaps it will be driving in a car and marveling at the amount of cooperation that exists in everyone driving on the road. Or it may be while you are enjoying a meal or when you are talking to a friend. Your conscious mind may recognize that you are connecting to this very same feeling at those times or it may be that your conscious mind will just feel very content and peaceful. I do not know which it will be. But I do know that you can attend more and more to these types of experiences in your life. As that occurs, you will be discovering how these feelings can make a positive difference in the way you feel about yourself and other people. [At this point, self-image thinking was used to help link the experience to feeling more connected with his wife and children.]

In addition to the therapeutic benefits of doing this type of procedure, there is an indirect suggestion that therapy is not just about processing trauma. It is also important to build positive states. Some heavily traumatized patients have trouble accessing any positive states. In fact, some "dark" or "bad" alters of DID patients report that they have never seen the sun or have never smelled a flower. It can be very useful to specifically allow these alters to have these "positive" experiences. Positive experiences of safety and boundaries can be built up via imagery or hypnosis. Sacerdote (1977) described the use of hypnotically created mystical states to help attenuate physical or emotional pain. He differentiated introverted and extroverted states. The extroverted state was built up by having patients make a difficult climb up a symbolic mountain. Once at the top of the mountain, patients are guided to seeing a valley followed by mountain ranges followed by a valley off in the distance. Suggestions are for an expanded sense of time and space. The introverted state is suggested by having the patient "surrounded in every direction by wider and wider transparent concentric luminous spheres of serenity and cheerful calmness" (Sacerdote, 1977, p. 314).

☐ Summary

The development or evolution of the holistic self is a process that occurs over time. It is cultivated within the therapeutic relationship as well as outside of it. Most of the tools described in this chapter are going to be used during the third phase of therapy. However, the principles underlying these tools are going to be present throughout treatment. Work with spiritual peak experiences will probably be foreshadowed with work on building a safe place. There is also going to be a dialectical movement between second phase memory work and third phase reconnection work. This is only to be expected. As patients process traumatic experiences that support their disconnection from others, it becomes more possible to connect with others. As people reconnect with a more resourceful and supportive world, they are more able to work on more sensitive issues.

Throughout this process the therapist can hold the knowledge for and with the patient that both of them are part of something far bigger than either can know (Gilligan, 1997). According to the concepts of morphic fields and the 100th monkey effect (Sheldrake, 1981, 1989), each time a survivor overcomes the effects of trauma it makes it a little easier for every other survivor of trauma throughout the world, now and in the future, to do the same thing.

CHAPTER

If You Meet the "Tool" on the Road, Leave It! Person-of-the-Therapist Issues

Throughout this book I have discussed the merits of learning tools that will help transform trauma. The tools framework is based on active skills that therapists can learn and can even teach their patients to use for themselves. It is based on mastery, competency, and resourcefulness. Most of the tools we have discussed have been focused on the patient. However, there is a danger in focusing our attention too much on learning tools that help *change* the patient. It tends to put us out of balance. It is too much on the *Yang* (active) side of the equation. We need to balance it with *Yin* (passivity). It also focuses too much attention on the individual patient as the focus of our attention. We need to also focus our attention on ourselves as part of the therapist–patient relationship. By the Yin or passive side, I am referring to the other end of the spectrum, such as passivity and receptivity, no action, accepting pain and suffering. As therapists we must not get stuck in either/or thinking. Effective therapy must be open to *both* action *and* inaction, both mastery and acceptance, both resourcefulness and helplessness. It is not that one must do all of these things at the same time. It is a matter of knowing which to do at what time with a given person. This, of course, is more in the nature of art rather than science.

As therapists we need to be aware of the fact that we are constantly making choices in our interactions with our patients. We choose to ask questions, stay silent, initiate a specific intervention, and so on. Each choice has the potential to influence the direction of the therapy. We need to be aware of our motivations for making a given intervention or not making a given intervention. We have spent considerable time focusing on our motivations in terms of what we are trying to achieve for the patient. We also need to be aware of our own motivations in terms of what we want for ourselves in the process. We also must be able to track our interventions over time to be able to make course corrections.

The Yin side of being a therapist focuses on several things:

1. There is an aspect of helplessness and suffering that no "tool" will fix. In fact, there is nothing really broken. It is only an illusion on the part of the patient (and perhaps the therapist) that the patient is damaged and broken.
2. The only "tool" of any use is the therapist himself or herself being emotionally present and acting as a witness and a loving presence that gently (and sometimes firmly) helps the patient experience his or her experiences and come through those events knowing that he or she is "OK."
3. Anything that moves the therapist away from the position of witness has a strong probability of being a defense against being present as a fellow human being (without the protection of the role of "therapist"). The emotional press in witnessing the impact of heinous and/ or highly traumatic acts can be very upsetting on a variety of dimensions (e.g., depression, despair, anger, helplessness, fear). The use of active tools can be a therapist defense against feeling these types of feelings.
4. Emphasizing competency skills tends to stimulate rescue fantasies for the therapist and "being rescued" fantasies for the patient. I will attempt to use a both/and approach in elaborating these ideas. Where possible I will try to operationalize the "doing" involved. We must acknowledge that these operational suggestions are only approximations at best.

☐ Therapist as Witness

As a witness, the therapist does not "do" anything. The therapist listens and serves as a witness to the experience of the patient. The witnessing can be carried out at several different levels. The therapist does not ask too many questions, does not use a tool or technique to solve the problem, does not interpret, and so on. The therapist listens and perhaps reflects or clarifies a few of the patient's points. The therapist uses Carl Rogers's magic trilogy of genuineness, warmth, and unconditional positive regard. The key skill involved for the therapist in being in this position is affect tolerance. Perhaps a better term would be affect resonance. Tolerance connotes gritting one's teeth and bearing it. Resonance connotes a more empathetic stance.

The more emotionally open a patient is in telling his or her experience, the more emotion will be stirred up in the therapist. It is not unlike good theater or cinema. When the story is told "well," the people in the audience feel/live the story. Resonating refers to the experience of empathically identifying with the characters in the story. In therapy, how well the story is told is defined by emotional vulnerability. Therapists, like all people, have different levels of capacity for how much general emotional intensity they can feel comfortably. Therapists also have specific levels of tolerance for specific emotions such as anger or sadness. On an even more idiosyncratic level, therapists will have differential capacities to witness specific topics or content areas because of their own personal issues.

It is not a problem for the therapy if the therapist's affect is aroused. Without affect, how can a therapist empathize? Some stories arouse a great deal of emotion. The issue becomes whether or not the feelings overwhelm the therapist or force the therapist to psychologically leave the room. In many instances the therapist must expend effort to contain the affect. The therapist must stay connected to sufficiently resourceful SoCs so that he or she can psychologically stay in the room and resonate with the patient's emotional experience. One simple strategy is to assume a resourceful posture (e.g., keep both feet on the floor and sit straight with a fairly erect spine) and take centering breaths. As the therapist stays in the moment with the patient, all kinds of possibilities open up. One can never know ahead of time what they will be. It may be that the main possibility that develops is that the patient feels fully heard and cared about. Thus, she or he can fully express their feelings and the meanings they had from their experience, so that the therapist can witness these more elaborated expressions of the patient's experience. As a result the patient feels even more fully heard and cared about. In this recursive loop of understanding and unconditional positive regard, a great deal of healing occurs. It may be that the therapist will understand something that he or she had not understood before and a new avenue of exploration will develop. It may be that the therapist will become clear on a specific piece of work for which one of the active tools can be used.

It can be a problem for the therapy if the therapist has to spend too much energy to cope with his or her feelings. It is definitely a problem if the therapist must defend against them. By defend, I mean resist, deny, dissociate, repress, and avoid. It is not feeling the affect that causes problems. It is the running away from the affect (by whatever psychological means) that prevents the healing of the trauma (just like it created the PTSD to begin with). To the extent that the therapist must spend effort to defend against his or her feelings, the therapist will not be present in the room.

To put it simply, if the therapist is busy taking care of himself, who is witnessing the patient? We ask our patients to face what happened to them. Can we avoid facing what is happening to us as we are present with our patients? This is not an all-or-nothing proposition. The process happens by degrees. If the therapist is aware he or she is struggling to be present, the situation is not so bad. The therapist can begin to correct the problem. It is when the therapist is unaware that he or she is fighting or avoiding his or her affect that a more serious situation arises. The therapist will give cues to the patient to stop talking about such emotionally laden material. The patient will also have some difficulty discussing the more affective material for his or her own reasons. So the patient will offer the therapist hints, or send up test balloons, to see if the therapist can tolerate the material. One way for the therapist to unconsciously focus the therapy away from the affective material is to fail to respond to the hints.

For instance, Anna, a relatively new patient with a dissociative disorder, was talking about the difficult time she had had with previous treatment. She herself had a great deal of awareness and could talk about how the psychiatric residents who had treated her had hid behind their roles as doctors. We talked about how she wanted to know that I would be present and real with her. Anna had a great deal of experience doing psychic readings, but had stopped. I had been encouraging her to take this up again as a way to make money, since she had no money. One day, Anna came in and said something to the effect that she could tell that I was having a bad day. She was in fact correct about this. This moment in time was interesting, because here I was exposed to her "seeing." I had been encouraging her to use her talents, although *not on me* necessarily. I was tempted to withdraw, but thought better of it. So, I stayed present and asked her about how she could tell that I was having a bad day. The discussion did not last long. However, she was very moved that I was willing to stay present and that only one other doctor had been able to do that with her. Anna started to talk about her problems with spirituality.

A number of sessions later, I even allowed Anna to read my aura. Not only was this surprisingly accurate, it again helped Anna feel that I was willing to be with her on her own terms rather than hiding behind the role of therapist. Make no mistake: It did raise some anxiety in me about allowing Anna to do this. What would she see? Would it jeopardize the doctor–patient relationship? Would it make things too intense for the patient and/or for me? It did none of these things. It did help Anna talk about the psychic and spiritual parts of her life, which were huge aspects of her experience.

The problem with the therapist moving the therapy to less intense areas is that the mistake tends to be noticeable only after you stop making it. If I had withdrawn from Anna, I doubt that she would have commented on it. If the therapist continues to make the mistake long enough and consistently enough, the patient may begin to either make bigger hints or act out the feelings that are being blocked. At this point, a therapist might begin to actively look for this type of error and find it.

What needs to be different may be a behavior, a consistent feeling state, or a pattern of thinking. Beginning on page 230 is a series of self-reflective assessments that the therapist can use. Each question leads to certain action steps that may lead toward a solution of the "problem."

☐ When the Therapy Goes Off Course

A riddle: If an airplane flies from New York to Los Angeles, how often is it off course? The answer: all the time. Airplanes must constantly make small course corrections along the way. If you are working with a single-event trauma in a time-limited fashion, these issues do not come up that often. There is an agreed upon goal. You do the work. You and the patient arrive at the desired place and therapy is over. The tools that have been covered in this book will be very helpful. When you are working with more chronic cases and the treatment is longer and more intense new variables sometimes rise to the surface. These variables always have to do with the therapeutic relationship.[1]

Issues of the therapeutic relationship only tend to come up when the therapy goes off course. It is relatively easy to blame the pathology of the patient for any problem. However, it is my contention that to do so is a grave mistake. A "difficulty" in the treatment should be construed by the therapist as feedback that something is amiss in the interaction. The patient is attempting to cooperate by giving the feedback. The therapist may not understand or like the feedback. The therapist may not even realize it is feedback. Remember the TOTE framework. When you hit the

---

[1]The therapeutic relationship is always a variable. In briefer therapy it usually does not become an issue. In brief therapy such as SFT, the specific interventions are actually crafted to work with and maintain a positive relationship.

nail and it bends, you do not blame the nail for not cooperating. (Well actually, we often do, don't we?) The therapist must assess which of the ongoing patterns of behavior, feeling, thinking, or theorizing in which he or she is engaging, as well as of the patient's reactions, that are not working. The "problem" may involve errors of omission and/or commission by the therapist. The important point to know is that going off course is part of the process. Therapists need a method to self-correct the course from time to time. We will do that in a minute. Let me first describe a few common problems to look for.

The first is not thinking that you are a substantial part of the problem. If you do not acknowledge this to yourself, you will not be in a position to correct your errors. You are also communicating a level of arrogance that is of little help to patients. If you are working with people who have been abused, the position that the problem is all in the patient is parallel to the position taken by the abuser and often by the other people in the family. At a minimum, you must acknowledge to yourself that you are part of the problem as well as part of the solution and make adjustments accordingly.

The second common mistake is not acknowledging and apologizing for mistakes to your patients. Abuse patients have had very little experience with people in positions of authority acknowledging and apologizing for their mistakes. When a therapist is able to apologize, it enhances trust and role-models nondefensiveness. It strengthens a patient's ego functioning to know that something she perceived and felt was in fact accurate and legitimate. When I work with patients who I believe will require more than brief therapy, I generally prepare them that I will make mistakes and that it will help me help them if they let me know they are upset with something I have done or said or not done or not said.

A third common problem is attributing negative motivations to patients. One of the creative challenges for therapists is to help elicit positive motivations underlying what may appear to be very negative behavior. A common example is the construction of "self-sabotage":

> Barbara was hospitalized and improving at a good rate. Then suddenly, she started having problems and backsliding. The therapist talked with Barbara about her self-sabotaging behavior. Barbara became upset and began to rapidly decompensate. A careful analysis of Barbara's pattern revealed that she was doing much better. Her expectations of herself increased beyond her ability to consistently meet them. Dissociative patients, and most other survivors of abuse, tend to be highly perfectionistic. She began to "fail." She began to try harder, which only decreased her performance. The label of "self-sabotage" had a number of meanings to Barbara. One of them was an implied command, "Try harder!" When it was suggested to Barbara that she was trying too hard and doing too much, she began to improve again.

Figure 8.1 is a chart that shows how therapists and helping others unwittingly cocreate a cycle of self-sabotaging behavior. It also shows how to take steps to transform this pattern of interaction. It should be noted that this pattern is equally applicable to therapists themselves in their own personal lives or as they are learning to become therapists.

1) Person makes a major improvement	1) Person makes a major improvement
2) Expectations rise (I will never feel depressed again)	2) Keep expectations low
3) Reality fails to meet expectations	3) Recognize that mistakes must occur and they are to be used as feedback
4) Person is very upset with themselves and begins to think that they are a failure	4) Be gentle with self & give self permission to make mistakes. Honestly look at information for making correction
5) They apply more pressure to themselves and try much harder, often berating and shaming themselves	5) TRY LESS HARD. TAKE A SMALLER STEP. LOWER EXPECTATION
6) This only backfires and the person starts to feel much worse and may begin to have symptoms again	6) Give the self credit for steps taken. You deserve credit and approval on the way to success, not only once you have arrived
7) Either the person himself/herself, a friend or therapist now makes some comment about self sabotage	7) Instead of self sabotage label, realize you usually try to do too much and the issue is perfectionism/shame
8) Now the person feels s/he is to blame (which is just like how s/he felt as a child)	8) There is no blame in feedback, just information. Resist the concept of "blame" and move toward the concept of Response-"able" to take new steps
9) So person feels less resourceful & symptoms get worse	9) Notice small successes & improvements due to changes made from new information (symptoms have not returned or have left again)
10) Label of self sabotage is more strongly applied and the downward spiral is firmly in place	10) Positive loop is established

Figure 8.1. 10 steps of turning perfectionism/shame into "self-sabotage" and the 10 counter practices.

☐ Acknowledging Powerlessness (Or, A Person's Got to Know His Limitations)

Taking a position of weakness has been a strategy often used in so-called paradoxical approaches. I am using it here in one very special circumstance, namely, when you, the therapist, have really lost it. For instance, many years ago as a young therapist, I was working with a woman who had experienced years of physical and emotional abuse. She had also been raped as a teenager. She had an extensive history of drug abuse and parasuicidal self-harming behavior. She had made numerous calls to me late at night. During these calls she was always suicidal and also refusing help. She had called one evening, threatening suicide and refusing hospitalization, etc. I got angry and yelled at her. She hung up. At the next session, I told her that I could handle her pain, depression, anger etc. But, I could not handle her calling me up threatening suicide and tying my hands. I needed her help. If she wanted me to be the best therapist I could be for her, she would have to not do this behavior.

I remember discussing this with my supervisor at the time. She thought I had given up too much power. I thought this was rather strange, because it was clear to me that I did not have any power. I could work on what buttons got pushed in me, but I knew that I had "lost it." It seemed to me that the only thing to do was acknowledge the way things really were. I have never forgotten the outcome of this intervention. The patient came to a couple more sessions and then dropped out of treatment. It looked like it was a treatment failure. About 10 months later, the patient called and wanted to come back for more treatment. She reported that she had moved out of the city and had been living in the country, which she felt was better for her. She had decided that she herself needed to get her act together. She had been using my hypnotic tapes during the whole time. She had read the book, *If You Meet the Buddha on the Road, Kill Him* (Knopp, 1988). She was never again suicidal. She never again took drugs. She did in fact get her life together.

The moral of this example is that when the therapist takes on more responsibility for patients than they are willing to take on for themselves (i.e., rescue fantasies), the therapy will not go well. Patients of chronic abuse and neglect tend to see the therapist as an all-powerful parent. They cannot imagine that you have problems, that you have limitations. They cannot imagine that anything they do can really affect you. If a patient is acting out and it is affecting you, why not let the patient know about this? Why not model some vulnerability? Why not invite the patient to use his or her power more constructively?

☐ When Therapists Cannot Manage Their Own Affect

To the extent that a therapist is going to work with more seriously traumatized individuals, he or she needs to fully acknowledge and own that there are going to be times when strong feelings will arise in the therapist. The issue is, will the need to cope with these feelings make the therapist behave in a manner that is not helpful to the patient? Or, to put it another way, will these issues reduce one's creativity and flexibility as a therapist in helping people solve their problems? We can classify these potential problems in one of two areas: (a) general problems with affective tolerance or (b) specific problems with affective tolerance. In the former, the problem occurs much of the time with many patients. In the latter, the problem occurs at specific times with specific patients.

Reasons for Insufficient General Affective Tolerance

1. *Instead of allowing feelings to be present, the therapist tries to get rid of feelings that are aroused, which only tends to increase affective pressure.* This issue is the same problem as described in chapter 7 on the holistic self. The antidote to this problem involves awareness that the problem is happening followed by the therapist allowing himself to feel the feelings during the session while remaining connected to a resourceful state of mind. It may be necessary to practice this skill after the session with or without the help of a colleague or supervisor.
2. *The therapist is under the conscious impression that he or she should not have feelings aroused, so he or she feels like he or she is doing something wrong. This leads to a less resourceful state, which will lead to increased inability to cope with feelings.* The main correction here is to learn that it is normal to have these feelings. It is important to be understanding and forgiving of oneself for having these feelings, then to learn how to stay present with this feelings. See Figure 8.1 on dealing with perfectionism and self-sabotage.
3. *The therapist does not have skills of centering or mindfulness or equivalence.* The obvious answer here is to learn these skills.
4. *General unresolved personal issues around affect tolerance.* This is a serious problem that must be dealt with if the therapist wants to remain in

the field. Undoubtedly the previous problem is also present. Personal therapy and or person-of-the-therapist supervision[2] are required.

5. *The therapist is burnt out or has been traumatized by dealing with too much trauma.* Assuming there are no other problems and the therapist is burnt out, he or she needs to either take a vacation, reduce the number of trauma patients in his or her caseload and/or start cultivating a better life through more enjoyable activities (see chapter 7). If the therapist is traumatized, in addition to the above, he or she should get some focused therapy (e.g., see TFT or TRC) or supervision that will help process the trauma.

Reasons for Insufficient Specific Affective Tolerance

1. *The therapist's ego is too wrapped up in the patient getting better.* The therapist consciously or unconsciously feels injured if the patient does not get better.

2. *The therapist does not like to feel helpless.* Lets address problems one and two at the same time since they often occur together. The issue that is usually happening in this situation is that the therapist is more invested in the patient's "getting better" than the patient. To be more precise, the therapist and the patient usually have very different ideas about what getting better means or what the goals of therapy are. So, the first move is to take a time out and review the goals of treatment. The patient may even say that he or she wants to "get better" or "be happy." The problem is that his or her idea of what that "better" or "happy" looks like and how to achieve it are usually very different from the therapist's ideas. Many times the patient's concept of "better" and his or her method for getting there will simply not be achievable. These issues must be clarified.

A related issue may be that the therapist is not providing firm enough direction, structure, or limits. In many cases this actually increases the anxiety of the patient. It often puts the therapist in a position of first attempting to rescue the "victim" patient. After some time the therapist begins to feel victimized. This pattern is known as the Karpman

---

[2]Person-of-the-therapist supervision is a family therapy modality that emphasizes looking at the issues of the person as they apply to how he or she is coping in the therapy with patients. It is similar to personal therapy in that it focuses on personal feelings, conflicts, and family-of-origin issues. It is different from personal therapy, because the focus is always on how the issues affect the choices the therapist makes in the room.

triangle of victim, rescuer, and persecutor (Karpman, 1968). Another aspect to this dynamic is that the therapist's sense of being OK is dependent on the patient getting better. If the patient does not get better, the therapist feels that he or she is not OK and begins to feel dysphoric affect. If the therapist cannot manage this on his own, supervision or personal therapy is required. One final aspect of this dynamic is that the patient is replaying his or her own issues of feeling like a victim and wanting to be rescued. However, the dynamic is being played out with the therapist. The therapist gets to feel the helplessness of the patient. Sometimes, if the therapist becomes aware of this dynamic and then works with the patient on it, the situation can correct itself.

3. *The therapist is unprepared to deal with specific existential issues that carry tremendous affective voltage such as "good and evil" that the patient is trying to express.* Patients who have been seriously or sadistically abused have had to cope with horrific crimes. Just listening to these stories can short-circuit the affective system of the unprepared therapist. In addition to the intensity of the stories themselves, highly charged existential questions are often in the background. For instance, "Where was God?" or "What do you do when you have been touched by evil?"

4. *The patient is working on issues that are unresolved sore spots for the therapist.* There is a saying: "We get the patients that we need." This saying refers to the phenomena that we seem to synchronystically attract patients that are relevant for our own life issues. If this is happening for you, then see it as a gift and take the appropriate steps. There are two basic choices. The first is personal therapy. The second is person-of-the-therapist supervision that is specifically aimed at your personal issues and how they are activated in therapy. My personal recommendation is the latter. Intensive supervision that includes these issues tends to be more focused and gets to the point quicker. It can be possible to use the problems that one is having with a patient as an entry point into life issues so that some personal work is actually done. For instance, a therapist could use TFT with the feelings that come up with the patient as well as tracing back the issue to its original source and using TFT with that as well.

5. *The patient is directly challenging the therapist in some way, such as confronting the therapist on a "mistake."* Any emotional reaction to this type of problem is a reflection of the therapist's own issues. It may be your own insecurity. It may be no one ever taught you how to deal with this type of thing as a therapist. If the advice below does not solve the problem and you remain anxious, defensive, or even indignant (e.g., the patient should not be challenging me this way), you need to get

supervision and/or personal therapy. I have rarely ever made a mistake that did not lead to some very good therapy as a result. You must be able to access the holistic self in order to get the most out of these events. If the patient has the moxy to actually confront you on a perceived mistake, you should be congratulating the patient for doing so. Then you should be encouraging the patient to fully explain what you did wrong. As they are doing this, you should be listening for important themes in the patient's life and really trying to understand what you did or did not do that was painful or problematic. How were you not emotionally present? Attempt to resonate with everything the patient is saying about you and imagine that you are in the patient's shoes. You will become aware of something useful.

☐ The Survivor–Therapist

A significant number of therapists who work with trauma (between 30% and 50%) are themselves survivors of physical or sexual abuse. It is important to put this statistic in some type of context. According to Miller (1982), virtually all therapists had emotional trauma in their childhoods. Nobody would be drawn to the profession unless they had some experience with being injured. The fact that a therapist has or does not have a history of abuse is neither good nor bad. It just is. It is what you do with your history that matters. For instance, a history of abuse might make it easier for a person to empathically resonate with a patient. It may make it easier to trust that the patient will come through a certain problem because the therapist has also come through that problem. It may also make it more difficult to stay present in the room because the patient's issues will stir up too much emotional material for the therapist.

Over the years I have noticed that a large percentage of therapists who are survivors of abuse do not talk about this part of their life openly in professional circles. Many people have told me that they are concerned that if their colleagues knew that they were survivors they would be treated in a less desirable manner. To me there is ample evidence within the professional community to justify such concerns. For instance, in professional circles a history of abuse is usually described as a liability to be overcome. It is rarely treated as a potential resource. My point here is that I am concerned that there is a dissociative (either/or) split between the survivor and nonsurvivor aspects of the therapeutic community. This split creates a context that is not helpful for anyone. There is plenty of discourse on the liabilities and pitfalls of one's own abuse for one's work as a therapist. There needs to be more discourse on the positive or resourceful aspects of being a survivor in the role of therapist. Therapists who are survivors should not be invited by the therapist community to feel shame simply because of their history.

If you have a history of abuse and you are working with survivors of trauma and abuse, I would like to suggest that you do the following:

1. Take stock in the resources and strengths that your history gives you in dealing with patients. Who do you have in your life to remind you of, or amplify, these strengths?
2. Take stock in the potential weaknesses and problems your trauma history gives you. What types of problems do you need to be on guard against? Who do you have in your life to help you with these problems?
3. Take stock in how you have been invited by the professional community to feel bad (or good) about your history and to what extent this influences the previous questions. Take some time and write your answers down and meditate on them for a period of time.
4. Based on the results of the above questions, what changes would you make?

☐ Three Tools for Working With the Therapist–Patient Relationship

It is well known that the therapist–patient relationship is a crucial part of treatment. However, it is less well known how to manage the relationship. There is a great deal of information on how to help patients grow. But there is considerably less information on how to help therapists grow. What follows are three different methods to help you either grow as a therapist or manage the therapeutic relationship. These elucidations are not meant to be reified as the truth. They are simply attempts to operationalize what good therapists usually do. I am postulating that the more flexible and creative you are as a therapist, the easier it will be to manage the therapeutic relationship.

The "Countertransference" Question List: A Tool for Checking Yourself

The goal of this list is to give you a series of questions that you can use to check yourself when you are having problems with a patient. To use it most effectively (at least in the beginning), schedule 30–50 minutes for you to go over these questions. Literally write it in your schedule calendar! In answering these questions you want to consider several variables: (a) Your own thinking on the matter. (b) Things the patient has said. Assume they are comments on these questions. With that assumption in mind, does it suggest any answers to you? (c) Things the patient has done in therapy or outside of therapy. Assume they are comments on these questions. With that assumption in mind, does it suggest any answers to you? (d) Specific problems that have occurred in session between you and the patient. What is the pattern? If the pattern could talk, what might it say with regards to these questions? Another way to gather information regarding these issues is through the use of the tool-aligning perceptual positions (see chapter 7). Once you have found some likely problem spots, the next step is to determine what you need to do differently to come back into balance for yourself and for the patient.

1. What is your habitual error? (Everyone has at least one. Are you too active, too passive, etc.?). Have I been making this error?
2. What is your habitual error with this particular patient? Have I been making this error?
3. What is the usual interpersonal pattern (transference/countertransference) between you and this patient?
4. To what extent am I trying to "rescue" the patient?
5. Am I being a witness a sufficient amount of the time?
6. To what extent am I more invested in the patient getting better than he or she is?
7. To what extent am I not keeping the boundaries in the therapy, either too distant and walled off or too close, too soft, and unboundaried.
8. Do I want a goal for the patient that he or she does not actively endorse?
9. To what extent is the patient dealing with issues that are similar to my own issues (especially if those issues stem from your own trauma and abuse)?
10. Have I really explored the previous questions 8 and 9 thoroughly?
11. Have I been having trouble tolerating ambiguity?
12. Have I been too tough (expecting too much too fast) or too enabling (doing for the patient what he needs to be doing for himself, e.g., validating past events)?
13. Am I pushing the therapy too fast (i.e., is the patient not feeling safe? Is it too intense? What stage of treatment are we really in?)?
14. Am I feeling strong emotion (afraid, angry, annoyed, worried) about something that the patient is doing or not doing (e.g., not leaving an abusive situation), talking about, or has done? How is this influencing my behavior? Why am I feeling this? Why am I not centered? How would I be behaving if I were more centered?

15. Am I feeling strong emotions about the abusers? What am I doing with these feelings? How is this influencing my behavior? Why am I not being less judgmental? How would I be behaving if I were more centered?

16. Am I feeling relatively detached, dissociated, numbed, or bored with the patient? What is this about?

17. How am I feeling with this patient?

18. What negative motivations have I been attributing to this patient? What would be a more positive frame?

19. Have I avoided certain topics, actively or simply by not picking up on material the patient is talking about?

20. Is what I am experiencing with this patient at this given moment in time similar to what the patient has talked about in his or her life?

21. Am I feeling de-skilled? If I am at a point where I am lost, have I asked for help? If not, is this a usual pattern for me to not ask for help? If so I definitely need to get some help with my problem of not asking for help.

22. Am I burned out or overworked?

23. Have I focused sufficient attention on building the positive?

24. Have I colluded in helping the patient avoid dealing with his or her feelings, thoughts or actions? This might include:
    • avoiding pointing out the consequences and effects of the patient's acting out (e.g., the patient will not get better with any speed);
    • hanging onto unrealistic wishes, (e.g., one day my abusive parents will love me the way I wanted);
    • blaming themselves in order to avoid dealing with loss and helplessness;
    • avoiding difficult cognitive/affective states or levels of meaning: helplessness, rage, revenge, sadism, evilness, and shame.

25. Think about the patient and focus your attention on your body. What sensations do you feel? Focus more attention on those sensations. What else do you become aware of?

Some Additional Countertransference Questions to Ask If You Are Working with Dissociative Patients

1. Have I been treating each part respectfully and accountably?

2. Have I been asking for guidance from the entire system?

3. Have I held the whole system accountable for problems?

4. Have I been involving parts in an intervention that need to be kept out of the intervention for now?

5. Am I in communication with all of the key alters involved in the

"problem"? A variant on this is, Am I talking to the part in charge of the problematic issue?[3]

6. Have I been attributing positive motivations to parts that do appear to be doing destructive behavior?
7. Have I been favoring certain aspects of the system (e.g., child alters over angry alters)?
8. Have I been assuming that the patient/part actually understands what I am saying in the way that I mean it?
9. Have I not been following the dictum *where "either/or" thinking was, "both/and" thinking shall be*? This is in terms of both the patient and myself.

A Solution-Oriented Decision Tree Model for Correcting Problems in Treatment

This approach differs from the first in several important manners. First, it looks much more at the interaction between the therapist and the patient, rather than just focusing on the therapist. Second, it gives priority to looking for when things have gone well as potential solutions for solving the problematic pattern. You can use this model (see Figure 8.2) to work with a problem situation or to attempt to increase the effectiveness of the treatment.

Recently, I was stuck with a long-term dissociative patient. For a variety of reasons I chose to go with the patient to get a consult. The consult was very effective. One of the key things that came out of the consult was that the patient talked about how safe she had felt with the consultant because he was so firm and directive. What was immediately apparent to me was that the answer to the first question on the solution-oriented decision tree was that things went better with this patient when I had been much more firm and strict. I had not been doing that for some time. So we discussed it. I am once again much more firm and strict. It has made things better.

Solution-Oriented Checklist for Therapist Development

The solution-oriented checklist for therapist development (see Figure 8.3) can help you discover areas in which you have strengths and areas that need development. As you will undoubtedly notice, the questions

---

[3]I am indebted to Dr. Richard Kluft, who pointed out this crucial intervention.

No ↓	Can you identify when things have gone well (a solution pattern)? (Spend some time on this. You should be able to come up with something. If not you have waited far too long to use this approach.)	Yes →	Do more of that. Go to last step
Yes ↓	Can You identify the problem pattern? Can you imagine the relationship from patient's point of view? (Do aligning perceptual positions yourself. (See chapter 7. The other is the patient.)	No →	Consultation with patient or others
No ↓	Does this point of view give you new information about the patient and how your actions are problematic to the patient?	Yes →	Go to *
Yes ↓	Have you consulted with the patient about either when things have gone well/better or about the problem and asked for his/her input or advice?	No →	Do it. Then go down 1 step
Yes ↓	Have you followed the patient's input or advice?	No →	Try their advice
Yes Go to END	Was it helpful?	No →	Go to next step
Yes ↓	Has the patient's advice given you new information?	No →	Consultation
Yes ↓	*With this Information, can you imagine what a solution would look and sound like and feel like?	No →	Consultation. New skill development
Yes ↓	What steps can you take to make that happen? What would support you taking those steps?	None →	Consultation
Yes ↓	Put steps into action. Do they make a difference?	No →	Do something different, go back to previous steps or get consultation
END	Do more of those things. Reflect with self and/or patient about the impact and meaning of those changes. What needs to happen to make you more consistent or more flexible		

Figure 8.2. A solution-oriented decision tree model for correcting problems in treatment.

parallel ideas that I have described in this book. Once you have answered the questions you may notice areas that need improvement. You can then create specific goals for yourself. For example, if you scored a "4" on the item regarding praising the patient for making small steps, write down a specific behavior that would let you know that you were at the level of a "5" and then another goal for "level 6" and so on. Put this list of goals in some place that you would see them regularly (e.g., in your calendar, on

Below are 34 behavior patterns that as a therapist you may or may not do when treating clients who are recovering from trauma. Please rate the occurrence of each item according to the following 0 to 10 scale where 10 = 100% of the time when it is appropriate 5 = 50% of the time when appropriate, 0 = not at all. If you are not sure, just put what feels accurate at this point in time.

Date _____

	0–10			0–10	
1		Able to notice small positive changes even though no large one	19		Can talk with client about the consequences of dysfunctional coping skills without labeling
2		Looks for strengths and resources of client	20		Can give direction and structure to client
3		Can help client focus on angry feelings	21		Able to feel comfortable while feeling angry at abusers
4		Can help client focus on sad feelings	22		Able to feel comfortable while being asked to solve ambiguity
5		Can help client focus on fearful feelings	23		Able to reflect ambiguity back toward client
6		Can help client focus on spiritual feelings	24		Able to feel comfortable dealing with angry/hurtful aspects of client
7		Can help client focus on joyful feelings	25		Able to feel comfortable dealing with childlike aspects of client
8		Can recognize a negative interactional pattern	26		Tolerates constructive criticism from client well
9		Can do something different to change a negative interactional pattern	27		Accepts praise from client well
10		Shows sense of humor when appropriate	28		Believes that the client can live a "good enough" life
11		Can feel "OK" even when client is doing poorly	29		Able to construct positive motivations for symptoms
12		Gives client praise for taking small steps	30		Acknowledges pain and weaknesses of client
13		Can acknowledge that "I" made a mistake	31		Can suspend judgment
14		Can apologize to the client for that mistake	32		Can be forgiving of client's actions and/or problems
15		Able to listen to details of abuse & remain centered & present	33		Can be forgiving of abuser
16		Able to be comfortable while feeling sad or crying with client	34		Can be forgiving of yourself when you make mistakes (as a therapist or in your life)
17		Able to feel comfortable while feeling angry with client			Other
18		Can set limits well			Other

Figure 8.3. Solution-oriented checklist for therapist development.

your desk, on your computer screen). Do not work on too many goals at one time. After a period of time, reassess yourself. Save your previous checklists so you can see your improvement.

When Is It Time to Get a Consult or Supervision?

Frankly, this is probably the most underutilized resource that therapists have. For the most part, if you were even considering the option, that is a sign that you and your patient would benefit from supervision. The problem that is more likely to occur is that the therapist does not realize that he or she could use supervision or at least a consult. It is a good idea to have a colleague who has more experience to act as a supervisor or a consultant. A supervisory relationship is more regularly scheduled. Supervision is important as therapists are learning new skills or moving into new areas of expertise. It is also important if therapists are running into problems on a more regular basis.

There are three types of consultant relationships. A consultant relationship is scheduled on an as-needed basis. The first type of consultation is with the therapist alone. This is essentially a brief, intermittent supervisory relationship on a case-by-case basis. The second type of consult is with the patient alone. This is like a second opinion. The third type of consultation is with the therapist and the patient. A great deal of time may be spent interviewing the patient, or there may be a lot of three-way dialogue. Feedback is given to both the patient and the therapist. It is my opinion that this is by far the most powerful option.

The effects of trauma and abuse increase when people do not have sufficient support systems. It is important that therapists have sufficient resources to help transform the trauma. Supervision and consultation are vital resources for therapists. It is crucial to understand that there is no shame in getting a consult (also known as asking for help). First, it is good modeling for the patient in asking for help. It demonstrates to the patient that you need help from time to time. Second, it does not matter how skilled you are. Sometimes, in intensive therapy, we get to close to the problem. It is often helpful to have a fresh pair of eyes. Third, a consult can act as a minicrisis to break negative patterns that have developed. It makes everyone stop and think a bit. It is far less costly than a hospitalization. It is usually more effective than a change in medication.

Here are some general guidelines for when it is time for a consult:

1. The patient is becoming more dysfunctional in day-to-day living (increased self-harm or suicidality, problems at work, problems raising children, increased acting out) over a period of several weeks. If the therapist can account for these problems and the patient and therapist are working on them within some reasonable parameters, the

need for a consult is less paramount. If the therapist believes that the patient is becoming increasingly dysfunctional because she is in the middle of working through traumatic memories more caution is advised. While dealing with painful abuse can cause regression, too much regression becomes a new problem. It may be that the patient cannot handle the trauma, which would indicate an adjustment toward slowing down. It might also be that the therapist cannot deal with the amount of affect being raised. In this case, supervision is most certainly needed.

2. The therapy is not going anywhere. There is little change in the patient who appears stuck.
3. The therapist feels stuck.
4. The patient is upset with the therapist and it does not appear to be resolving in a reasonable time frame.

☐ Summary

Most of our countertransference mistakes stem from our own anxieties. We are fallible human beings dealing with a difficult situation. It is not a matter of "if our own issues come up." It is a matter of "when our issues come up." Survivors need to be able to face "that what is and that what was" in a resourceful manner. We can do no less. The tools presented in this chapter can help therapists maintain a resourceful therapeutic relationship and keep the therapy on course. On the other hand, if we are looking for the newest tool to "fix" the patient and we find it on our therapeutic "road," then perhaps we need to follow Knopp's (1988) advice and "kill it." Another way to describe the message in this chapter is that it is the person-of-the-therapist himself or herself that is the "tool for healing." The other tools that I have described in this book are merely useful. I have attempted to make them as explicit as possible so that they can be mastered completely. Once these techniques have been learned to such a degree that we do not have to think about them consciously, we can keep ourselves fully present with our patients. In that presence we can witness their pains and sorrows that have deluded our patients into believing that they are unacceptable and unlovable. We, too, must recognize that to the extent we believe the same illusion for ourselves or others, albeit at an unconscious level, we will be less able to help our patients. In all cases we must help each other to remember the truth that we are all lovable and acceptable.

INTEGRATION AND SUMMARY: BEYOND TOOLS AND TRAUMA

As clinicians we carry around our toolbag. A significant part of this book has been to expand the number of tools in the bag and provide a rationale for their use. In addition to describing the different tools in detail, I have provided guidelines about how to use these tools during the different phases of trauma treatment. Certainly, there are more tools than those described in this book that can be of use to people who have been traumatized. The reader is encouraged to practice and learn the tools in this book as well as other tools. Furthermore, I have attempted to place these tools within a systemic framework that included looking at the role of the therapist in the process of treatment.

I have saved one last tool until now. This tool requires no action. It has no steps. It does not even "work" in the usual meaning given to the idea that a tool works. The tool is a belief and awareness. It is simply this. When we work with people who come to us for help, we must keep in our awareness that there is nothing wrong with this person. We must keep in our awareness that this person is a perfect child of God. The only problem this person has is that he or she believes that there is something wrong with them. To put it another way, the patient believes that he or she is defined or limited by trauma. This is of course an illusion. It is an illusion that we share about ourselves as well. We are all more than we think we are.

How do you use this "tool"? The first thing you do is just keep this awareness present in your mind. It will do two things. It will help you not become hypnotized and disheartened by the negative hypnosis of the patient's story about her own "damagedness." Second, and more importantly, when you see the person in front of you as being completely "OK," it will help move that person to a place where she comes to believe that she is completely OK. It may not happen instantly, but she will get there quicker than if you see her as damaged. The only reason she does not believe it immediately is because she does not want to take the chance to believe it. Letting go of her old belief system is too scary. Third, you may even share this point of view with your patient explicitly. If you do, you do not do it to change her mind about her illusory belief. Any intention of helping a person change actually implies that there is something wrong with the person. So if you choose to share this idea, then you need to do it with the intention of simply sharing a vision, or offering an invitation to see this vision. From a hypnotic perspective the suggestion is as follows:

> At the moment your conscious mind believes that you are damaged and that you are limited. But at a deeper level, your unconscious mind knows that there is more to you than the effects of this trauma. Your conscious mind may think that you have lost yourself, but your unconscious mind knows that this is a temporary state of affairs. I know that for now you are not going to believe me when I tell you that you are more than who you think you are. I know that at this moment in time it would be very hard for you to believe all the way inside that you are lovable and deserving of every good thing. Nevertheless, this is the absolute truth, and even if you do not see it, consciously or even at somewhat of an unconscious level, I see it and your soul knows it. So we will continue to work together. And gradually the truth of these statements will be revealed to you. The speed at which it will be revealed to you is directly proportional to the degree that you want to believe it. You need to be open to believing it. You do not see the plant growing underground from the seed. It may take some time for the sprout to force its way out from the heavy soil. But all the while it is growing underground. Then, when you least expect it, it becomes a reality.

Fourth, even when you use the tools of change described in the preceding chapters, you continue to hold the idea that there is nothing wrong or broken about the patient. Finally there is a fifth course of action. The therapist can use energy work to strengthen this belief (see Durlacher, 1994; and/or Gallo, 2000). The purpose of the tools is to generate an experience in which the patient has an opportunity to experience something different that may help him or her wake up to the fact that there is nothing wrong with him or her. The tools also help wake the therapist up from thinking or believing negatively.

☐ DID as a Microcosm of a Global Illusion

Back in chapter 6, I raised the issue that DID is the perfect metaphor for the problems that we are having on a global level. The human species lives in a dissociative state, believing that we are separate from each other. From a humanistic perspective it is clear that we are either going to survive and thrive as a single planet or be doomed to conflict and war. From the spiritual perspective described in *A Course in Miracles* (Foundation for Inner Peace, 1975) and even the Jewish Mystical Kabbalah, the illusion we all live in is even greater. From this perspective, there is only one mind. Our illusion of separateness makes all the problems of the world possible. Is this not precisely the issue that MPD/DID clients must confront? The alters of a dissociative client fight like crazy to maintain their separateness for fear of death. Is this not the same illusion that we are so different from other countries and cultures?

So, when we are working with people to help them integrate the disowned aspects of themselves, let us remember that we have our own work to do as well. Let us remember that perhaps the work these "patients" are doing is a preamble to the work that we all must do.

EPILOGUE: TOOLS FOR TRANSFORMING TERRORISM[1]

The goal of terrorism is not to destroy property or harm people. These things happen, but they are a means to achieving the goal. The goal of terrorism is to disconnect people from resourceful positive states of consciousness and to connect them instead to non-resourceful fearful states of consciousness. As fear grips a person he or she tends to withdraw from life, avoid activities and other people. This further disconnects a person from resourceful SoCs. Terrorists engage in these activities to achieve some sort of political goal (at least that is the story). In a terrorist incident there are two factors that increase the probability that a person will develop PTSD. The first is the perceived likelihood of death or serious bodily harm (Kilpatrick et al., 1989). The second is the fact that the incident was man made with a harmful intent (Peterson, Prout, & Schwarz, 1991). One factor that may help to mitigate the probability of PTSD is the fact that the event was experienced by a community and that community can respond as a whole (Quarantelli, 1985).

After a terrorist incident the people who were directly involved, who become symptomatic can be treated with many of the tools in this book such as trauma reassociative conditioning, thought field therapy as well as other approaches, such as EMDR. Obviously families who have lost loved ones require many different levels of support. The people who are directly affected need to be treated similarly to other victims of violence such as crime and war.

I want to direct most of the comments in this section to all of the people who are more indirectly influenced by terrorism or the threat of it. I want to focus attention on the community response to terrorism

---

[1]This chapter was written in response to the events that occurred after September 11, 2001. It is not meant to be by any means an exhaustive review of the literature. I had only a brief amount of time to write this due to the publishing schedule of the book. Nevertheless I felt it was important to start to say something of use for therapists who may need to be dealing with this phenomenon.

including how therapists can treat and/or support the vast majority of the population who were not directly involved, but who rapidly become affected due to the immediate flow of information in our culture. In virtually every case of trauma related fear and anxiety with whom I worked after the September 11th attack on the World Trade Center and the anthrax attack that followed, the person was almost obsessively watching television. Not only was the person watching television a great deal, the person watched TV in a very specific manner. It was as if the person turned off every filtering mechanism they had and was just trying to absorb meaning and understanding from the TV. They had questions and were looking for answers. Instead of going to the good parent, the rabbi, the minister or whomever, the person went to trustworthy news anchor-person. The problem is that the person takes in whole all of the fear based images and messages without even being aware of them or attempting to process them. This process appears to be similar to van der Kolk's (1996c) ideas about traumatic memories being stored visually in eidetic store rather than verbally processed. These images then continue to assert influence on the brain.

The news media have great difficulty resisting the temptation to sensationalize. The sensationalism is created through sound bites and visual pictures. Sound bites are designed to go in whole and uncritically digested. Visual images are designed to be emotionally evocative. In fact these images are often used as a "background" for the print and the story. Since they are background the person watching is less likely to screen out its impact. In fact these images are not unlike Erickson's interspersal technique (1980c). In one example of this technique Erickson would tell a story about a tomato plant to a pain patient. He would talk about how the tomato plant could *rest comfortably* in the ground. The words in italics were suggestions interspersed throughout the dialogue. Erickson pointed out that the patient is looking for help from the hypnotist. It is the placing of the hypnotist in the position of power that makes the patient particularly susceptible to this type of suggestion that bypasses most conscious control. Unfortunately this is a very similar relationship that many people have with news sources. People are looking toward these outlets for help and meaning. They leave themselves open for influence. Let me give several examples from the anthrax scare the followed the WTC bombing. On one local news program they were doing a story on anthrax. The announcer was describing the events of the day including comments about how people should remain calm. However, the background graphic included a very large skull and cross bones in dark green and blackish shades. It was a strong fear-evoking image. So the person watching starts to unconsciously react to the image. Then the announcer says to remain calm. Now the person watching begins to feel worse about himself because he is failing at remaining calm. Another example was a *US News and World* cover story of all this mail in a vortex that was reminiscent of Hitchcock's *Vertigo*. The image alone could make you a bit dizzy. Then there were the words on top of the image "DEATH BY MAIL." One of my patients who both works with trauma and is herself a trauma survivor commented on the fact that the news media was simply engaging in the same trauma re-enactment that individual patients engage in. The main difference is that the news media have the ability to influence a much larger audience than individual patients.

The first intervention with individual's who are becoming increasingly fearful after a terrorist event is to educate that person about what is happening (Schwarz & Prout, 1991) and to get them to turn off the TV. A second intervention is to help individuals remain in resourceful SoCs when they engage the media. Therapists can educate people that while it is common and normal to be fearful after a traumatic event, it is not required. People can learn to take control of their own experience. This can take a number of forms. All of these forms include maintaining some type of boundary between themselves and the media. Individuals can use the bubble technique described in chapter 4. They can be helped to remain active and become aware of fear evoking images and be able to verbally name it (e.g., "Look at that scary skull and cross bones in the back ground") and choose to reject its influence (e.g., "It is just a scary graphic that some art director thought would capture my attention . . . I am not going to react to that.) A third intervention would be to use TRC or TFT on the news-watching event or on the experience of thinking about the terrorist event. A fourth intervention is to allow people to talk about their concerns and worries. This is particularly important in group-settings such as middle schools, high schools, and colleges. Unfortunately, there is often a temptation to go into denial and numbing. Administrators and teachers are often ill prepared to handle these types of events. They themselves may be traumatized. They do not want to make things worse for themselves or their charges. This strategy usually makes things worse. Talking about what is happening helps to provide mastery of the experience. The only caveat here is that leaders of these groups need to prevent a contagion of fear by providing sufficient structure, information and guidance. It is not a good idea to just let people talk about their worst fears. It is important to begin to guide people towards some method of coping. For instance, asking people to compare and contrast the different ways they can choose to react to events is a crucial question. This intervention was discussed in chapter 7. Fear based responses such as avoidance and withdrawal will be raised. It is vital to help people understand the consequences of avoiding and withdrawing from life. First it does not really help reduce fear or increase mastery. In fact it tends to reinforce fear and undermine mastery. People need support in adjusting to the somewhat increased level of risk in a reasoned fashion. For instance, the real level of increased risk from an anthrax letter when compared to all of the other potential dangers in life was actually negligible for the population at large. You would never have guessed this from the level of near panic that was being reported. Therapists, doctors and others need to provide real data for people so they are less susceptible to fear.

Another group method would be a modification of the tool "Yes, and" (see chapter 7). The group can be asked to acknowledge the negative event that has happened and then each person can be asked to think of several things that are positive in his or her life. These can then be shared as a group. Common themes can be developed for the positive resources. The actual technique can be done with the individuals in the group setting. The goal in this approach is to help people stay connected to their resources while they also acknowledge the trauma.

When children are younger, my opinion is that it is more important to shield them from these events than it is to have them talk about it. Obviously in directly effected communities this would be impossible. In certain parts of the world such as Israel this may also be difficult. But where it is possible, I see little benefit of forcing younger children to face the difficulties the world. In many instances the only reason that a child is becoming overly aware of a terrorist incident is the parents or other adults are not sufficiently containing their own affect that it spills over into the children. Young children should not be allowed to see trauma-based pictures that are played over and over on the news. To the extent that a child has been exposed to the stories of what is happening the child needs to be reassured that they will be protected.

An intervention on a larger social level is for therapists to be voices in the community to advocate that the news media and other community leaders have an important responsibility to help the community remain or return to a resourceful SoC. I have already mentioned the need not to pander to the lowest common denominator of fear. As mentioned in chapter 7 the need to cultivate a resourceful life is paramount on a community wide level. People appear to naturally understand this. The desire to volunteer to provide help and assistance is one of the best ways to combat helplessness and resourcelessness and disconnection. On a community level the important phases of intervention are phases 1 and 3 of trauma treatment. Our leaders have to provide a sense of safety by resisting the temptation to overreact and sensationalize. Our leaders need to support the sense of connectedness to each other. Within a social context of connectedness and a sense of control and safety people can naturally process what they need to with or without the help of professionals.

Finally, if we are to stop trauma and violence throughout the world, we will need to recognize that we cannot continue to live in the black and white world of the so called "good guys" and the so called "evil doers." This does not work for treating individual people and it certainly does not work on a global level. Every major spiritual practice advises the same solution. This cannot be an accident. Just like the individual patient with DID, we need to look at the long-term consequences of the choices and beliefs that we have. We are one world and we are one. Continuing to pretend otherwise is folly.

REFERENCES

American Psychiatric Association. (1980). *Diagnostic and statistical manual* (3rd ed.). Washington, DC: Author.

American Psychiatric Association. (1994). *Diagnostic and statistical manual* (4th ed.). Washington, DC: Author.

Bandler, R., & MacDonald, W. (1988). *An insider's guide to sub-modalites.* Cupertino, CA: Meta Publications.

Barrett, M. J. (1994, November). *Working with families when the issue of false memories has been raised.* Presented at the 3rd Annual Conference on Advances in Treating Survivors of Abuse. Baltimore, MD: Audio Cassette # G250-25AB available from Infomedix: 1-800-367-9286.

Beahrs, J.O. (1982). *Unity and multiplicity.* New York: Brunner/Mazel.

Becker, R., & Selden, G. (1985). *The body electric.* New York: Morrow.

Berne, E. (1972). *What do you say after you say hello.* New York: Grove Press.

Berne, E. (1977). *Intuition and ego states: The origins of transactional analysis.* San Francisco: TA Press.

Bernstein, E. M., & Putnam F. W. (1986). Development reliability and validity of a dissociation scale. *Journal of Nervous and Mental Disease, 174,* 727–735.

Blanchard, K., & Johnson, S. (1982). *The one minute manager.* New York: William Morrow.

Bloom, S. (1997). *Creating sanctury: Toward the evolution of sane societies.* London: Routledge.

Bohm, D. (1980). *Wholeness and implicate order.* London: Routledge & Keegan Paul.

Bradshaw, J. (1992). *Homecoming: Reclaiming and championing your inner child.* New York: Doubleday.

Briere, J., N. (1988). Long term clinical correlates of childhood sexual victimizaiton. *Annals of the New York Academy of Sciences, 528,* 327–334.

Briere, J., N. (1992). *Child abuse trauma: Theory and treatment of the lasting effects.* Thousand Oaks, CA: Sage.

Briere, J., & Conte, J. (1993). Self-reported amnesia for abuse in adults molested as children. *Journal of Traumatic Stress, 6,* 21–31.

Brown, D. P., Scheflin, A. W., & Hammnond, D. C. (1998). *Memory, treatment and the law.* New York: Norton.

Burgess, A. W., Hartmann, C. R., & Baker, T. (1995). Memory representations of childhood sexual abuse. *Journal of Psychosocial Nursing, 33*(9), 9–16.

Burgess, A. W., Hartmann, C. R., & McCormick, A. (1987). Abused to abuser: Antecedents of socially deviant behavior. *American Journal of Psychiatry, 144,* 1431–1436.

Callahan, R., & Perry, P. (1991). *Why do I eat when I am not hungry?* New York: Double Day.

Callhan, R. (1981). Psychological reversal. In *Collected papers of the International College of Applied Kineseology.*

Calof, D. (1993a). An interview with Pamela Freyd, co founder & executive director, the False Memory Syndrome Foundation Part I. *Treating Abuse Today: The International Newsjournal of Abuse Survivorsship and Therapy, 3*(3), 26–33.

Calof, D. (1993b). An interview with Pamela Freyd, co founder & executive director, the False Memory Syndrome Foundation Part II. *Treating Abuse Today: The International Newsjournal of Abuse Survivorsship and Therapy, 3*(4), 26–33.

Calof, D. (1994a). From traumatic dissociation to repression: Historical origins of the "false memory syndrome" hypothesis. *Treating Abuse Today: The International Newsjournal of Abuse Survivorsship and Therapy, 4*(4), 24–37.

Calof, D. (1994b). An interview with Michael Yapko, PhD Part I. *Treating Abuse Today: The International Newsjournal of Abuse Survivorsship and Therapy, 4*(6), 21–40.

Calof, D. (1994c). An interview with Michael Yapko, PhD Part II. *Treating Abuse Today: The International Newsjournal of Abuse Survivorsship and Therapy, 4*(5), 33–44.

Calof, D. F. (1995a) Chronic self-injury in adult survivors of abuse: Sources, motivations and functions of self injury (Part 1). *Treating Abuse Today, 5*(3), 11–17.

Calof, D. (1995b, March). *Compassionate alternatives to direct validation of memories.* Presented at the 3rd Annual Conference on Advances in Treating Survivors of Abuse. Audio Cassette # H129 available from Info-medix: 1-800-367-9286.

Calof, D. L., & Schwarz, R.A (1994, March). *Indirect suggestion, unwitting therapist influence & other iatrogenic issues in trauma work.* Presented at Advances in Treating Survivors of Sexaul Abuse: Empowering the Healing Process II. Audiotape available from Info-medix: 1-800-367-9286.

Cheek, D., & Lecron, L. (1968). *Clincal hypnotherapy.* New York: Grune & Stratton.

Cho, Z. H., Chung, S. C., Jones, J. P., Park, J. B., Park, H. J., Lee, H. J., Wong, E. K., & Min, B. (1998). New findings of the correlation between acupoints and corresponding brain cortices using functional MRI. *Proceedings of the National Academy of Sciences, 95,* pp. 2670–2673.

Coustois, C. A. (1988). *Healing the incest wound.* New York: W. W. Norton.

Covey, S. R. (1990). *The 7 habits of highly effective people.* New York: Fireside.

Danieli, Y. (1985) The treatment and prevention of long-term effects and intergenerational transmission of victimization. In C. R. Figley (Ed.), *Trauma and its wake: The study and treatment of posttraumatic stress disorder.* New York: Brunner/Mazel.

deMause, L. (1991) The universality of incest. *Journal of Psychohistory, 19*(2), 1–21.

de Shazer, S. (1985). *Keys to solution in brief therapy.* New York: Norton

de Shazer, S. (1988). *Clues: Investigating solutions in brief therapy.* New York: Norton.

Diamond, J. (1980a). *Life energy.* New York: Dodd, Mead & Co.

Diamond, J. (1980b). *Your body does not lie.* New York: Warner Books.

Dilts, R. (1980). *Neuro linguistic programming.* Cupertino, CA: Meta Publications.

Dilts, R. (1990). *Changing belief systems with NLP.* Cupertino, CA: Meta Publications.

Dolan, Y. M. (1991). *Resolving sexual abuse: Solution focused therapy and Ericksonian hypnosis for adult survivors.* New York: Norton.

Dolan, Y. M. (1998). *One small step: Moving beyond trauma and therapy to a life of joy.* Watsonville, CA: Papier-Mache Press.

Dollard, J., & Miller, N. E. (1950). *Personality and psychotherapy.* New York: McGraw Hill.

Durlacher, J. V. (1994). *Freedom from fear forever.* Tempe, AZ: Van Ness.

Durrant, M., & White, C. (1990). *Ideas for therapy of sexual abuse.* Adelaide, Australia: Dulwhich Centre Publications.

Epstein, S. (1990). Beliefs and symptoms in maladaptive resolutions of the traumatic neurosis. In D. Ozer, J. M. Healy, & A. J. Stewart (Eds.), *Perspectives on personality, Vol. 3.* London: Jessica Kingsley Publishers.

Epston, D. (1988). *Collected papers.* Adelaide, Australia: Dulwhich Centre Publications.

Epston, D., & White, M. (1992). *Experience contradiction narrative & imagination: Selected papers of David Epston and Michael White*. Adelaide, Australia: Dulwhich Centre Publications.

Erickson, M. H. (1980a). *The collected papers of Milton H. Erickson on hypnosis* (E. L. Rossi, Ed.). New York: Irvington.

Erickson, M. H. (1980b). Deep hypnosis and its induction. In E. L. Rossi (Ed.), *The collected papers of Milton H. Erickson on hypnosis* (vol. 1, pp. 139–167). New York: Irvington. (Original work published 1952)

Erickson, M. H. (1980c). Further clinical techniques of hypnosis: Utilization techniques 4. In E. L. Rossi (Ed.), *The collected papers of Milton H. Erickson on hypnosis* (vol. 1, pp. 177–205). New York: Irvington. (Original work published 1959)

Erickson, M. H. (1980d). The interspersal hypnotic technique for symptom correction and pain control. In E. L. Rossi (Ed.), *The collected papers of Milton H. Erickson on hypnosis* (vol. 4, pp. 262–278). New York: Irvington. (Original work published 1967)

Erickson, M. H. (1980e). Pseudo-orientation in time as a hypnotherapeutic procedure. In E. L. Rossi (Ed.), *The collected papers of Milton H. Erickson on hypnosis* (vol. IV, pp. 397–423). New York: Irvington. (Original work published 1954)

Erickson, M. H., & Rossi, E. L. (1979). *Hypnotherapy: An exploratory casebook*. New York: Irvington.

Erickson, M. H., Rossi, E. L., & Rossi, S. I. (1976). *Hypnotic realities: The induction of clinical hypnosis and forms of indirect suggestion*. New York: Irvington.

Figley, C. R., & Carbonell, J. (1995). *The "Active ingredient" project: The systematic clinical demonstration of the most efficient treatments of PTSD, a research plan*. Tallahassee: Florida State University Psychosocial Stress Research Program and Clinical Laboratory.

Figley, C. R. (Ed.). (1985). *Trauma and its wake: The study and treatment of posttraumatic stress disorder*. New York: Brunner/Mazel.

Fine, C. (1990). The cognitive sequelae of incest. In R. O. Kluft (Ed.), *Incest-related syndromes of adult psychopathology* (pp. 85–109). Washington, DC: American Psychiatric Press.

Foundation for Inner Peace. (1975). *A course in miracles*. New York: Viking.

Foundation for Inner Peace. (1996). *Supplements to a course in miracles*. New York: Viking.

Frankle, V. (1990). *Keynote address at the Second Evolution of Psychotherapy Conference*. Phoenix, AZ: The Milton H. Erickson Foundation.

Freedman, J., & Combs, G. (1996). *Narrative therapy: The social construction of preferred realities*. New York: Norton.

Furman, F., & Gallo, F. (2000). *The neurophysics of human behavior: Explorations at the interface of the brain, mind, behavior, and information*. New York: CRC Press

Gallo, F. (1999). *Energy psychology*. New York: CRC Press.

Gallo, F. (2000). *Energy diagnostic and treatment methods*. Norton: New York

Gilligan, S. (1987). *Therapeutic trances: The cooperation principle in Ericksonian hypnotherapy*. New York: Brunner/Mazel.

Gilligan, S. (1997). *The courage to love: Principles and practices of self-relations psychotherapy*. New York: Norton.

Glass, J. M. (1993). *Shattered selves: Multiple personality in a postmodern world*. Ithaca, NY: Cornell University Press.

Goulding, M. M., & Goulding, R. L. (1979). *Changing lives through redecision therapy*. New York: Brunner/Mazel.

Gray, J. (1992). *Men are from mars, women are from venus*. New York: HarperCollins.

Gray, J. (1999). *Having what you want and wanting what you have*. New York: HarperCollins.

Green, B. L., Wilson, J. P., & Lindy, J. D. (1985). Conceptualizing post traumatic stress disorder: A psychosocialframework. In C. R. Figley (Ed.), *Trauma and its wake: The study and treatment of posttraumatic stress disorder* (pp. 53–69). New York: Brunner/Mazel.

Grove, D. R. (1993). Ericksonian therapy with multiple personality clients. *Journal of Family Psychotherapy, 4*(2), 13–18.

Hall, E. T. (1990). *The hidden dimension.* New York: Anchor Press

Hammond, D. C. (Ed.). (1990). *Handbook of hypnotic suggestions and metaphors.* New York: Norton.

Hammond, C. D. (1995). *Clinical hypnosis and memory: Guidelines for clinicians and for forensic hypnosis.* ASCH Committee on Hypnosis & Memory. Des Plaines, IL: Asch Press.

Hammond, D. C., & Cheek, D. B. (1988). Ideomotor signaling: A method for rapid unconscious exploration. In D. C. Hammond (Ed.), *Hypnotic induction and suggestion: An introductory manual* (pp. 90–97). Des Plaines, IL: American Society of Clinical Hypnosis.

Hawkins, D. (1995). *Power versus force.* Sedona, AZ: Veritas Publishing.

Herman, J. L. (1992). *Trauma and recovery: The aftermanth of violence-from domestic abuse to political terror.* New York: Basic.

Herman, J. L., Perry, J. C., & van der Kolk, B. A. (1989). Childhood trauma in borderline personality disorder. *American Journal of Psychiatry, 146,* 490–495.

Herman, J. L., & Schatzow, E. (1987). Recovery & verification of memories of childhood sexual trauma. *Psychoanalytic Psychology, 4*(1), 1–14.

Herman, J. L., & van der Kolk, B. A (1987). Traumatic origins of borderline personality disorder. In B. A. van der Kolk (Ed), *Psychological trauma* (pp. 116–126). Washington, DC: APA Press.

Horowitz, M. J. (1973). *Stress response syndromes.* New York: Jason Aronson

Horowitz, M. J. (1986). *Stress response syndromes* (2nd ed.). New York: Jason Aronson.

Hoyt, M. F. (1996a). Postmodernism, the relational self, constructive therapies, and beyond: A conversation with Kenneth Gergen in M. F. Hoyt (Ed.), *Constructive therapies, Volume 2* (pp. 87–123). New York: Guilford.

Hoyt, M. F. (1996b). Welcome to possibilityland: A conversation with Bill O'Hanlon. In M. F. Hoyt (Ed.), *Constructive therapies, Volume 2* (pp. 87–123). New York: Guilford.

James, T., & Woodsmall, W. (1988). *Time line therapy and the basis of personality.* Cupertino, CA: Meta Publications.

Janet, P. (1889). *L'automatisme psychologique.* Paris. Alcan.

Janet, P. (1919). *Psychological healing. Vol 1.* New York: Macmillan.

Janoff-Bulman, R. (1985). The aftermath of victimization: Rebuilding shattered assumption. In C. R. Figley (Ed.), *Trauma and its wake: The study and treatment of posttraumatic stress disorder.* New York: Brunner/Mazel.

Janoff-Bulman, R. (1992). *Shattered assumptions: Towards a new psychology of trauma.* New York: The Free Press.

Jenkins, A. (1990). *Invitations to responsibility: The therapeutic engagement of men who are violent and abusive.* Adelaide, Australia: Dulwhich Centre Publications.

Karpman, S. B. (1968). Fairy tales and script drama analysis. *Transactional Analysis Bulletin, 7*(26), 39–43.

Kilpatrick, D. G., Saunders, B. E., Amick-McMullan, A., Best, C. L., Veronen, L. J., & Resnick, H. S. (1989). Victims and crime factors associated with the development of crime related post-traumatic stress disorder. *Behavior Therapy, 20,* 199–214.

Knopp, S. H. (1988). *If you meet the Buddha on the road, kill him.* New York: Bantam Books.

Kluft, R. P. (1984). Treatment of multiple personality disorder: A study of 33 cases. *Psychiatric Clinics of North America, 7*(1),9–29.

Kluft, R. P. (1990a). The fractionated abreaction technique. In D. C. Hammond (Ed.), *The handbook of hypnotic suggestions and metaphors.* New York: Norton.

Kluft, R. P (Ed). (1990b) *Incest-related syndromes of adult psychopathology.* Washington, DC: American Psychiatric Press.

Kluft, R. P. (1991). Clinical presentation of multiple personality disorder. In R. L. Lowenstein (Ed.), *Psychiatric clinics of North America—Multiple personality disorder, 14*(3), 605–630.

Kluft, R. P. (1994). Treatment trajectories in multiple personality disorder. *Dissociation, 7*(1), 63–76.

Lankton, S. R. (1985). A state of consciousness model of Ericksonian hypnosis. In S. R. Lankton (Ed.), *Ericksonian monographs Vol. 1. Elements and dimensions of an Ericksonian approach,* 26–41.

Lankton, S. R., & Lankton, C. (1983). *The answer within: A clinical framework of Ericksonian hypnotherapy.* New York: Bruner/Mazel.

Lankton, S. R., & Lankton C. (1987). *Enchantment and intervention.* New York: Brunner/Mazel.

LeGuin, U. K. (1991). *A wizard of earthsea.* New York: Atheneum Press.

Linehan, M. M. (1983a). *Cognitive-behavioral treatment of borderline personality disorder.* San Francisco: Guilford.

Linehan, M. M. (1983b). *Skills training manual for treating borderline personality disorder.* San Francisco: Guilford.

Litz, T. L., & Weathers, F. W. (1994). The diagnosis and assessment of post-traumatic stress disorder in adults. In M. B. Williams & J. F. Sommer (Eds.), *Handbook of post traumatic therapy.* Westport, CT: Greenwood Press.

Loftus, E. F. (1975). Leading questions and the eyewitness report. *Cognitive Psychology, 7,* 560–572.

Loftus, E. F. (1993). The reality of repressed memories. *American Psychologist, 48*(5), 518–537.

Loftus, E., & Ketchum, K. (1994). *The myth of repressed memory: False memories and allegations of sexual abuse.* New York: St Martin's Press.

Loftus, E. F., Polonsky, S., & Fullilove, M. T. (1994). Memories of childhood sexual abuse: Remembering and repressing. *Psychology of Women Quarterly, 18,* 67–84.

Loftus, E., & Zanni, G. (1975). Eyewitness testimony: The influence of wording of a question. *Bulletin of the Psychonomic Society, 5,* 86–88.

Lynn, S. J., Milano, M., & Weeks, J. R. (1991). Hypnosis and pseudo-memories. *Journal of Personality & Social Psychology, 60*(2), 318–326.

Maltz, W. (1992). *The sexual healing journey: A guide for survivors of sexual abuse.* New York: Harper.

Maslow, A. H. (1970). *Religions, values and peak experiences.* New York: Penguin.

McCann, I. L., & Pearlman, L. A. (1990). *Psychological trauma and the adult survivor: Theory therapy and transformation.* New York: Brunner/Mazel.

McCann, T. E., & Sheehan, P. W. (1988). Hypnotically induced pseudomemories—sampling their conditions among hypnotizable subjects. *Journal of Personality & Social Psychology, 54*(2), 339–346.

McConkey, K., Labelle, L., Bibb, B., & Bryant, R. (1990). Hypnosis and suggested pseudomemory. The relevance of test contest. *Australian Journal of Psychology, 42,* 197–206.

McConkey, K., & Sheehan, P. (1980). Inconsistency in hypnotic age regression and cue structure as supplied by the hypnotist. *International Journal of Clinical and Experimental Hypnosis, 28,* 394–408.

Miller, A. (1981). *Prisoners of childhood.* New York: Basic Books. (Reissued in paperback as *The drama of the gifted child.* Basic Books: New York.)

Murrey, G. J. Cross, H. J., & Whipple, J. (1992). Hypnotically create pseudo-memories: Further investigations into the "memory distortion or response Bias" question. *Journal of Abnormal Psychology, 101*(1), 75–77.

Nathanson, D. (1994). *Shame and pride: Affect, sex, and the birth of the self.* New York: Norton.

Ochberg, F. M. (Ed.). (1988). *Post-traumatic therapy and victims of violence.* New York: Brunner/ Mazel.

Ofshe, R. (1992). Inadvertent hypnosis during interrogation: False confession due to dissociative state, misidentified multiple personality, and the satanic cult hypothesis. *International Journal of Clinical and Experimental Hypnosis, 40,* 125–156.

O'Hanlon, W. H., & Weiner-Davis, M. (1989). *In search of solutions: A new direction in psychotherapy.* New York: Norton.

Orne, M. T. (1969). Demand characteristics and the concept of quasi-controls. In R. Rosenthal & R. l. Rosnow (Eds), *Artifacts in Behavioral Research.* New York: Academic Press.

Pare, D., & Tavano, N. (1996). Mining for intent: Bringing forward values with sexual abuse perpetrators and victims in a family context. *Therapeutic Conversations 3* (June 27). Sponsored by the Institute for Advanced Clinical Training, Boulder, CO.

Peterson, C., Prout, M., & Schwarz, R. (1991). *Post-traumatic stress disorder: A clinicians guidebook.* New York: Plennum Press.

Phillips, M., & Frederick, C. (1995). *Healing the divided self: Clinical and Ericksonian hypnotherapy for post-traumatic and dissociative conditions.* New York: Norton.

Piaget, J. (1962). *Play dreams and imitation in childhood.* New York: Norton.

Premack, D. (1976). *Intelligence in ape and man.* New York: Erlbaum.

Putnam, F. W. (1989). *Diagnosis and treatment of multiple personality disorder.* New York: Guilford.

Pynoos, R. S., Frederick, C. J., Nader, K., Arroyo, W., Steimberg, A., Nunez, F., & Fairbanks, I. (1987). Life threat and posttraumatic stress in school age children. *Archives of General Psychiatry, 44,* 1057–1063.

Quarantelli, E. L. (1985) An assessment of conflicting views on mental health: Consequences of traumatic events. In C. R. Figley (Ed.), *Trauma and its wake.* New York Brunner/Mazel.

Ross, C. A. (1989). *Multiple personality disorder: Diagnosis, clinical features and .treatment.* New York: Wiley.

Ross, C. A. (1992). *Keynote address presented at the Third Eastern Regional Conference on Abuse and Multiple Personality.* Alexandria, VA.

Ross, C. A. (1995). *Satanic ritual abuse: Principles of treatment.* Toronto: University of Toronto Press.

Rossi, E. L., & Check, O. B. (1988). *Mind-body therapies: Idedynamic healing in hypnosis.* New York: Norton.

Sacerdote, P. (1977). Applications of hypnotically elicited mystical sates to the treatment of physical and emotional pain. *International Journal of Clinical and Experimental Hypnosis, 25*(4), 309–324.

Salter, A. C. (1995). *Transforming trauma.* Thousand Oaks, CA: Sage.

Schwarz, R. A. (1994). Hypnotic approaches in treating PTSD: An Ericksonian framework. In M. B. Williams & J. F. Sommer (Eds.), *The handbook of post traumatic stress* (pp. 401–417). Westport, CT: Greenwood Press.

Schwarz, R. A. (1995). Clinical treatment strategies to reduce distortions of memory and action in trauma work. *Innovations in clinical practice, Vol. 14.* Sarasota, FL: Professional Resource Press.

Schwarz, R. A. (1998). From "either-or" to "both-and": Collaborative approaches to treating dissociative disorders. In M. Hoyt (Ed), *Constructive therapies 3.* San Francisco: Guilford.

Schwarz, R. A., & Calof, D. (1994, March). *Indirect suggestion, unwitting therapist influence & other iatrogenic issues in trauma work.* Presented at Advances in Treating Survivors of Sexaul Abuse: Empowering the Healing Process II. Available from Info-medix: 1-800-367-9286.

Schwarz, R. A., & Dolan, Y. (1995). *Strategies of successful thrivors.* Unpublished manuscript.

Schwarz, R. A., & Prout, M. F. (1991). Integrative approaches in the treatment of post-traumatic stress disorder. *Psychotherapy, 28,* 364–372.

Schwarz, R. A., & Gilligan, S. (1995, March/April). The devils is in the details: A review of *The myth of repressed memory: False memories and allegations of sexual abuse, suggestions of abuse: True and false memories of childhood sexual trauma, unchained memories: True stories of traumatic memories lost and found. Family Therapy Networker,* 21–23.

Scurfield, R. (1985). Post trauma stess assessment and treatment: Overview and formulations. In C. R. Figley (Ed.), *Trauma and its wake: The study and treatment of posttraumatic stress disorder.* New York: Brunner/Mazel.

Shapiro, F. (1995). *Eye movement desensitization and reprocessing: Basic principles, protocols and practices.* New York: Guilford.

Sheldrake, R. (1981). *A new science of life.* ??????, VT: Park Street Press.

Sheldrake, R. (1989). *The presence of the past.* New York: Vintage.

Shor, R. E. (1959). Hypnosis and the concept of the generalized reality orientation. *American Journal of Psychotherapy, 13,* 582–602.

Spiegel, D., & McHugh, P. (1995). The pros and cons of dissociative identity (multiple personality) disorder. *Journal of Practical Psychiatry and Behavioral Health, 1*(13), 158–166.

Tart, C. T. (1975). *States of consciousness.* New York: Dutton.

Terr, L. (1994). *Unchained memories: True stories of traumatic memories lost and found.* New York: Basic Books.

Trepper, T. S., & Barrett, M. J. (1989). *Systemic treatment of incest.* New York: Brunner/Mazel.

van der Kolk, B. A. (1988). *Psychological trauma.* Washington, DC: APA Press.

van der Kolk, B. A. (1989). The compulsion to repeat trauma: Revictimization, attachment and masochism. *Psychiatric Clinics of North America, 12,* 389–411.

van der Kolk, B. A (1996a). The complexity of adaptation to trauma: Self regulation, stimulus discrimination and characterological development. In B. A. van der Kolk (Ed.), *Posttraumatic stress disorder: Psychological and biological sequelae.* Washington, DC: American Psychiatric Press.

van der Kolk, B. A (1996b). Trauma and memory. In B. A. van der Kolk (Ed.), *Posttraumatic stress disorder: Psychological and biological sequelae.* Washington, DC: American Psychiatric Press.

van der Kolk, B. A. (1996c). The body keeps the score: Approaches to psychobiology of posttraumatic stress disorder. In B. A. van der Kolk, A. C. McFarlane, & L. Weisaeth (Eds.), *Traumatic stress: The effects of overwhelming experience on the mind, body and society* (pp. 214–241). New York: Guilford Press.

van der Kolk, B. A., & Ducey, C. (1994). The psychological processing of traumatic experience: Rorschach patterns in PTSD. *Journal of Traumatic Stress, 2*(3), 259–274.

van der Kolk, B. A., & Greenberg, M. S. (1987). The psychobiology of the trauma response: Hyperarousal, constriction and addiction to traumatic reexposure. In B.A. van der Kolk (Ed.), *Psychological trauma.* Washington, DC: American Psychiatric Press.

van der Kolk, B. A., Greenberg, M. S., Boyd, H., & Krystal, J. H. (1985). Inescapable shock neurotramsitters and addiction to trauma: Towards a psychobiology of post traumatic stress. *Biological Psychiatry, 20,* 314–325.

van der Kolk, B. A., & McFarlane, A. C. (1996). The black hole of trauma. In B. A. van der Kolk, A. C. McFarland, & L. Weisaeth (Eds.), *Traumatic stress: The effects of overwhelming experience on the mind, body and society* (pp. 3–23). New York: Guilford Press.

van der Kolk, B. A., McFarlane, A. C., & van der Hart, O. (1996). A general approach to treatment of posttraumatic stress disorder. In B. A. van der Kolk, A. C. McFarlane, &

L. Weisaeth (Eds.), *Traumatic stress: The effects of overwhelming experience on the mind, body and society* (pp. 417–440). New York: Guilford Press.

van der Kolk, B. A., McFarlane, A. C., & Weisaeth, L. (Eds.). (1996). *Traumatic stress: The effects of overwhelming experience on the mind, body and society.* New York: Guilford Press.

van der Kolk, B. A., & Saporta, J. (1993). Biological response to psychic trauma. In J. L Wilson & B. Raphael (Eds.), *International handbook of traumatic stress syndromes* (pp. 25–34). New York: Plennum.

van der Kolk, B. A., van der Hart, O., & Marmer, C. R. (1996). Dissociation and information processing in posttraumatic stress disorder. In B. A. van der Kolk (Ed.), *Posttraumatic stress disorder: Psychological and biological sequelae.* Washington, DC: American Psychiatric Press.

Wade, A. (1996, June). *Small acts of living: Resistance to violence and other forms of oppression.* Presented at Therapeutic Conversations 3 Conference, Denver, CO. Audiotape available from Info-medix: 1-800-367-9286.

Watkins, J. G. (1971). The affect bridge a hypnoanalytic technique. *International Journal of Clinical and Experimental Hypnosis, 19,* 21–27.

Watkins, J., & Watkins, H. (1997). *Ego states theory and practice.* New York: Norton.

Watkins, S. G. (1992). *The practice of clinical hypnosis, Vol. II: Hypnoanalytic techniques.* New York: Irvington.

Watzlawick, P., Weakland, J. H., & Fisch, R. (1974). *Change: Principles of problem formation and problem resolution.* New York: Norton.

White, M., & Epston, D. (1990). *Narrative means to therapeutic ends.* New York: Norton.

Whitfield, C. L. (1990). *Healing the child within: Discovery and recovery for adult children of dysfunctional families.* New York: Health Communications.

Williams, L. (1994). Recall of childhood trauma: A prospective study of women's memories of childhood sexual abuse. *The Journal of Consulting and Clinical Psychology, 62*(6), 1167–1176.

Williams, M. B., & Sommer, J. F. (Eds.). (1994). *The handbook of post traumatic stress.* Westport, CT: Greenwood Press.

Wilson, J., & Keane, T. (1997) *Assessing psychological trauma and PTSD.* New York: Guilford.

Yapko, M. (1994). *Suggestions of abuse: True and false memories of childhood sexual trauma.* New York: Simon & Schuster.

Zeig, J. K. (1985). *Experiencing Erickson: An introduction to the man and his work.* New York: Brunner/Mazel.

Zimmerman, J. L., & Dickerson, V. C. (1996). *If problems talked.* San Francisco: Guilford.

INDEX

OTHER RESOURCES

☐ Tools for Mastering Trauma: A Self-Help Audio-Tape Series for Survivors

The purpose of this series is to provide people who are recovering from the effects of trauma a cost-effective manner to learn a variety of psychological tools that will help them master the debilitating effects of trauma. This series has been specifically designed to meet the needs of trauma survivors. The tools taught in these tapes have actually been used by clients with successful results. The tools are designed to enhance a person's ability to cope and function in the world. These tools are also designed to be used in conjunction with psychotherapy. On the first side of each tape the tool is taught in steps to allow for a wide range of learning styles and patterns. On the reverse side of the tape, the process is streamlined and taken further. The listener is coached on how to use the tools in a variety of situations.

Volume 1: Developing Internal Safety and a Safe Place

Contents of This Tape: Survivors of trauma and abuse often lose internal feelings of safety. In addition to suffering from past abuse and trauma, research has shown that the nervous systems of survivors remain hyperaroused after daily stresses when compared to nontraumatized individuals. In this tape the listener will learn how to develop internal feelings of safety and visual imagery of a safe place. This tape is specifically designed to help alleviate the hyperarousal that often accompanies trauma and abuse. It restores the survivor's ability to calm down after being stressed.

Volume 2: Developing Boundaries/The Energy Shield

Contents of This Tape: Survivors of trauma and abuse often have difficulties maintaining boundaries. In this tape the listener will learn how to develop an energy bubble or shield that works as a boundary. This tool allows a person to remain more resourceful in situations that had been considered stressful. After learning the tool on side A, the listener may use side B to rehearse and practice the energy shield/bubble in increasingly difficult situations.

☐ Professional Quality Video Demonstration of Trauma Re-association Conditioning with a Vietnam Vet

This tape is an excellent example of TRC. It shows the fine points of the tool, for instance how to negotiate a resource. Dr. Schwarz demonstrates how the tool is weaved into a Neo-Ericksonian therapy session. There are examples of creating well-formed outcomes, solution oriented questions, indirect suggestion, and utilization principles.

For information on how to purchase these resources, or to arrange for seminars, consultations, or supervision, contact Dr. Schwarz at the address, phone number, or email address below:

Robert A. Schwarz, Psy.D., PC
349 W. Lancaster Avenue
Haverford, PA 19041
Phone: (610) 642-0884 Fax (610) 853-9561
email: *iactinc@aol.com*
www.Doctor-bob.net